ILS
INSTITUTE FOR LANGUAGE STUDY
P9-DFC-752

Russian

IN A NUTSHELL

Titles in This Series

•

SPANISH IN A NUTSHELL
FRENCH IN A NUTSHELL
GERMAN IN A NUTSHELL
ITALIAN IN A NUTSHELL
MODERN GREEK IN A NUTSHELL
JAPANESE IN A NUTSHELL
RUSSIAN IN A NUTSHELL
INGLES EN EL BOLSILLO
(ENGLISH IN A NUTSHELL)

Russian

IN A NUTSHELL

by MARSHALL D. BERGER, Ph.D.
The City College of New York

THIRD EDITION

INSTITUTE FOR LANGUAGE STUDY, MONTCLAIR, N.J. • 1966
Exclusive Distributors to the Book Trade
DOUBLEDAY & COMPANY, INC. • GARDEN CITY, N. Y.

Library of Congress Catalog Card Number: 60-9758

PRINTED IN U.S.A.

GETTING THE MOST OUT OF YOUR COURSE

The world is growing smaller every day. Far-sighted people who recognize the value of speaking a second language will reap the benefits of more traveling enjoyment, finer social relationships, and deeper cultural understanding.

"Russian in a Nutshell" will unlock for you the treasure house of language with a fresh, new approach — without monotonous drills. Before you know it, you'll be speaking your new language easily and without embarrassment. You will be able to converse with fascinating people from other lands and read books and magazines from their country in the original language.

Much research and painstaking study has gone into the "Record Time" method of learning a new language as easily as possible. This Course is the result of that research, and for the reader's convenience it is divided into several basic, closely related sections:

The KEY TO PRONUNCIATION explains the sounds of the language. Each sentence is accompanied by a phonetic transcription to help you learn the pronunciation. This method has been tested extensively and has been found to be the best way of helping students to associate sounds with written forms.

The BASIC SENTENCE PATTERNS incorporate the very latest approach to sentence construction. Here you will find the sentence patterns which are needed in general conversation. On these basic patterns you can build sentences to suit your own particular needs.

The EVERYDAY CONVERSATIONS form the main section of this book. Here you will find a large number of situations useful for general language learning and traveling purposes. You will learn the hundreds upon hundreds of conversational sentences you may need to make yourself understood. Even more important, the material is so organized as to afford the widest latitude in varying the vocabulary and the composition of the sentences. The only limits are your own interest and ingenuity.

The OUTLINE OF GRAMMAR provides a rapid understanding

of the grammatical structure of Russian. The Basic Sentence Patterns are closely correlated with this section to give you a quick knowledge of your new language.

The two-way DICTIONARY of over 6500 entries includes all the words used in the Everyday Conversations and contains another 3000 frequently used words and expressions. It thus forms a compact and invaluable tool for the student.

Here are the tools. Use them systematically, and before you know it you will have a "feeling" for the language. The transcriptions furnish authentic reproduction of the language to train your ear and tongue to the foreign sounds; thus you can SEE the phrase, SAY the phrase, HEAR the phrase, and LEARN the phrase.

Remember that repetition and practice are the foundation stones of language learning. Repeat and practice what you have learned as often as you can. You will be amazed (and your friends will, too) how quickly you acquired a really practical knowledge of Russian.

THE EDITORS

ACKNOWLEDGEMENT

I wish to express my thanks to Dr. Zoya Yurieff and Mr. Hans ter Laan for their valuable assistance in the preparation of the dictionary; to my wife Gale Dashuck Berger and to Anton and Ludmila Kolomatsky for their invaluable help in assuring the idiomatic accuracy of the Russian text; and most of all to the editors of the Institute for Language Study, my good friend and colleague Dr. George C. Pappageotes and Mr. Benedict Kolthoff, for their careful and conscientious editorial work.

M. D. B.

Many of the Russian sentences in the Everyday Conversations have been based on materials found in the *Language Guide* by S. Abrahm and Ph. Silpert (Moscow: Mezhkniga, 1934). The phonetic transcription is entirely the author's.

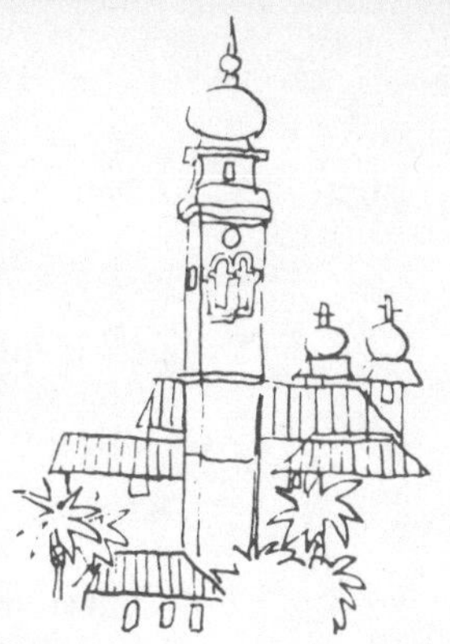

TABLE OF CONTENTS

KEY TO RUSSIAN PRONUNCIATION

RUSSIAN PRONUNCIATION AND SPELLING

Russian spelling is not consistently phonetic. One cannot simply read off the approximate English equivalents of each Russian letter to arrive at a good, or even understandable, pronunciation of Russian.

For this reason, one must resort to the use of a system of phonetic writing. Such a system represents the basic sounds and sound combinations of the language as simply and consistently as possible. In such a system, each symbol stands for one sound, and one sound only. There are no exceptions.

RUSSIAN CONSONANT SOUNDS

Russian consonant sounds, with a very few exceptions, come in pairs. Of each pair, one member is *plain* and the other *palatalized.* *

1. Plain Consonants

A listing of plain consonant phonetic symbols and Russian letters follows:

PHONETIC SYMBOL	DESCRIPTION	RUSSIAN LETTER	EXAMPLE	
b	For all practical purposes, identical with the equivalent English sounds.	**б**	бас	(bass [voice])
m		**м**	мáма	(mama)
g		**г**	газ	(gas)
f		**ф**	факт	(fact)
v		**в**	вáза	(vase)
s		**с**	сорт	(sort)
z		**з**	зóна	(zone)
p	Same as the English sounds except that they are produced with less force of breath.	**п**	пáпа	(papa)
t		**т**	такт	(tact)
k		**к**	кáрта	(card)

* The traditional Russian term for *palatalized* is "soft." For *plain* the traditional term is "hard."

PHONETIC SYMBOL	DESCRIPTION	RUSSIAN LETTER	EXAMPLE
t **d** **n** **l**	Same as the English sounds but with the tongue tip placed lower, i.e. on the backs of the upper teeth.	т д н л	такт (tact) да (yes) нос (nose) ла́мпа (lamp)
r	Trilled by vibrating the tongue tip against the upper gum ridge.	р	ра́са (race [of people])
ḥ	Similar to the English *h* sound but breathier. Somewhat like the sound produced when "clearing the throat."	х	халва́ (halva [candy])
sh	Similar to the English sound but in Russian the tongue tip is curled up toward the roof of the mouth, producing a "thicker," "deeper," "harder" sound.	ш	шок (shock)
zh	This symbol stands for the sound of *z* in *seizure* with the same tongue curling described for *sh* and with the same "thick" effect.	ж	жанда́рм (gendarme)
ts	Same as in English but it comes at the beginning of Russian words as well as medially and finally.	ц	царь (tsar)

A preliminary note about Russian vowels

In the Russian words given above, the reader will note that the familiar vowel letters **a** and **o** are used. As in many languages other than English, these letters have their so-called continental values, i.e., the *ah* sound of *father,* but shorter and more clipped, and the *aw* sound of *law* or *sort,* but shorter and more strongly lip-rounded.

Another basic Russian vowel, not shown in any of the earlier examples, is like the *oo* of *food,* but is shorter and has a "deeper" quality. This sound is represented in Russian spelling by the letter **у**:

суп (soup) **футбóл** (football)

2. Palatalized Consonants

Palatalized consonants are formed in the same manner as plain consonants, i.e. with the same organs and in the same places in the mouth, but with a simultaneous raising of the front of the tongue toward the roof of the mouth or hard palate.

This produces the effect of a *y*-sound (as in *yes*) being attached to the basic consonant sound. At first blush, this may not seem like much, since the initial sounds of such English words as *beauty, music* and *few* are made in a similar manner.

In English, however, there are three fairly distinct movements from the first consonant to the *y*-sound to the vowel sound of long *u,* whereas in Russian the basic consonant and the *y*-sound are made in one simultaneous movement with the vowel sound coming tumbling after.

A possible representation of this pronunciation might well be p^y, t^y, l^y, d^y, s^y and the like, but since so many *y*'s would be rather difficult to read and even harder to print we have used an apostrophe instead: *p', t', l', d', s',* etc. The apostrophe, then, is the equivalent of such a small *y*.

There are a few Russian consonants which do not have either plain or palatalized counterparts:

1) The sounds represented by the letters **ш**, **ж** and **ц** are always plain (see earlier discussion).

2) Russian *ch* (spelled **ч**) and *shch* (spelled **щ**) are always palatalized, even though in our transcription the palatalizing apostrophe is omitted.

3) Palatalized *zh'zh'* occurs in the word уезжáть (to go away) and a few others.

4) The sound of *y* (as in *yes*) itself is a full-fledged Russian sound, and—although it is palatal, not really palatal*ized*—it clearly belongs with the palatalized group in any sensible system of classification.

Spelling of the y-sound and other palatalized consonants

The sound of *y* coming at the beginning of a word or syllable is not represented by a separate letter in Russian. For the common sequences *ya, ye, yo,* and *yu* (continental values of the vowel letters), Russian uses the single letters **я**, **е**, **ё**, and **ю**:

я (I)
ел (ate)
ёлка (fir tree)
юг (south; cf. *Yu*goslavia)

The same single letters are used to indicate that a preceding consonant letter represents a palatalized rather than a plain sound. Note the following three-way contrast:

ёлка [YOL-kə], fir tree
тёлка [T'OL-kə], heifer
толк [tolk], sense

Two-way contrasts:

он знал [on znal], he knew
нос [nos], nose
лук [luk], onion
он снял [on sn'al], he took off
нёс [n'os], was carrying
люк [l'uk], trapdoor

At the end of words or syllables, palatalization is indicated by a special symbol called a "soft sign" and spelled **ь**:

сталь [stal'], steel
брать [brat'], to take
пальма [PAL'-mə], palm tree

In some cases a *plain* consonant or a *palatalized* one may make all the difference between one possible meaning and another. At the very least, proper placement of these consonants is essential to correct pronunciation:

стал [stal], became **брат** [brat], brother **палка** [PAL-kə], stick

FURTHER DISCUSSION OF VOWELS: SOUNDS AND LETTERS

Like я, ё, and ю, the Russian letter **е** also appears after consonant letters to indicate the palatalized character of the preceding consonant sound:

тень [t'en'], shade, shadow
нет [n'et], no
где [gd'e], where

Strange to say, the sound of [e] after *plain* consonants is represented by the same letter:

шесть [shest'], six	**теннис** [TE-n'is], tennis *
жест [zhest], gesture	**купе** [ku-PE], train compartment *
центр [tsentr], center	

The letter **э**, which also stands for [e], is never used after consonant letters, but is restricted to the initial position of words or syllables:

это [E-tə], this, that	**дуэт** [du-ET], duet
эхо [E-ḥə], echo	**поэт** [pa-ET], poet

The vowel [i] as in *machine,* but somewhat shorter, is found only after *palatalized* or "soft" consonants, or at the very beginning of words. The letter **и** is used to represent the vowel sound and, if necessary, to indicate the palatalized character of the preceding consonant sound:

бить [b'it'], to beat	**эти** [E-t'i], these, those
и [i], and	**лифт** [l'ift], elevator

After *plain* or "hard" consonants an *i*-type of sound does occur, but it undergoes an important change. Since the front of the tongue cannot rise toward the palate after a plain consonant (such a movement would convert it into a palatalized consonant), the middle or even the back of tongue rises instead. The result is a special form of *i,* which may sound or feel strange to the non-Russian, but is not difficult to make if the *plain* or "hard" consonant is produced properly in all basic respects (review earlier discussion of plain consonants). The consonant conditions the quality of the vowel.

Considering that this vowel is a centralized *i,* the phonetic symbol [ɨ] is used to represent it. The Russian spelling is **ы**, except after ш and ж, where **и** is used in spite of the pronunciation. After ц, both **и** and **ы** are found:

дым [dɨm], smoke	**жить** [zhɨt'], to live
быть [bɨt'], to be	**цирк** [tsɨrk], circus
сын [sɨn], son	**отцы** [at-TSƗ], father

DIPHTHONGS

The sound of *y* (as in *yes*) can combine with any Russian vowel to form a diphthong. The *y*-sound in this position usually is represented by the letter **й**:

* Recent borrowings from English and French.

[ay]	as in **дай**, give!		(like *die,* but shorter)
[ey]	„ „ **ей,** to her		(like *yay,* but tenser)
[iy]	„ „ **кий,** billiard cue		(like *key,* but tenser and longer)
[ɨy]	„ „ **милый,** dear		(like *mealy,* but with a "harder" l)
[oy]	„ „ **бой**, battle		(like *boy,* but shorter)
[uy]	„ „ **фуй,** * faugh!		(like *phooey,* but much shorter)

VOWELS IN UNSTRESSED SYLLABLES

Russian words, no matter how long, have only one stress. There are almost no secondary stresses. Consequently, vowel sounds in unstressed syllables tend to be obscured or merged with one another. There are similar tendencies in English.

For this reason, the spelling and pronunciation rules for vowels taken up in the preceding sections are valid only for the stressed syllables of plurisyllabic words.

In the unstressed syllables of words of more than one syllable. two basic mergers take place:

1) After *plain* consonants, [a] and [o] fall together into [a].

сама [sa-MA], herself **дома** [da-MA], houses

2) After *palatalized* consonants, [a], [e], and [i] fall together into [i].

восемь [VO-s'im'], eight **девять** [D'E-v'it'], nine

3) [u] remains unchanged.

культуру [kul-TU-ru], culture (accus. case)

In unstressed syllables other than the one directly before the stressed syllable of the word, [a] is further weakened to [ə] (a neutral, murmured vowel identical with the first vowel sound of *along* and the last one of *sofa*):

хорошо [ḥə-ra-SHO], good, well **понимаю** [pə-n'i-MA-yu], I understand

можно [MOZH-nə], possible **спасибо** [spa-S'I-bə], thank you

These rules apply to all Russian words and names. Be especially careful about the pronunciation of familiar words such as the Russian counterparts of telephone, American, and officer:

телефон	[t'i-l'i-FON]	(*not*: te-lə-FON)
американец	[a-m'i-r'i-KA-n'its]	(*not*: a-me-rə-KA-nəts)
офицер	[a-f'itSER]	(*not*: o-fə-SER)

---

* Фу, however, is much more commonly used.

MUTUAL CONSONANT INFLUENCES

Russian spelling does not mirror faithfully and consistently the influences that neighboring consonant sounds in a word or phrase exert upon one another:

1) Russian permits only voiced or voiceless consonant sequences. The determining consonant is the last one in the sequence, i.e. only [g] can precede [z], never [k]; only [k] can precede [s], etc.:

вокзал [vag-ZAL], railroad station
футбол [fud-BOL], football (soccer)
в кино [f k'i-NO], in the movies
завтра [ZAF-trə], tomorrow
в городе [v GOR-ə-d'i], in the city

2) Final consonants before a pause (the very end of the word with only silence following) are voiceless. The pause may be said to have the force of a voiceless consonant:

багаж [ba-GASH], baggage **город** [GOR-ət], city **зуб** [zup], tooth

3) Palatalized consonants sometimes occur in groups, too, notably those which contain *t', d', n', s'* and *z'* before another palatalized consonant. Russian spelling usually shows the palatalization only of this last consonant:

здесь [z'd'es'], here **шесть** [shes't'], six **кончил** [KON'-chil], finished

In the text of this book the palatalizing apostrophe is generally placed after the last member of a consonant group, as in Russian spelling. There are a few instances, however, where extra apostrophes have been inserted to help the learner along.

MISCELLANEOUS SOUND AND LETTER PROBLEMS

The letter **ч** stands for [sh] instead of the normal [ch] in a few words:

что [shto], what **конечно** [ka-N'ESH-nə], of course

The letter **г** stands for [v] instead of the normal [g] in genitive endings:

его [yi-VO], him, his
ничего [n'i-chi-VO], nothing (*lit.*: of nothing)
сегодня [s'i-VOD'-n'ə], today (*lit.*: of this day)

The endings **-ся** and **-тся** are pronounced [sə] and [tsə], respectively, instead of [s'ə], [t's'ə] or [ts'ə]:

называться [nə-zɨ-VAT-sə], to be called

называется [nə-zɨ-VA-yit-sə], is called

заблудился [zə-blu-D'IL-sə], got lost, lost one's way

In certain common conversational words, sounds are omitted:

пожалуйста [pə-ZHA-lə-stə], please

здравствуйте [ZDRAST-vuy-t'i], hello!

STRESS

Stress in Russian cannot be reduced to simple rules. In this book, placement of stress is indicated by the capitalizing of the stressed syllable, e.g. **сказать** [ska-ZAT'], to say. * Monosyllables are often capitalized, too, to indicate the stresses necessary for the rhythm of the particular sentence. Moreover, rhythms may vary from context to context:

Я американец.
YA a-m'i-r'i-KA-n'its or *ya a-m'i-r'i-KA-n'its.*
I am an American.

SYLLABICATION

Each word of more than one syllable is broken up into syllables by means of hyphenation. The syllabication is not necessarily Russian, however. In many cases, the hyphen was placed where it would be helpful to the native speaker of English, even though the rules of Russian syllabication might be violated.

* In the Grammar and Dictionary sections at the end of this book, an acute accent is used to indicate the stressed syllable of a word, for instance as in **сказáть**. The letter **ё** always represents a stressed sound, as in **ёлка** [YOL-kə], fir tree.

THE RUSSIAN ALPHABET

PRINTED	WRITTEN	NAME OR VALUE
А а	А а	[a]
Б б	Б б	[be]
В в	В в	[ve]
Г г	Г г	[ge]
Д д	Д д, д	[de]
Е е	Е е	[ye]
Ё ё	Ё ё	[yo]
Ж ж	Ж ж	[zhe]
З з	З з, з	[ze]
И и	И и	[i]
Й й	Й й	short [i]
К к	К к	[ka]
Л л	Л л	[el]
М м	М м	[em]
Н н	Н н	[en]
О о	О о	[o]
П п	П, П п	[p]
Р р	Р р	[er]
С с	С с	[es]
Т т	Т т, т̄, Т	[te]
У у	У у	[u]
Ф ф	Ф ф	[ef]
Х х	Х х	[ḥa]

PRINTED	WRITTEN	NAME OR VALUE
Ц ц	Ц ц	[tse]
Ч ч	Ч ч	[che]
Ш ш	Ш ш, ш	[sha]
Щ щ	Щ щ	[sh'cha]
Ъ ъ	ъ	separative sign
Ы ы	ы	[ɨ]
Ь ь	ь, ь	soft sign
Э э	Э э	reversed [e]
Ю ю	Ю ю	[yu]
Я я	Я я	[ya]

SAMPLE OF RUSSIAN HANDWRITING

Я тоже не беспокоилась бы много, если бы знала, что мой сын жив и здоров.

Ну, я отдохнул и чувствую себя лучше. Теперь, не спеша, пойду домой. До свидания, Анна Петровна. Желаю вам скорее получить хорошие новости от вашего сына.

Я то́же не беспоко́илась бы мно́го, е́сли бы зна́ла, что мой сын жив и здоро́в.

I, too, would not worry much if I knew that my son is alive and in good health.

Ну, я отдохну́л и чу́вствую себя́ лу́чше. Тепе́рь, не спеша́, пойду́ домо́й. До свида́ния, А́нна Петро́вна. Жела́ю вам скоре́е получи́ть хоро́шие но́вости от ва́шего сы́на.

Well now, I have rested and am feeling better. Now I shall go home without hurrying. Good-by, Anna Petrovna. I hope that you will get good news from your son as soon as possible.

BASIC SENTENCE PATTERNS
AND
EVERYDAY CONVERSATIONS

BASIC SENTENCE PATTERNS

In each language there are a few types of sentences which are used more often than others in everyday speech.

On the basis of such sentences, one can form many others simply by replacing one or two of the words of each of these basic sentences. The sentences selected to illustrate the basic patterns are short, useful and easy to memorize. Learning them before you enter the main section of Everyday Conversations will automatically give you an idea of the structure of the language. Through them, you will also learn indirectly some of the most important grammatical categories and their function in the construction of sentences. This is in fact the natural way of learning a language — the way a child absorbs its native language by hearing, repeating and using the words and constructions in actual practice.

Cross references have been supplied to establish a correlation between the Basic Sentence Patterns and the Outline of Russian Grammar in this book. The grammatical knowledge you will acquire from the basic sentences can thus be related to the systematic presentation of Russian grammar.

SIMPLE DECLARATIVE SENTENCES

(See Grammar 6.1-4; 1.0-1; 2.0-2)

Russian has no separate words for the verb forms *am, is* and *are*. Also, there are no equivalents for the articles *a* or *an* and *the*. The meanings of these words are derived from the context. Similarly, the context tells whether это means *this* or *that*.

Affirmative

Я понимаю по-русски.
ya pə-n'i-MA-yu pa-RU-sk'i.
I understand Russian.

Он говорит по-русски.
on gə-va-R'IT pa-RU-sk'i.
He speaks Russian.

Мы возьмём это.
mi vaz'-M'OM E-tə.
We'll take this (*or* that).

Вы заказали комнату.
vi zə-ka-ZA-l'i KOM-nə-tu.
You ordered a room (*or* the room).

Я американец.
ya a-m'i-r'i-KA-nits.
I am an American.

Суп пересолен.
SUP p'i-r'i-SO-l'in.
The soup is oversalted.

Это нужно.
E-tə NUZH-nə.
This is necessary.

Моя фамилия Петров.
ma-YA fa-M'IL'-yə p'i-TROF.
My surname is Petrov.

Я хочу сесть.
YA ḥa-CHU S'EST'.
I want to sit down.

Иван будет завтракать.
i-VAN BU-d'it ZAF-trə-kət'.
John is going to have breakfast.

Он англичанин.
on an-gl'i-CHA-n'in.
He is an Englishman.

Это можно.
E-tə MOZH-nə.
That is possible (permissible).

Это правильно.
E-tə PRA-v'il'-nə.
That is correct.

Negative

Я не понимаю по-русски.
ya n'i pə-n'i-MA-yu pa-RU-sk'i.
I don't understand Russian.

Мы не возьмём это.
mi n'i vaz'-M'OM E-tə.
We won't take this.

Вы не заказали комнату.
vi n'i zə-ka-ZA-l'i KOM-nə-tu.
You didn't order a room.

Я не американец.
ya n'i a-m'i-r'i-KA-n'its.
I am not an American.

Суп не пересолен.
SUP n'i p'i-r'i-SO-l'in.
The soup is not oversalted.

Это не нужно.
E-tə n'i NUZH-nə.
This is not necessary.

Моя фамилия не Петров.
ma-YA fa-M'IL'-yə n'i p'i-TROF.
My surname is not Petrov.

Он не говорит по-русски.
on n'i gə-va-R'IT pa-RU-sk'i.
He doesn't speak Russian.

Я не хочу сесть.
ya n'i ḥa-CHU S'EST'
I don't want to sit down.

Иван не будет завтракать.
i-VAN n'i BU-d'it ZAF-trə-kət'.
John is not going to have breakfast.

Он не англичанин.
on n'i an-gl'i-CHA-n'in.
He is not an Englishman.

Это нельзя.
E-tə n'il-Z'A.
That is not possible (permissible).

Это не правильно.
E-tə n'i PRA-v'il'-nə.
That is not correct.

SIMPLE QUESTIONS

With interrogative words

(See Grammar 4.5-6)

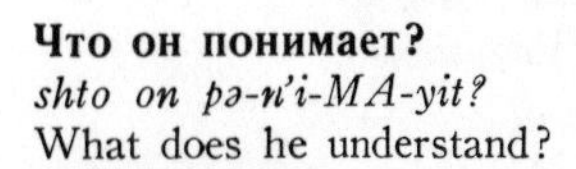

Что он понимает?
shto on pə-n'i-MA-yit?
What does he understand?

Кто говорит по-русски?
kto gə-va-R'IT pa-RU-sk'i?
Who speaks Russian?

Где Иван будет завтракать?
GD'E i-VAN BU-d'it ZAF-trə-kət'?
Where is John going to have breakfast?

Что это такое?
shto E-tə ta-KOY-ə?
What is that? (*lit.,* what that such?)

Что нужно?
SHTO NUZH-nə?
What is necessary?

Как ваша фамилия?
KAK VA-shə fa-M'IL'-yə?
What is your surname? (*lit.,* how ...?)

Что вы возьмёте?
shto vɨ vaz'-M'O-t'i?
What will you take?

Куда вы хотите сесть?
ku-DA vɨ ḥa-T'I-t'i S'EST'?
Where do you want to sit?

Кто он такой?
kto on ta-KOY?
Who is he? (*lit.,* who he such?)

Как это можно?
KAK E-tə MOZH-nə?
How is that possible?

Где комната?
GD'E KOM-nə-tə?
Where is the room?

Yes-or-no questions

(See Grammar 4.1, 4.4; 7.1)

The simplest and most common way of forming such questions in Russian is by the addition of an interrogative intonation to the declarative sentence. This intonation is often quite different from that heard in English, in that it consists of simply raising very high the most prominent syllable in the phrase or sentence. To English ears this sounds like a very emphatic statement, but it is nevertheless the commonest Russian way of asking a yes-or-no question. The English type of final-rising inflection is heard also.

Он понимает по-русски?
on pə-n'i-MA-yit pa-RU-sk'i?
Does he understand Russian?

Он не говорит по-русски?
on n'i gə-va-R'IT pa-RU-sk'i?
Doesn't he speak Russian?

Мы возьмём это?
mi vaz'-M'OM E-tə?
Will we take this?

Иван не будет завтракать?
i-VAN n'i BU-d'it ZAF-trə-kət'?
Isn't John going to have breakfast?

Суп пересолен?
SUP p'i-r'i-SO-l'in?
Is the soup oversalted?

Это можно?
E-tə MOZH-nə?
Is this possible (permissible)?

Ваша фамилия Петров?
VA-shə fa-M'IL'-yə p'i-TROF?
Is your name Petrov?

Вы заказали комнату?
vi zə-ka-ZA-l'i KOM-nə-tu?
Did you order a room?

Он англичанин?
on an-gl'i-CHA-n'in?
Is he an Englishman?

Это нужно?
E-tə NUZH-nə?
Is that necessary?

Это правильно?
E-tə PRA-v'il'-nə?
Is this correct?

An alternative, though less common, way of forming yes-or-no questions is by reversing verb and subject:

Понимает он по-русски?
pə-n'i-MA-yit on pa-RU-sk'i?
Does he understand Russian?

Нужно это?
NUZH-nə E-tə?
Is this necessary?

More commonly, the particle ли is added:

Понимает ли он по-русски?
pə-n'i-MA-yit l'i on pa-RU-sk'i?
Does he understand Russian?

Англичанин ли он?
an-gl'i-CHA-n'in l'i on?
Is he an Englishman?

Нужно ли это?
NUZH-nə l'i E-tə?
Is this necessary?

MORE COMPLEX DECLARATIVE SENTENCES

Indirect quotations

(See Grammar 6.5; 5.1-2)

Note use of ли as in yes-or-no questions type 3:

Я не знаю, понимает ли он по-русски.
YA n'i ZNA-yu pə-n'i-MA-yit l'i on pa-RU-sk'i.
I don't know if (= whether) he understands Russian.

Я не знаю, хочу ли я сесть.
YA n'i ZNA-yu ḥa-CHU l'i ya S'EST'.
I don't know if I want to sit down.

Я не знаю, англичанин ли он.
YA n'i ZNA-yu an-gl'i-CHA-n'in l'i on.
I don't know if he is an Englishman.

Я не знаю, нужно ли это.
YA n'i ZNA-yu NUZH-nə l'i E-tə.
I don't know if that is necessary.

Other types:

Я не знаю, что он понимает.
ya n'i ZNA-yu shto on pə-n'i-MA-yit.
I don't know what he understands.

Я спрошу, где комната.
YA spra-SHU gd'e KOM-nə-tə.
I'll ask where the room is.

Я не знаю, что нужно.
YA n'i ZNA-yu shto NUZH-nə.
I don't know what is necessary.

Я спрошу, что это такое.
ya spra-SHU shto E-tə ta-KOY-ə.
I'll ask what that is.

Он понимает, что я говорю по-русски.
on pə-n'i-MA-yit shto ya gə-va-R'U pa-RU-sk'i.
He understands what I am saying in Russian. }*
He understands that I am speaking Russian. }

Мы возьмём, что нужно.
MƗ vaz'-M'OM shto NUZH-nə.
We'll take what is necessary.

Он говорит, что он хочет сесть.
ON gə-va-R'IT shto on ḤO-chit S'EST'.
He says that he wants to sit down.

Мы знаем, что он американец.
mɨ ZNA-yim shto on a-m'i-r'i-KA-n'its.
We know that he is an American.

Мы говорим по-русски потому, что это нужно.
mɨ gə-va-R'IM pa-RU-sk'i pə-ta-MU-shtə E-tə NUZH-nə.
We are speaking Russian because it is necessary.

---

* Depending on intonation что means *what* or *that*.

Так как это нужно, мы говорим по-русски.
tak kak E-tə NUZH-nə mɨ gə-va-R'IM pa-RU-sk'i.
Since it is necessary, we speak Russian.

Если можно, он возьмёт это.
YE-sl'i MOZH-nə on vaz'-M'OT E-tə.
If possible, he'll take that.

Если он захочет, я поговорю с ним об этом.
YE-sl'i on za-ḤO-chit, ya pə-gə-va-R'U sn'im a-BE-təm.
If he wishes (*lit.*, if he will want), I'll speak with him about this.

Я американец, который говорит по-русски (*or* говорящий по-русски).
YA a-m'i-r'i-KA-n'its ka-TOR-ɨy gə-va-R'IT pa-RU-sk'i (or *gə-va-R'ASH'-chiy pə-RU-sk'i*).
I am an American who speaks Russian (*or lit.*, speaking Russian).

(See Grammar 2.6; 7.2)

The foregoing simple sentences can be expanded into the longer and more expressive sentences of normal, everyday speech by the mere addition of more words:

Adverbs

Я хочу сесть сюда.
YA ḥa-CHU S'EST' su-DA.
I want to sit here.

Я спрошу, кто там.
ya spra-SHU KTO tam.
I'll ask who's there.

Он хорошо говорит по-русски.
on ḥə-ra-SHO gə-va-R'IT pa-RU-sk'i.
He speaks Russian well.

Кто тут говорит по-русски?
KTO tut gə-va-R'IT pa-RU-sk'i?
Who speaks Russian here?

Это очень нужно.
E-tə O-chin NUZH-nə.
This is very necessary.

Negatives

Я ничего не понимаю.
ya n'i-chi-VO n'i pə-n'i-MA-yu.
I don't understand anything.

Мы ничего не возьмём.
mɨ n'i-chi-VO n'i vaz'-M'OM.
We won't take anything.

Иван никогда не будет завтракать.
i-VAN n'i-kag-DA n'i BU-d'it ZAF-trə-kət'.
John is never going to have breakfast.

Object pronouns

Я его понимаю.
YA yi-VO pə-n'i-MA-yu.
I understand him.

Вы заказали её.
VƗ zə-ka-ZA-l'i yi-YO.
You ordered it (*lit., her,* referring to *room* [fem.]).

Это мне нужно.
E-tə mn'e NUZH-nə.
I need that (*lit.*, that is necessary to me).

Он знает меня.
on ZNA-yit m'i-N'A.
He knows me.

Infinitives

Это нужно знать.
E-tə NUZH-nə ZNAT'.
That is necessary to know.

Как можно узнать?
KAK MOZH-nə uz-NAT'?
How can one find out? (*lit.,* How is it possible to find out?)

Как можно пройти туда?
KAK MOZH-nə pray-T'I tu-DA?
How can one get there?

PREPOSITIONAL PHRASES

(See Grammar 1.2-6)

With nouns

Иван будет завтракать в гостинице.
i-VAN BU-d'it ZAF-trə-kət' vga-ST'I-n'itsɨ.
John is going to have breakfast in the hotel.

Он говорит по-русски с Иваном.
on gə-var-R'IT pa-RU-sk'i sɨ-VA-nəm.
He is speaking Russian with John.

Я хочу сесть у окна.
YA ha-CHU S'EST' u ak-NA.
I want to sit by the window.

Как можно пройти на вокзал?
KAK MOZH-nə pray-T'I nə-vag-ZAL?
How can one get to the railroad station?

With pronouns

Я поговорю с ним.
ya pə-gə-va-R'U sn'im.
I'll speak with him.

Я поговорю с ним об этом.
ya pə-gə-va-R'U sn'im a-BE-təm.
I'll speak with him about that.

Мы возьмём это с собой.
mɨ vaz'-M'OM E-tə ssa-BOY.
We'll take this with us (*lit.,* with self).

Я спрошу у него карандаш.
YA spra-SHU u n'i-VO kə-ran-DASH.
I'll ask him for a pencil (*lit.,* I'll ask by him a pencil).

FORMS OF THE VERB БЫТЬ (TO BE)

(See Grammar 6.1)

As shown earlier, Russian does not have forms for the meanings of *is, am* and *are,* but it does have such words as *to be, was, were, will be,* and *there is, are.* The normal way of saying *I have, you have,* etc., is *by me there is, by you there is,* etc.

Он был англичанин.
ON bɨl an-gl'i-CHA-n'in.
He was an Englishman.

Его фамилия была Петров.
yi-VO fa-M'IL'-yə bɨ-LA p'i-TROF.
His surname was Petrov.

У меня есть спички.
u m'i-N'A yest' SP'ICH-k'i
I have matches (*lit.,* by me there are matches).

Суп был пересолен.
SUB bɨl p'i-r'i-SO-l'in.
The soup was oversalted.

Это будет нужно.
E-tə BU-d'it NUZH-nə.
That will be necessary.

Есть у вас словарь?
YEST' u vas sla-VAR'?
Do you have a dictionary?

WORD ORDER IN RUSSIAN SENTENCES

Word order in Russian is not so strict as in English because there is little possibility of misinterpreting the function or meaning of a word, regardless of its position in the sentence. Since each function is marked by a special ending of some sort, Russian words may be either strung out in an order that is not very different from that of English or they may be transposed in various ways to produce important stylistic effects or emphases.

ELLIPSIS

In familiar Russian conversation, subject and object pronouns, certain impersonal forms and even certain verbs are put in or left out of sentences at the speaker's option.

The following examples illustrate both transposition of words and ellipsis:

"Normal"	*Modified*
Я не говорю по-русски. *ya n'i gə-va-R'U pa-RU-sk'i.* I don't speak Russian.	**По-русски не говорю.** *pa-RU-sk'i n'i go-va-R'U.*
Я хочу сесть. *YA ḥa-CHU S'EST'.* I want to sit down.	**Сесть хочу.** *S'EST' ḥa-CHU.*
Как мне нужно итти? *KAK mn'e NUZH-nə i-T'I?* How should I go?	**Как нужно итти?** **Как мне итти?** *KAK [NUZH-nə] [mn'e] i-T'I?*

In some cases, the "normal" example is simply more common than the "modified" one, and requirements of emphasis and intonation determine which one is used at a particular moment:

У вас есть словарь? *u VAS yest' sla-VAR'?* Do you have a dictionary?	**Есть у вас словарь?** *YEST' u vas sla-VAR'?*
Он меня знает. *on m'i-N'A ZNA-yit.* He knows me.	**Он знает меня.** *on ZNA-yit m'i-N'A.*
Как можно туда пройти? *kak MOZH-nə tu-DA pray-T'I?* How can one get there?	**Как можно пройти туда?** **Как туда пройти?** *KAK MOZH-nə pray-T'I tu-DA?* *KAK tu-DA pray-T'I?*

BASIC QUESTIONS AND ANSWERS

(See Grammar 2.3-5; 4.3)

Он понимает по-русски? *on pə-n'i-MA-yit pa-RU-sk'i?* Does he understand Russian?	**Да, понимает.** *DA, pə-n'i-MA-yit.* Yes, he does.
Не говорит ли он по-русски? *n'i gə-va-R'IT l'i on pa-RU-sk'i?* Doesn't he speak Russian?	**Нет, не говорит.** *N'ET, n'i gə-va-R'IT.* No, he doesn't.
Что вы возьмёте с собой? *SHTO vɨ vaz'-M'O-t'i ssa-BOY?* What will you take with you?	**Возьмём эти вещи.** *vaz'-M'OM E-t'i V'ESH'-chi.* We'll take these things.

Куда хотите сесть?
ku-DA ḥa-T'I-t'i S'EST'?
Where do you want to sit down?

Я хочу сесть сюда.
YA ḥa-CHU S'EST' su-DA.
I want to sit down here.

Где комната?
GD'E KOM-nə-tə?
Where is the room?

Комната там.
KOM-nə-tə TAM.
The room is there.

Это нужно?
E-tə NUZH-nə?
Is that necessary?

Это очень нужно.
E-tə O-chin' NUZH-nə.
It is very necessary.

Как ваша фамилия?
KAK VA-shə fa-M'IL'-yə?
What is your surname?

Моя фамилия Петров.
ma-YA fa-M'IL'ye p'i-TROF.
My name is Petrov.

Кто он такой?
KTO on ta-KOY?
Who is he?

Он американец.
on a-m'i-r'i-KA-n'its.
He is an American.

Есть у вас словарь?
YEST' u vas sla-VAR'?
Do you have a dictionary?

Да, у меня есть.
DA, u m'i-N'A YEST'.
Yes, I have one.

EVERYDAY CONVERSATIONS

BASIC EXPRESSIONS

Да.
DA.
Yes.

Нет.
N'ET.
No.

Хорошо.
ḥə-ra-SHO.
All right.

Это.
E-tə.
This one.

Нет, не это.
N'ET, n'i E-tə.
No, not this one.

Вот он.
VOT ON.
Here he is.

Вот она.
VOT a-NA.
Here she is

Вот оно.
VOT a-NO.
Here it is.

Когда?
kag-DA?
When?

Где?
GD'E?
Where?

Который?
ka-TOR-ɨy?
Which?

Почему?
pə-chi-MU?
Why?

Что это такое?
SHTO E-tə ta-KOY-ə?
What is this?

Вы готовы?
vɨ ga-TO-vɨ?
Are you ready?

Поспешите!
pə-sp'i-SHɨ-t'i!
Hurry!

Это всё?
E-təf-S'O?
Is that all?

Сколько?
SKOL'-kə?
How much?

Я американец.
ya a-m'i-r'i-KA-n'its.
I am an American. (masc.)

Я американка.
ya a-m'i-r'i-KAN-kə.
I am an American. (fem.)

Я англичанин.
ya an-gl'i-CHA-n'in.
I am an Englishman.

Я англичанка.
ya an-gl'i-CHAN-kə.
I am an Englishwoman.

Я иностранец.
ya i-na-STRA-n'its.
I am a foreigner. (masc.)

Я иностранка.
ya- i-na-STRAN-kə.
I am a foreigner. (fem)

Я из Нью Йорка.
ya iz n'yu YOR-kə.
I am from New York

По-русски не говорю.
pə-RU-sk'i n'i gə-va-R'U.
I don't speak Russian.

Как ваша фамилия?
kak VA-shə fa-M'IL'-yə?
What is your name?

Моя фамилия . . .
ma-YA fa-M'IL'-yə . . .
My name is . . .

Вот мой паспорт.
vot moy PAS-pərt.
Here is my passport.

Я живу в Нью Йорке.
ya zhɨ-VU vn'yu YOR-k'i.
I live in New York.

Кто тут говорит по-английски?
KTO tut gə-va-R'IT pə-an-GL'IY-sk'i?
Who speaks English here?

Я в затруднении.
yav-zə-trud-N'E-n'i-i.
I am in trouble.

Я бы хотел кое что об'яснить вам.
ya-bɨ-ha-T'EL KOY-ə-shtə ab-jis-N'IT' vam.
I would like to explain something to you.

Как это называется по-русски?
KAK E-tə nə-zɨ-VA-yit-sə pa RU-sk'i?
What is that called in Russian?

Я понимаю.
ya pə-n'i-MA-yu.
I understand.

Я не понимаю.
ya n'i-pə-n'i-MA-yu.
I don't understand.

Понимаете?
pə-n'i-MA-yi-t'i?
Do you understand?

Доброе утро.
DO-brə-yə U-trə.
Good morning.

Добрый день.
DO-brɨy D'EN'.
Good afternoon.

Добрый вечер
DO-brɨ-y V'E-chir.
Good evening.

Спокойной ночи.
spa-KOY-nəy NO-chi.
Good night.

До свидания.
də-s'v'i-DA-n'i-yə.
Good bye.

Как поживаете?
kak pə-zhɨ-VA-yi-t'i?
How are you?

Благодарю вас, хорошо.
blə-gə-da-R'U-vas, ḥə-ra-SHO.
Very well, thanks.

С удовольствием.
su-da-VOL'-s'-t'v'i-im.
With pleasure.

Извините.
iz'-v'i-N'I-t'i.
Excuse me.

Пожалуйста.
pa-ZHA-lə-stə.
Please.

Большое спасибо.
bal'-SHOY-ə spa-S'I-bə.
Thank you very much.

Вы очень любезны.
vɨ O-chin l'u-B'EZ-nɨ.
You are very kind.

Ничего!
n'i-chi-VO!
It does not matter.

Это очень неприятно.
E-tə O-chin n'i-pr'i-YAT-nə.
It's very annoying.

Я выхожу.
ya-vɨ-ḥa-ZHU.
I am about to go out.

Идите скорее.
i-D'I-t'i ska-R'EY-ə.
Go at once.

Помогите мне.
pə-ma-G'I-t'i mn'e.
Help me.

Принесите мне...
pr'i-n'i-S'I-t'i mn'e...
Bring me...

Дайте мне...
DAY-t'i mn'e...
Give me...

Несите это.
n'i-S'I-t'i E-tə.
Carry this.

Идите за мной.
i-D'I-t'i za-MNOY.
Follow me.

GETTING TO KNOW YOU

Можно вас познакомить с гражданином Петровым?
MOZH-nə vas pəz-na-KO-m'it' zgrazh-da-N'I-nəm p'i-TRO-vɨm?
May I introduce you to Citizen Petrov?

Это моя жена.
E-tə ma-YA zhi-NA.
This is my wife.

А это мой сын (моя дочка).
a E-tə moy SɨN (ma-YA DOCH-kə).
This is my son (my daughter).

Вы, повидимому, говорите по-русски.
vɨ, pa-V'I-d'i-mə-mu, go-va-R'I-t'i pa-RU-sk'i.
You speak Russian, I see.

Да, немножко.
DA, n'im-NOSH-kə.
Yes, a little.

Вы очень скромны.
vɨ O-chin SKROM-nɨ.
You're very modest.

Это ваша первая поездка в Советский Союз?
E-tə VA-shə P'ER-və-yə pa-YEST-kə fsa-V'ET-sk'iy sa-YUS?
Is this your first trip to the Soviet Union?

Вы довольны своей поездкой?
vɨ da-VOL'-nɨ sva-YEY pa-YEST-kəy?
Are you enjoying your trip?

Очень, ваша страна мне очень нравится.
O-chin, VA-shə stra-NA mn'e O-chin NRA-v'it-sə.
Very much, I like your country very much.

Где вы живёте в Соединённых Штатах?
gd'ə vɨ zhi-V'O-t'i fsə-yi-d'i-N'ON-nɨḥ SHTA-təḥ?
Where do you live in the United States?

Я живу в Нью Йорке.
YA zhɨ-VU vn'yu YOR-k'i.
I live in New York.

Ах так, это очень интересно.
aḥ TAK, E-ta O-chin in-t'i-R'ES-nə.
Oh, is that so? That's very interesting.

Да, вы должны обязательно нас навестить когда вы будете в Америке.
Da, vɨ dalzh-Nɨ ab'i-ZA-t'il-nə nas nə-v'i-ST'IT' kag-DA vɨ BU-d'i-t'i va-M'E-r'i-k'i.
Yes, you must visit us when you come to America.

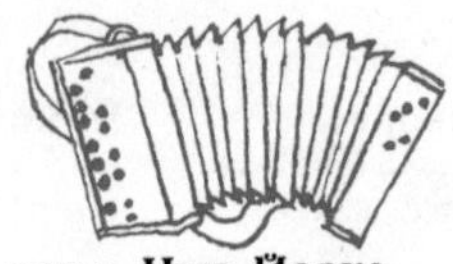

Очень мило с вашей стороны.
O-chin M'I-lə sVA-shəy stə-ra-NƗ.
That's very nice of you.

Непременно зайдём к вам когда мы будем в Нью Йорке.
n'i-pr'i-M'EN-nə zay-D'OM kvam kag-DA mɨ BU-d'im vn'yu YOR-k'i.
We'll certainly drop by to see you when we're in New York.

COUNTING

Cardinal Numbers

один
a-D'IN
one

два
DVA
two

три
TR'I
three

четыре
chi-TƗ-r'ə
four

пять
P'AT'
five

шесть
SHES'T'
six

семь
S'EM'
seven

восемь
VO-s'im'
eight

девять
D'E-v'it'
nine

десять
D'E-s'it'
ten

одиннадцать
a-D'I-nət-sət'
eleven

двенадцать
dv'i-NAT-sət'
twelve

тринадцать
tr'i-NAT-sət'
thirteen

четырнадцать
chi-TƗR-nət-sət'
fourteen

пятнадцать
p'it-NAT-sət'
fifteen

шестнадцать
shɨs-NAT-sət'
sixteen

семнадцать
s'im-NAT-sət'
seventeen

восемнадцать
və-s'im-NAT-sət'
eighteen

девятнадцать
d'i-v'it-NAT-sət'
nineteen

двадцать
DVAT-sət'
twenty

двадцать один
DVAT-sət' a-D'IN
twenty-one

двадцать два
DVAT-səd' DVA
twenty-two

двадцать три
DVAT-sət' TR'I
twenty-three

тридцать
TR'IT-sət'
thirty

сорок
SO-rək
forty

пятьдесят
p'i-d'i-S'AT
fifty

шестьдесят
shɨz-d'i-S'AT
sixty

семьдесят
S'EM'-d'i-s'it
seventy

восемьдесят
VO-s'im'-d'i-s'it
eighty

девяносто
d'i-v'i-NO-stə
ninety

сто
STO
a hundred

тысяча
Tɨ-s'i-chə
a thousand

миллион
m'i-l'i-ON
a million

сто тридцать пять
STO TR'IT-sət' P'AT'
one hundred and thirty-five

Ordinal Numbers

первый
P'ER-vɨy
the first

второй
fta-ROY
the second

третий
TR'E-t'iy
the third

четвёртый
chit-V'OR-tɨy
the fourth

пятый
P'A-tɨy
the fifth

шестой
shɨ-STOY
the sixth

седьмой
s'id'-MOY
the seventh

восьмой
vas'-MOY
the eighth

девятый
d'i-V'A-tɨy
the ninth

десятый
d'i-S'A-tɨy
the tenth

одиннадцатый
a-D'I-nəts-tɨy
the eleventh

двенадцатый
d'v'i-NATS-tɨy
the twelfth

тринадцатый
tr'i-NATS-tɨy
the thirteenth

четырнадцатый
chi-TɨR-nəts-tɨy
the fourteenth

пятнадцатый
p'it-NATS-tɨy
the fifteenth

шестнадцатый
shɨs-NATS-tɨy
the sixteenth

семнадцатый
s'im-NATS-tɨy
the seventeenth

восемнадцатый
və-s'im-NATS-tɨy
the eighteenth

девятнадцатый
d'i-v'it-NATS-tɨy
the nineteenth

двадцатый
dvat-SA-tɨy
the twentieth

двадцать первый
DVAT-sət' P'ER-vɨy
the twenty-first

двадцать второй
DVAT-sət' fta-ROY
the twenty-second

двадцать третий
DVAT-sət' TR'E-t'iy
the twenty-third

тридцатый
tr'it-SA-tɨy
the thirtieth

сороковой
sə-rə-ka-VOY
the fortieth

пятидесятый
p'i-t'i-d'i-S'A-tɨy
the fiftieth

шестидесятый
shɨ-s't'd'i-S'A-tɨy
the sixtieth

семидесятый
s'i-m'i-d'i-S'A-tɨy
the seventeenth

восьмидесятый
və-s'm'i-d'i-S'A-tɨy
the eightieth

девяностый
d'i-v'i-NO-stɨy
the ninetieth

сотый
SO-tɨy
the one hundredth

миллионный
m'i-l'i-ON-nɨy
the one millionth

тысячный
Tɨ-s'ich-nɨy
the one thousandth

сто тридцать пятый
STO TR'IT-sət' P'A-tɨy
the one hundred and thirty-fifth

Collective and Fractional Numbers

один раз
a-D'IN RAS
once

два раза
DVA RA-zə
twice

три раза
TR'I RA-zə
thrice

четыре раза
chi-Tɨ-r'i RA-zə
four times

пара
PA-rə
a couple, a pair

один
a-D'IN
single

двойной
dvay-NOY
double

дюжина
D'U-zhi-nə
a dozen

двадцать
DVAT-sət'
a score

четверть
CHET'-v'ir't'
a quarter

половина
pə-la-V'I-nə
a half

третья часть
TR'ET'-yə CHAS'T'
a third

пятая часть
P'A-tə-yə CHAS'T'
a fifth

восьмая часть
vas'-MA-yə CHAS'T'
an eighth

THE CLOCK AND THE CALENDAR

Который час?
ka-TOR-ɨy CHAS?
What's the time?

час
CHAS
One o'clock

два часа
DVA chi-SA
Two o'clock

три часа
TR'I chi-SA
Three o'clock

четыре часа
chi-Tɨ-r'i chi-SA
Four o'clock

пять часов
P'AT' chi-SOF
Five o'clock

шесть часов
SHES'T' chi-SOF
Six o'clock

семь часов
S'EM' chi-SOF
Seven o'clock

восемь часов
VO-s'im' chi-SOF
Eight o'clock

девять часов
D'E-v'it' chi-SOF
Nine o'clock

десять часов
D'E-s'it' chi-SOF
Ten o'clock

одиннадцать часов
a-D'I-nət-sət' chi-SOF
Eleven o'clock

двенадцать часов
d' v'i-NAT-sət' chi-SOF
Twelve o'clock

В котором часу?
fka-TO-rəm chi-SU?
At what time?

В три десять
f-TR'I D'E-s'it'
At 3:10

В три пятнадцать
f-TR'I p'it-NAT-sət'
At 3:15

В три двадцать
f-TR'I DVAT-sət'
At 3:20

В три тридцать
f-TR'I TR'IT-sət'
At 3:30

В три пятьдесят
f-TR'I p'i-d'i-S'AT
At 3:50

В четыре пятьдесят
f-chi-Tɨ-r'i p'i-d'i-S'AT
At 4:50

В восемь пятьдесят
v-VO-s'im' p'i-d'i-S'AT
At 8:50

Утром
U-trəm
In the morning

Днём
DN'OM
In the afternoon

Вечером
V'E-chi-rəm
In the evening

Ночью
NOCH-yu
At night

Days of the week

Какой сегодня день?
ka-KOY s'i-VOD'-n'ə D'EN?
What day is today?

Воскресенье
və-skr'i-S'EN'-yə
Sunday

Понедельник
pə-n'i-D'EL'-n'ik
Monday

Вторник
FTOR-n'ik
Tuesday

Среда
sr'i-DA
Wednesday

Четверг
chit-V'ERK
Thursday

Пятница
P'AT-n'it-sə
Friday

Суббота
su-BO-tə
Saturday

Выходной день
vɨ-had-NOY D'EN'
Off-day; day off

Months

Январь
yin-VAR'
January

Февраль
f'iv-RAL'
February

Март
MART
March

Апрель
a-PR'EL'
April

Май
MAY
May

Июнь
i-YUN'
June

Июль
i-YUL'
July

Август
AV-gust
August

Сентябрь
s'in-T'A-br'
September

Октябрь
ak-T'A-br'
October

Ноябрь
na-YA-br'
November

Декабрь
d'i-KA-br'
December

STRANGER IN TOWN

Я американец (*masc.*), **англичанин** (*masc.*).
ya a-m'i-r'i-KA-n'its, an-gl'i-CHA-n'in.
I am an American, Englishman.

Я американка (*femin.*), **англичанка** (*femin.*).
ya a-m'i-r'i-KAN-kə, an-gl'i-CHAN-kə.
I am an American, an Englishwoman.

Далеко отсюда Тверская улица?
də-l'i-KO at-SU-də tv'ir-SKA-yə U-l'itsə?
Is Tversky street far from here?

Как ближе пройти на Тверскую Улицу?
kak BL'I-zhə pray-T'I nə tv'ir-SKU-yu U-l'itsu?
Kindly tell me the shortest way to Tversky Street.

Это Красная Площадь?
E-tə KRAS-nə-yə PLOSH'-chit'?
Is this Red Square?

Извините, как пройти к Кремлю?
iz-v'i-N'I-t'i, kak pray-T'I kkr'im-L'U?
Pardon me, which is the way to the Kremlin?

Куда мне итти направо или налево?
ku-DA mn'e i-T'I, na-PRA-və I-l'i na-L'E-və?
Must I turn to the right or to the left?

Идите прямо.
i-D'I-t'i PR'A-mə.
Go straight ahead.

Второй поворот направо (налево).
fta-ROY pə-va-ROT na-PRA-və (na-L'E-və).
It is the second turn to the right (left).

Каким трамваем (автобусом) мне проехать на Кузнецский Мост?
ka-K'IM tram-VA-yim (af-TO-bu-səm) mn'e pra-YE-ḥət' na kuz-N'ETsk'iy MOST?
What streetcar (bus) will take me to Kuznetsky street (lit. bridge)?

Я заблудился (*masc.*), **заблудилась** (*fem.*).
ya zə-blu-D'IL-sə, zə-blu-D'I-ləs.
I have lost my way.

На какой улице находится Третьяковская галерея?
nə ka-KOY U-l'it-sɨ na-ḤO-d'it-sə tr'it'-yi-KOF-skə-yə gə-l'i-R'EY-ə?
On what street is the Tretyakov Gallery?

Куда ведёт эта дорога?
ku-DA v'i-D'OT E-tə da-RO-gə?
Where does this road lead to?

Там?
TAM?
Over there?

Дайте мне адрес, пожалуйста.
DAY-t'i mn'e A-dr'is, pa-ZHA-lə-stə.
Will you please give me the address?

Здесь живёт . . .?
ZD'ES' zhi-V'OT . . .?
Does... live here?

Проводите меня до ближайшей почты.
prə-va-D'I-t'i m'i-N'A də-bl'i-ZHAY-shəy POCH-tɨ.
Take me to the nearest post office.

Проводите меня в Госбанк.
prə-va-D'I-t'i m'i-N'A vgoz-BANK.
Take me to the State Bank.

Хочу пройти на Ленинский Стадион.
ḥa-CHU pray-T'I na L'E-n'in-sk'iy stə-d'i-ON.
I want to go to the Lenin Stadium.

Где ближайшая стоянка такси?
gd'e bl'i-ZHAY-shə-yə sta-YAN-kə tak-S'I?
Where is the nearest taxi stand?

Я потерял ключ.
ya pə-t'i-R'AL KL'UCH.
I have lost my key.

Не могу найти свой паспорт.
n'i-ma-GU nay-T'I svoy PAS-pərt.
I can't find my passport.

Это очень странно.
E-tə O-chin STRAN-nə.
It's very strange.

Утром я его здесь видел.
U-trəm ya yi-VO z'd'es' V'I-d'il.
I saw it here this morning.

Час тому назад он был у меня в руках.
CHAS ta-MU na-ZAT on BɨL u-m'i-N'A v-ru-KAḤ.
I had it an hour ago.

Нашёл! (нашла! *fem.*)
na-SHOL! (nash-LA!)
I've found it!

Идите вперёд.
i-D'I-t'i fp'i-R'OT.
Lead the way.

Позовите такси.
pə-za-V'I-t'i tak-S'I.
Call a taxi.

Закройте дверь.
za-KROY-t'i DV'ER'.
Close the door.

Закройте окно.
za-KROY-t'i ak-NO.
Close the window.

Войдите.
vay-D'I-t'i.
Come in.

Спасибо.
spa-S'I-bə.
Thank you.

Откройте дверь.
at-KROY-t'i DV'ER'.
Open the door.

Откройте окно.
at-KROY-t'i ak-NO.
Open the window.

Запишите.
zə-p'i-SHɨ-t'i.
Write it down.

Садитесь, пожалуйста.
sa-D'I-t'is, pa-ZHA-lə-stə.
Please sit down.

Пожалуйста.
pa-ZHA-lə-stə.
You are welcome.

Где находится Интурист?
gd'e na-ḤO-d'it-sə in-tu-R'IST?
Where is Intourist?

В этом доме находится Интурист?
vE-təm DO-m'i na-ḤO-d'it-sə in-tu-R'IST?
Is Intourist in this building?

Эту контору я ищу.
E-tu kan-TO-ru ya ish'-CHU.
This is the office I am looking for.

Прочтите это пожалуйста.
prach-T'I-t'i E-tə pa-ZHA-lə-stə.
Would you mind reading this for me, please?

Пожалуйста, проводите меня в метро.
pa-ZHA-lə-stə, prə-va-D'I-t'i m'i-N'A vm'i-TRO
Would you please show me the way to the subway?

Где вход?
GD'E f-ḤOT?
Where is the entrance?

Здесь вход на выставку?
ZD'ES' f-ḤOT na Vɨ-stəf-ku?
Is this the entrance to the exhibition?

Где бюро пропусков?
gd'e b'u-RO prə-pu-SKOF?
Where do they give out the admission passes?

Где справочный отдел?
gd'e SPRA-vəch-nɨy ad-D'EL?
Where is the information desk?

Где я могу получить справку?
gd'e ya ma-GU pə-lu-CHIT' SPRAF-ku?
Where can I have an inquiry answered?

Где можно получить пропуск?
gd'e MOZH-nə pə-lu-CHIT' PRO-pusk?
Where do you get a pass?

Я не говорю по-русски.
ya ni-gə-va-R'U pa-RU-sk'i.
I don't speak Russian.

Я иностранец.
ya i-na-STRA-n'its.
I am a foreigner. (masc.)

Я американец.
ya a-m'i-ri-KA-n'its.
I am an American. (masc.)

Я хочу подняться на шестой этаж.
ya ḥa-CHU pad-N'AT-sə nə shi-STOY i-TASH.
I want to go to the 6th floor.

Где лифт?
gd'e L'IFT?
Where is the elevator?

Мне нужно видеть директора.
mn'e NUZH-nə V'I-d'it' d'i-REK-tə-rə.
I want to see the manager.

Мне нужен секретарь.
mn'e NU-zhin s'i-kr'i-TAR'.
I want the secretary.

Мне нужен управляющий делами.
mn'e NU-zhin u-prav-L'A-yush'-chiy d'i-LA-m'i.
I want the business manager.

Мне нужен заведующий отделом.
mn'e NU-zhin za-V'E-du-yush'-chiy ad-D'E-ləm.
I want the department chief.

Мне нужно иностранное бюро.
mn'e NUZH-nə i-na-STRAN-nə-yə b'u-RO.
I want the foreign section.

Кто здесь говорит по английски?
KTO zd'es' gə-va-R'IT pə-an-GL'IY-sk'i?
Does anynone here speak English?

Мне нужен английский переводчик.
mn'e NU-zhin an-GL'IY-sk'iy p'i-r'i-VOT'-chik.
I need an English interpreter.

ABOARD SHIP

Где моя каюта?
GD'E ma-YA ka-YU-tə?
Where is my cabin?

Где первый класс?
gd'e P'ER-viy KLAS?
Where is the first class?

Где второй класс?
gd'e fta-ROY KLAS?
Where is the second class?

Где ресторан?
gd'e r'i-sta-RAN?
Where is the dining-room?

Где курительная?
gd'e ku-R'I-t'il'-nə-yə?
Where is the smoking room?

Хочу поговорить с капитаном.
ḥa-CHU pə-gə-va-R'IT' skə-p'i-TA-nəm.
I want to speak to the captain.

Принесите мне чаю в каюту.
pr'i-n'i-S'I-t'i mn'e CHA-yu fka-YU-tu.
Bring me some tea to my cabin.

Принесите мне горячей воды.
pr'i-n'i-S'I-t'i mn'e ga-R'A-chəy va-DI.
Bring me some hot water.

Где зал?
gd'e ZAL?
Where is the lounge?

Это зал первого класса?
E-tə ZAL P'ER-və-və KLA-sə?
Is this the first-class lounge?

Когда здесь обеды?
kag-DA zd'es' a-BE-di?
At what time is dinner served?

Когда здесь ужины?
kag-DA zd'es' U-zhi-ni?
At what time is supper served?

Когда отход?
kag-DA at-ḤOT?
When do we start?

Поставьте багаж сюда.
pa-STAF'-t'i ba-GASH su-DA.
Put my baggage here.

Откройте окно.
at-KROY-t'i ak-NO.
Open the window.

Закройте окно.
za-KROY-t'i ak-NO.
Close the window.

Принесите постельное бельё и полотенца.
pr'i-n'i-S'I-t'i pa-ST'EL'-nə-yə b'il'-YO i pə-la-T'ENT-sə.
Fetch me bedding and towels.

Дайте мне ключ от моей каюты.
DAY-t'i mn'e KL'UCH at ma-YEY ka-YU-ti.
Give me the key to my cabin.

Сколько мы здесь стоим?
SKOL'-kə mi zd'es' sta-YIM?
How long do we stay here?

Когда отходит пароход?
kag-DA at-ḤO-d'it pə-ra-ḤOT?
When does the boat sail?

Можно пройти на верхнюю палубу?
MOZH-nə pray-T'I na V'ERḤ-n'i-yu PA-lu-bu?
Are passengers permitted on the upper deck?

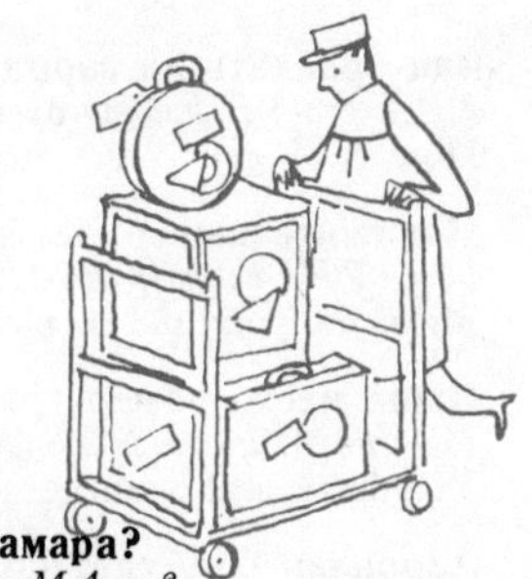

Хочу пройти на верхнюю палубу.
ḥa-CHU pray-T'I na V'ERḤ-n'i-yu PA-lu-bu.
I want to go to the upper deck.

Можно взять этот стул?
MOZH-nə VZ'AT' E-tət STUL?
May I take this chair?

Когда мы будем в Сталинграде?
kag-DA mɨ BU-d'im fstə-l'in-GRA-d'i?
When will we be in Stalingrad?

Как называется это место?
KAK nə-zɨ-VA-yit-sə E-tə M'E-stə?
What is the name of this place?

Это Самара?
E-tə sa-MA-rə?
Is this Samara?

Когда мы проедем Саратов?
kag-DA mɨ pra-YE-d'im sa-RA-təf?
At what time will we pass Saratov?

Пароход опаздывает?
pə-ra-ḤOT a-PAZ-dɨ-və-yit?
Is our boat late?

Где расписание?
gd'e rəs-p'i-SAN'-yə?
Where is the timetable?

Смотрите путеводитель по Волге.
sma-TR'I-t'i pu-t'i-va-D'I-t'il' pa VOL-g'i.
See Volga itinerary.

PLANE TRAVEL

Есть-ли аэроплан на Ленинград?
YEST'-l'i ay-ra-PLAN nə l'i-n'in-GRAT?
Is there a plane for Leningrad?

В котором часу улетает?
fka-TOR-əm chi-SU u-l'i-TA-yit?
What time does it leave?

Сколько стоит билет?
SKOL'-kə STOY-it b'i-L'ET?
What is the fare?

Сколько времени займёт полёт?
SKOL'-kə VR'E-m'i-n'i zay-M'OT pa-L'OT?
How long is the flight?

Дайте пожалуйста место у окна.
DAY-t'i pa-ZHA-lə-stə M'E-stə u ak-NA.
A window seat, please.

Будет-ли обед в этом полёте?
BU-d'it-l'i a-B'ET vE-təm pa-L'O-t'i?
Will lunch be served on this flight?

Сколько весит мой багаж?
SKOL'-kə V'E-s'it moy ba-GASH?
How much does my baggage weigh?

Ваш багаж весит пять фунтов сверх нормы.
vash ba-GASH V'E-s'it P'AT' FUN-təf sv'erḥ NOR-mɨ.
Your baggage is five pounds overweight.

Как проехать на аэродром?
KAK pra-YE ḥət' nə ay-ra-DROM?
How do I get to the airport?

Покажите ваш билет пожалуйста.
pə-ka-ZHɨ-t'i vash b'i-L'ET pa-ZHA-lə-stə.
Show me your ticket, please.

Ваше место номер тридцать.
VA-shə M'E-stə NO-m'ir TR'IT-sət'.
You have seat number 30.

Аэроплан прибудет по расписанию?
ay-ra-PLAN pr'i-BU-d'it pə rəs-p'i-SAN'-yu?
Will the plane arrive on schedule?

По расписанию мы должны быть в Ленинграде через час.
pə-rəs-p'i-SAN'-yu mɨ dalzh-Nɨ bɨt' vl'i-n'in-GRA-d'i chi-r'is-CHAS.
We are scheduled to arrive in Leningrad in one hour.

ALL ABOARD

Это Ярославский вокзал?
E-tə yi-ra-SLAF-sk'iy vag-ZAL?
Is this the Yaroslavsky station?

Позовите носильщика.
pə-za-V'I-t'i na-S'IL'-sh'chi-kə.
Call a porter.

Носильщик!
na-S'IL'-sh'-chik!
Porter!

Снимите эти вещи.
sn'i-M'I-t'i E-t'i V'ESH'-chi.
Take these things down.

Здесь не все вещи.
zd'es' n'i-FS'E V'ESH'-chi.
Not all the things are here.

Поставьте багаж сюда.
pa-STAF'-t'i ba-GASH su-DA.
Put my baggage here.

Когда отходит поезд в Загорск?
kag-DA at-ḤO-d'it POY-ist vza-GORSK?
When does the train for Zagorsk leave?

Это скорый поезд?
E-tə SKO-rəy POY-ist?
Is it a fast train?

Это беспересадочный поезд?
E-tə b'is-p'i-r'i-SA-dəch-nɨy POY-ist?
Is it a through train?

Есть-ли в этом поезде вагон-ресторан?
YES'T-l'i v-E-təm POY-iz-d'i va-GON r'i-sta-RAN?
Is there a dining-car on this train?

Где касса?
GD'E KAS-sə?
Where is the ticket window?

Дайте мне билет первого класса.
DAY-t'i mn'e b'i-L'ET P'ER-və-və KLAS-sə.
Give me a first class ticket.

Билет второго класса.
b'i-L'ET fta-RO-və KLAS-sə.
A second class ticket.

Хочу взять билет в Ленинград.
ḥa-CHU VZ'AT' b'i-L'ET vl'i-n'in-GRAT.
I want to take a ticket for Leningrad.

Хочу получить место в спальном вагоне.
ḥa-CHU pə-lu-CHIT' M'E-stə f-SPAL'-nəm va-GO-n'i.
I want to have a berth in a sleeping car.

Сколько стоит спальное место?
SKOL'-kə STOY-it SPAL'nə-yə M'E-stə?
What is the charge for a sleeping berth?

Есть-ли в этом поезде спальный вагон?
YES'T'-l'i v-E-təm POY-iz-d'i SPAL'-nɨy va-GON?
Is there a sleeping car in this train?

Я хочу это сдать в багаж.
ya ḥa-CHU E-tə ZDAT' vba-GASH.
I want these registered.

Сколько мне платить за излишек багажа?
SKOL'kə mn'e pla-T'IT' za iz-L'I-shɨk bə-ga-ZHA?
How much must I pay for excess baggage?

Когда поезд отходит?
kag-DA POY-ist at-ḤO-d'it?
When will the train leave?

Снесите это в камеру хранения.
sn'i-S'I-t'i E-tə f KA-m'i-ru ḥra-N'EN'-yə.
Put these in the baggage room.

Какой номер моего вагона?
ka-KOY NO-m'ir mə-yi-VO va-GO-nə?
What is the number of my car?

Какой номер моего места?
ka-KOY NO-m'ir mə-yi-VO M'E-stə?
What is the number of my berth?

С какой платформы отходит поезд в Ленинград?
ska-KOY plat-FOR-mɨ at-ḤO-d'it POY-ist vl'i-n'in-GRAT?
From which platform will the train leave for Leningrad?

Мне нужен вагон для (не)курящих.
mn'e NU-zhɨn va-GON dl'ə (n'i)ku-R'ASH'-chiḥ.
I want a (non-)smoker.

Поставьте это в мое купэ.
pa-STAF'-t'i E-tə v-ma-YO ku-PE.
Put these in my compartment.

Возьмите этот багаж.
vaz'-M'I-t'i E-tət ba-GASH.
Take this baggage, please.

Несите осторожно.
n'i-S'I-t'i a-sta-ROZH-nə.
Handle it carefully.

Поставьте эти вещи в мой вагон.
pa-STAF'-t'i E-t'i V'ESH'-chi vmoy va-GON.
Put these things into my car.

Когда мы прибудем?
kag-DA mɨ pr'i-BU-d'im?
What time shall we arrive?

Извините, это мое место.
iz-v'i-N'I-t'i, E-tə ma-YO M'E-stə.
Excuse me, this is my seat.

Это купе для курящих?
E-tə ku-PE dl'ə-ku-R'ASH'-chih?
Is this a smoking compartment?

Мне нужно постельное бельё.
mn'e NUZH-nə pa-ST'EL'-nə-yə b'il'-YO.
I want to have bedding.

Приготовьте постель.
pr'i-ga-TOF'-t'i pa-ST'EL'.
Fix up my bed for me, please.

Пожалуйста, принесите чаю.
pa-ZHA-lə-stə pr'i-n'i-S'I-t'i CHA-yu.
Please get me some tea.

Как называется это место?
kak nə-zɨ-VA-yit-sə E-tə M'E-stə?
What is the name of this place?

Сколько мы здесь стоим?
SKOL'-kə mɨ z'd'es' sta-YIM?
How long do we stop here?

Много остановок будет по дороге?
MNO-gə a-sta-NO-vək BU-d'it pə da-RO-g'i?
Are there many stops on the road?

Успею сойти?
u-SP'E-yu say-T'I?
Have I time to get out?

Какая ближайшая большая станция?
ka-KA-yə bl'i-ZHAY-shə-yə bal'-SHA-yə STANTsɨ-yə?
What is the next big stop?

Что это за фабрика?
SHTO E-tə za FA-br'i-kə?
What factory is that?

Что здесь сеют?
SHTO z'd'es' S'E-yut?
What do they cultivate here?

Где пересадка?
gd'e p'i-r'i-SAT-kə?
Where shall we have to change?

Когда мы будем в Минске?
kag-DA mɨ BU-d'im vM'IN-sk'i?
When shall we be at Minsk?

Можно получить немного кипячёной воды?
MOZH-nə pə-lu-CHIT' n'im-NO-gə k'i-p'i-CHO-nəy va-Dɨ?
May I have some boiled water?

Где уборная?
GD'E u-BOR-nə-yə?
Where is the toilet?

Дайте, пожалуйста, подушку.
DAY-t'i, pa-ZHA-lə-stə, pa-DUSH-ku.
Will you get me a pillow, please.

Закройте, пожалуйста, окно.
za-KROY-t'i, pa-ZHA-lə-stə, ak-NO.
Please close the window.

Покажите ваш билет.
pə-ka-ZHɨ-t'i vash bi-L'ET.
Show me your ticket, please.

Ваш билет на этот поезд не годится.
vash bi-L'ET na E-tət POY-ist n'i-ga-D'IT-sə.
Your ticket is not good for this train.

Вы не на тот поезд сели.
vɨ n'i na TOT POY-ist S'E-l'i.
You are on the wrong train.

Как мне попасть на поезд в Минск?
KAK mn'e pa-PAS'T' na POY-ist vM'INSK?
How am I to get to the Minsk train?

Где мне слезть?
gd'e mn'e SL'ES'T'?
Where do I get out?

На какой станции?
nə-ka-KOY STANTsɨy?
At what station?

Пожалуйста, откройте окно.
pa-ZHA-lə-stə at-KROY-t'i ak-NO.
Please open the window.

Где проводник?
GD'E prə-vad-N'IK?
Where is the porter?

Я хочу нижнее спальное место.
ya ḥa-CHU N'IZH-n'i-yə SPAL'-nə-yə M'E-stə.
I want to have a lower sleeping berth.

Это мое купе?
E-tə ma-YO ku-PE?
Is this my compartment?

Это мое место?
E-tə ma-YO M'E-stə?
Is this my berth?

GOING THROUGH CUSTOMS

Где таможня?
gd'e ta-MOZH-n'ə?
Where is the Customs House?

Где осматривают багаж?
gd'e a-SMA-tr'i-və-yut ba-GASH?
Where do they examine the baggage?

Будете осматривать мой багаж?
BU-d'i-t'i a-SMA-tr'i-vət' moy ba-GASH?
Will you examine my baggage?

Что у вас подлежит оплате?
SHTO u-VAS pəd-l'i-ZHɨT a-PLA-t'i?
Have you anything to declare?

У меня нет инчего подлежащего оплате.
u-m'i-N'A N'ET n'i-chi-VO pəd-l'i-ZHASH'-chi-və a-PLA-t'i.
I have nothing to declare.

Да, у меня есть.
DA, u m'i-N'A YEST'.
Yes, I have...

Вот мой багаж.
VOT moy ba-GASH.
That is my baggage.

Нужно ли открыть этот чемодан?
NUZH-nə-l'i at-KRɨT' E-tət chi-ma-DAN?
Must I open this trunk?

За это взимается пошлина?
za E-tə vz'i-MA-yit-sə POSH-l'i-nə?
Is this dutiable?

Это для собственного потребления.
E-tə dl'a SOPST'-v'i-nə-və pə-tr'i-BL'EN'-yə.
These articles are for my own use.

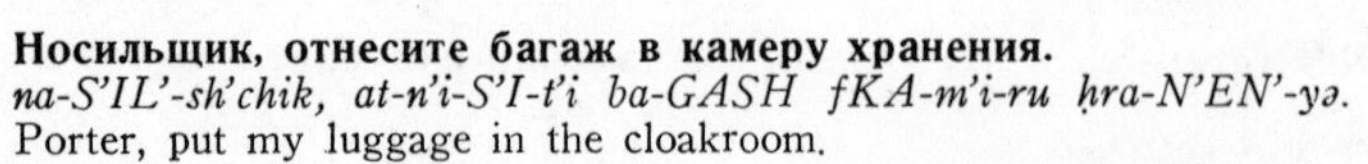

Носильщик, отнесите багаж в камеру хранения.
na-S'IL'-sh'chik, at-n'i-S'I-t'i ba-GASH fKA-m'i-ru ḥra-N'EN'-yə.
Porter, put my luggage in the cloakroom.

Носильщик!
na-S'IL'-sh'chik!
Porter!

Вот мой багаж.
VOT moy ba-GASH.
Here is my baggage.

Несите осторожно.
n'i-S'I-t'i ə-sta-ROZH-nə.
Handle them carefully.

Не ставьте на землю.
n'i-STAF'-t'i na Z'EM-l'u.
Do not put them on the ground.

Снесите это в такси.
sn'i-S'I-t'i E-tə ftak-S'I.
Take this bag to a taxi.

Позовите такси.
pə-za-V'I-t'i tak-S'I.
Call a taxi.

Покажите мне как пройти.
pə-ka-ZHɨ-t'i mn'e kak pray-T'I.
Show me how to get there.

Я возьму эти вещи с собой.
ya vaz'-MU E-t'i V'ESH'-chi s sa-BOY.
I will take these packages with me.

Поезжайте в гостиницу „Метрополь".
pə-yizh'-ZHAY-t'i vga-ST'I-n'itsu m'i-tra-POL'.
Take me to the Metropole hotel.

Сколько вам следует?
SKOL'-kə vam SL'E-du-yit?
How much do I owe you?

Везите меня в Интурист.
v'i-Z'I-t'i m'i-N'A vin-tu-R'IST.
Take me to the Intourist Office.

Я американский турист.
ya a-m'i-r'i-KAN-sk'iy tu-R'IST.
I am an American tourist.

Я английский турист.
ya an-GL'IY-sk'iy tu-R'IST.
I am an English tourist.

Мне нужен носильщик.
mn'e NU-zhɨn na-S'IL'-sh'chik.
I want a porter.

Это не мои вещи.
E-tə n'i-ma-YI V'ESH'-chi.
These are not mine.

Подождите немного.
pə-dazh-D'I-t'i n'im-NO-gə.
Wait a bit.

Снимите этот багаж.
sn'i-M'I-t'i E-tət ba-GASH.
Get this baggage down.

Вот мой чемодан на полке над дверью.
VOT moy chi-ma-DAN na POL-k'i nad D'V'ER'-yu.
There is my trunk, above the door, on the shelf.

Там остался ещё один чемодан.
tam a-STAL-sə yish'-CHO a-D'IN chɨ-ma-DAN.
There is still one trunk up there.

Возьмите это.
vaz'-M'I-t'i E-tə.
Take this.

Сколько времени будем ехать до гостиницы?
SKOL'-kə VR'E-m'i-n'i BU-d'im YE-ḥət' də ga-ST'I-n'i-tsɨ?
How long will it take to the hotel?

Сколько возьмёте?
SKOL'-kə vaz'-M'O-t'i?
How much will you charge?

Положите багаж сюда.
pə-la-ZHɨ-t'i ba-GASH su-DA.
Put my baggage here.

Хочу сесть сюда.
ḥa-CHU S'ES'T' su-DA.
I want to sit here.

STREETCAR AND BUS

Куда идёт этот трамвай (автобус)?
ku-DA i-D'OT E-tət tram-VAY (af-TO-bus)?
Where does this streetcar (bus) go?

Где конечная станция этой линии?
GD'E ka-N'ECH-nə-yə STANTsɨ-yə E-təy L'I-n'i-i?
Where is the last stop of the line?

Автобус № 4 идёт от площади Свердлова до Серебряного Бора.
af-TO-bus NO-m'ir chi-Tɨ-r'i i-D'OT at PLOSH'-chi-d'i sv'ird-LO-və də-s'i-R'E-br'i-nə-və BO-rə.
The No. 4 bus route begins at Sverdlov Square and ends at Silver Wood.

Я хочу проехать в Большой Театр.
ya ḥa-CHU pra-YE-ḥət' vbal'-SHOY t'i-AT-r.
I want to go to the Bolshoi Theater.

Какой автобус идёт в центр города.
ka-KOY af-TO-bus i-D'OT fTSENT-r GOR-ə-də?
What bus do we take to get to the center of the city?

Сколько стоит билет?
SKOL'-kə STOY-it b'i-L'ET?
What is the fare?

Когда начинается трамвайное движение?
kag-DA nə-chi-NA-yit-sə tram-VAY-nə-yə dv'i-ZHEN'-yə?
When do the cars start running?

В шесть часов утра и до двенадцать часов ночи.
fSHEST' chi-SOF u-TRA i də dv'i-NAT-sət' chi-SOF NO-chi.
At 6 o'clock in the morning and until 12 o'clock midnight.

Вход только с задней площадки.
f-ḤOT TOL'-kə zZAD-n'iy plash'-CHAT-k'i.
Remember to enter only through the rear door.

Выход только с передней площадки.
Vɨ-ḥət TOL'kə sp'i-R'ED'-n'iy plash'-CHAT-k'i.
Always get off through the front door.

На ходу не входить.
nə-ḥa-DU n'if-ḥa-D'IT'.
Don't jump on the car while it is moving.

Не высовывайтесь.
n'i-vɨ-SO-vɨ-vəy-t'is.
Don't lean out.

Не плевать.
n'i pl'i-VAT'.
No spitting.

Место кондуктора.
M'E-stə kan-DUK-tə-rə.
Conductor's seat.

Где можно узнать о вещах, потерянных в трамвае?
GD'E MOZH-nə uz-NAT' a v'ish'-CHAḤ pa-T'E-r'i-nɨḥ ftram-VA-yə?
What is the address of the Lost and Found Office?

Всё что кондуктор находит остаётся на хранении на конечной станции в течение одного дня.
FS'O shtə kan-DUK-tər na-ḤO-d'it a-sta-YOT-sə nə-ḥra-N'EN'-yi nə-ka-N'ECH-nəy STANTsɨ-i ft'i-CHEN'-yi ad-na-VO DN'A.
Anything found by the conductor remains at the office of the terminus station the first day.

После этого срока надо обратиться в контору.
PO-sl'i E-tə-və SRO-kə NA-də a-bra-T'IT-sə fkan-TO-ru.
If you inquire later, you must apply at the office.

Вы здесь сходите?
vɨ Z'D'ES' s-ḤO-d'i-t'i?
Do you get off here?

Пропустите, пожалуйста.
prə-pu-S'T'I-t'i, pa-ZHA-lə-stə.
Please let me pass.

Я схожу.
ya s-ḥa-ZHU.
I am getting off.

Я еду в Сокольники.
ya YE-du fsa-KOL'-n'i-k'i.
I'm going to Sokolniki Park.

Где пересадка?
GD'E p'i-r'i-SAT-ka?
Where should I change?

Сколько отсюда езды до финского вокзала?
SKOL'-kə at-SU-də yiz-DƗ da F'IN-skə-və vag-ZA-lə?
How much does it take to get to the Finnish station?

Мы проедем Красную площадь?
mɨ pra-YE-d'im KRAS-nu-yu PLOSH'-chit'?
Will we pass Red Square?

Что это?
SHTO E-tə?
What is that?

Садитесь, пожалуйста.
sa-D'I-t'is, pa-ZHA-lə-stə.
Sit down, please.

Дайте мне сесть.
DAY-t'i mn'e S'ES'T'.
Let me sit down.

Вы сходите, да?
vɨ s-ḤO-d'i-t'i, DA?
You are getting off, aren't you?

Как проехать на финский вокзал?
KAK pra-YE-ḥət' na F'IN-sk'iy vag-ZAL?
How do I get to the Finnish station?

AT THE HOTEL

Я заказал по телеграфу одну комнату.
ya zə-ka-ZAL pə t'i-l'i-GRA-fu ad-NU KOM-nə-tu.
I have reserved one room by telegraph.

. . . Две комнаты . . .
. . . d'v'e KOM-nə-tɨ . . .
. . . two rooms . . .

Мне нужна комната.
mn'e nuzh-NA KOM-nə-tə.
I want to reserve a room.

Номер из двух комнат.
NO-m'ir iz DVUḤ KOM-nət.
Two connecting rooms.

Мне нужна большая комната.
mn'e nuzh-NA bal'-SHA-yə KOM-nə-tə.
I require a large room.

Мне нужен номер с ванной.
mn'e NU-zhɨn NO-m'ir sVAN-nəy.
I want a room with a private bath.

Этот номер слишком мал.
E-tət NO-m'ir SL'ISH-kəm MAL.
This room is too small.

Покажите другой номер.
po-ka-ZHƗ-t'i dru-GOY NO-m'ir.
Show me another room.

Номер с двумя кроватями.
NO-m'ir z dvu-M'A kra-VA-t'i-m'i.
A room with two beds.

Мне нужен номер поменьше.
mn'e NU-zhɨn NO-m'ir pa-M'EN'-shə.
A smaller room will suit me.

Сколько стоит в день (неделю, месяц)?
SKOL'-kə STOY-it vD'EN' (vn'i-D'E-l'u, vM'E-s'its)?
What is the charge per day (week, month)?

Это включает услуги?
E-tə fkl'u-CHA-yit u-SLU-g'i?
Does it include service?

... Эти номера.
... E-t'i nə-m'i-RA.
... these rooms.

Я возьму этот номер.
ya vaz-MU E-tət NO-m'ir.
I will take this room.

Где лифт?
gd'e L'IFT?
Where is the elevator?

Пожалуйста, пришлите багаж.
pa-ZHA-lə-stə pr'ish-L'I-t'i ba-GASH.
Please have my baggage sent up.

Поставьте багаж в мой номер.
pa-STAF'-t'i ba-GASH v moy NO-m'ir.
Put this baggage into my room.

Какой номер моей комнаты?
ka-KOY NO-m'ir ma-YEY KOM-nə-tɨ?
What is the number of my room?

Я не буду столоваться в гостинице.
ya n'i-BU-du stə-la-VAT-sə vga-ST'I-n'it-sɨ.
I will eat out.

Я буду завтракать в гостинице.
ya BU-du ZAF-trə-kət' vga-ST'I-nit-sɨ.
I will take breakfast at the hotel.

Я буду обедать.
ya BU-du a-B'E-dət'.
I will take dinner.

Я буду ужинать.
ya BU-du U-zhɨ-nət'.
I will take supper.

Подайте завтрак ко мне в номер.
pa-DAY-t'i ZAF-trək kam-N'E vNO-m'ir.
I will have breakfast served in my room.

Можно получить завтрак в десять часов?
MOZH-nə pə-lu-CHIT' ZAF-trək vD'E-s'it' chi-SOF?
Can I get breakfast at 10 o'clock?

Где ресторан?
gd'e r'i-sta-RAN?
Where is the restaurant?

Я хочу поговорить с заведующим.
ya ḥa-CHU pə-gə-va-R'IT' zza-V'E-du-jush'-chim.
I want to speak to the manager.

У кого можно оставить ценные бумаги на хранение?
u-ka-VO MOZH-nə a-STA-v'it' TSEN-nɨ-yə bu-MA-g'i nə-ḥra-N'EN-yə.
Where can I deposit my valuable papers?

Часы, кольцо.
chi-SƗ, kal't-SO.
Watch, ring.

Могу я сдать это вам?
ma-GU ya ZDAT' E-tə vam?
Can I put this in your charge?

Вы мне дадите квитанцию?
vi mn'e da-D'I-t'i kv'i-TANTsɨ-yu?
Will you give me a receipt for this?

Вот мой паспорт.
VOT moy PAS-pərt.
Here is my passport.

Дайте мне ключ от номера.
DAY-t'i mn'e KL'UCH at NO-m'i-rə.
Give me the key to my room.

Почистите мне башмаки.
pa-CHI-st'i-t'i mn'e bəsh-ma-K'I.
Will you polish my boots?

Почистите мне одежду (пальто).
pa-CHI-st'i-t'i mn'e a-D'EZH-du (pal'-TO).
Brush my clothes (overcoat).

Погладьте одежду.
pa-GLAT'-t'i a-D'EZH-du.
Press my clothes.

Когда пулучу это обратно?
kag-DA pə-lu-CHU E-tə a-BRAT-nə?
When can I have them back?

Мне это нужно через три дня.
mn'e E-tə NUZH-nə chi-r'is TR'I DN'A.
I must have them in three days.

Мне это нужно завтра утром.
mn'e E-tə NUZH-nə ZAF-trə U-trəm.
I want them tomorrow morning.

Хочу отдать бельё в стирку.
ḥa-CHU ad-DAT' b'il'-YO f ST'IR-ku.
I want my linen washed.

Где ванная комната?
gd'e VAN-nə-yə KOM-nə-tə?
Where is the bathroom?

Принесите горячей воды.
pr'i-n'i-S'I-t'i ga-R'A-chəy va-DƗ.
Bring me hot water.

Приготовьте мне тёплую ванну.
pr'i-ga-TOF'-t'i mn'e T'O-plu-yu VAN-nu.
I want a warm bath.

Принесите мыло и полотенце.
pr'i-n'i-S'I-t'i MƗ-lə i pə-la-T'ENTsə.
Bring me some soap and towels.

Принесите воды для питья.
pr'i-n'i-S'I-t'i va-DƗ dl'a p'it'-YA.
Get me some drinking water.

Поставьте здесь (там).
pa-STAF'-t'i Z'D'ES' (TAM).
Put it here (there).

Дайте другое одеяло.
DAY-t'i dru-GOY-ə a'-d'i-YA-lə.
Give me another blanket.

Кровать очень жесткая.
kra-VAT' O-chin ZHOST-kə-yə.
My bed is hard.

Дайте иголку с ниткой.
DAY-t'i i-GOL-ku sN'IT-kəy.
Give me a needle and thread.

Дайте белую нитку.
DAY-t'i B'E-lu-yu N'IT-ku.
Give me white thread.

Дайте чёрную нитку.
DAY-t'i CHOR-nu-yu N'IT-ku.
Give me black thread.

Принесите бумагу, чернила и перо.
pr'i-n'i-S'I-t'i bu-MA-gu, chir-N'I-lə i p'i-RO.
Bring me paper, ink, and pen.

Мне нужны марки на эти письма.
mn'e nuzh-NI MAR-k'i na E-t'i P'IS'mə.
I need stamps for these letters.

Отправьте эти письма.
at-PRAF'-t'i E-t'i P'IS'-mə.
Mail these letters.

Где парикмахер?
gd'e pə-r'ik-MA-h'ir?
Where is the hairdresser?

Пришлите парикмахера в мой номер.
pr'ish-L'I-t'i pə-r'ik-MA-h'i-rə v moy NO-m'ir.
Send the barber to my room.

Принесите мне чай (кофе, шоколад).
pr'i-n'i-S'I-t'i mn'e CHAY (KO-f'i, shə-ka-LAT).
Bring me tea (coffee, chocolate).

Где ресторан?
GD'E r'i-sta-RAN?
Where is the restaurant?

Разбудите меня в восемь часов.
rəz-bu-D'I-t'i m'i-N'A vVO-s'im' chi-SOF.
Call me at 8 o'clock.

Я буду есть у себя в комнате.
ya BU-du YES'T' u-s'i-B'A fKOM-nə-t'i.
I will eat in my room.

Как ваша фамилия?
kak VA-shə fa-M'IL'-yə?
What is your name?

Принесите меню.
pr'i-n'i-S'I-t'i m'i-N'U.
Bring me the menu.

Мне не здоровится.
mn'e n'iz-da-RO-v'it-sə.
I don't feel well.

Пошлите за доктором.
pash-L'I-t'i za-DOK-tə-rəm.
Send for a doctor.

Пошлите в аптеку.
pash-L'I-t'i vap-T'E-ku.
Send to the pharmacy.

Пусть сделают это лекарство.
pus't' ZD'E-lə-yut E-tə l'i-KARST-və.
Get this prescription made up.

Не беспокойтесь.
n'i-b'i-spa-KOY-t'is.
Don't trouble yourself.

Нет ли мне писем?
N'ET-l'i-mn'e P'I-s'im?
Have you any mail for me?

Никто меня не спрашивал?
n'ik-TO m'i-N'A n'i-SPRA-shi-vəl?
Has anyone called me?

Я жду одного гражданина (*masc.*)
ya ZHDU ad-na-VO grəzh-da-N'I-nə.
I am expecting a visitor (*lit.*, citizen).

Я жду одну гражданку (*fem.*).
ya ZHDU ad-NU grazh-DAN-ku.
I am expecting a visitor.

Если кто меня спросит, скажите, что я буду обратно в шесть часов.
YES'-l'i KTO m'i-N'A SPRO-s'it, ska-ZHɨ-t'i shtə ya BU-du a-BRAT-nə fSHES'T' chi-SOF.
If anyone calls for me say that I will be back at 6 o'clock.

Попросите его (её) подождать.
pə-pra-S'I-t'i yi-VO (yi-YO) pə-dazh-DAT'.
Ask him (her) to wait.

Я сейчас буду внизу.
ya s'i-CHAS BU-du vn'i-ZU.
I will be down right away.

Пошлите его (её) наверх.
pash-L'I-t'i yi-VO (yi-YO) na-V'ERḤ.
Send him (her) up.

Он (она) не сказал(а) своего имени?
on (a-NA) n'i-ska-ZAL(a) svə-yi-VO I-m'i-n'i?
Did he (she) give his (her) name?

Он (она) оставил(а) записку?
on (a-NA) a-STA-v'i-l(ə) za-P'I-sku?
Did he (she) leave a note?

В котором часу он (она) приходил(а)?
fka-TOR-əm chi-SU on pr'i-ḥa-D'IL?
At what time did he (she) come?

Я уезжаю сегодня (завтра).
ya u-yizh'-ZH'A-yu s'i-VOD'-n'ə.
I am leaving today (tomorrow).

Поездом.
POY-iz-dəm.
By train.

Дайте счёт, пожалуйста.
DAY-t'i SH'CH'OT, pa-ZHA-lə-stə.
Please have my bill made out.

Здесь ошибка в счёте.
Z'D'ES' a-SHɨP-kə f-SH'CH'O-t'i.
Here is an error in my bill.

Можете вы мне рекомендовать гостиницу?
MO-zhi-t'i vɨ mn'e r'i-kə-m'in-da-VAT' ga-ST'I-n'it-su?
Can you recommend a hotel to me?

Письма на мое имя отправляйте по этому адресу.
P'IS'-mə nə-ma-YO I-m'ə at-prav-L'AY-t'i pa E-tə-mu A-dr'i-su.
Please forward my mail to this address.

Когда отходит поезд на Кавказ?
kag-DA at-ḤO-d'it POY-ist nə kaf-KAS?
When does the train leave for the Caucasus?

Я хочу побывать в Крыму.
ya ḥa-CHU pə-bɨ-VAT' fkrɨ-MU.
I want to visit the Crimea.

Какая лучшая гостиница в этом городе?
ka-KA-yə LUCH-shə-yə ga-ST'I-nit-sə vE-təm GOR-ə-d'i?
Which is the best hotel in this town?

Сколько времени туда ехать?
SKOL'-kə VR'E-m'i-n'i tu-DA YE-ḥət'?
How long does it take to get there?

Покажите на карте где Ялта.
pə-ka-ZHƗ-t'i na KAR-t'i gd'e YAL-tə.
Show me on the map where Yalta is.

Сколько времени нужно ехать от Москвы?
SKOL'-kə VR'E-m'i-n'i NUZH-nə YE-ḥət' at mask-VƗ?
How long does it take to go from Moscow?

Где это место?
GD'E E-tə M'E-stə?
Where is the place?

Хочу получить место в спальном вагоне.
ḥa-CHU pə-lu-CHIT' M'E-stə fSPAL'-nəm va-GO-n'i.
I want to have a berth in a sleeping car.

С какого вокзала мне ехать на Кавказ?
ska-KO-və vag-ZA-lə mn'e YE-ḥət' na kaf-KAS?
From what station must I leave for the Caucasus?

Как лучше проехать на Курский вокзал?
KAK LUCH-shə pra-YE-ḥət' na KUR-sk'iy vag-ZAL?
Which is the best way to the Kursk station?

По дороге в Крым я хочу провести несколько дней в Харькове.
pə da-RO-g'i fKRƗM ya ḥa-CHU prə-v'i-ST'I N'E-skəl'-kə DN'EY fḤAR'-kə-v'i.
On my way to the Crimea I want to spend some days in Kharkov.

Позовите такси.
pə-za-V'I-t'i tak-S'I.
Call a taxi.

Снимите эти вещи.
sn'i-M'I-t'i E-t'i V'ESH'-chi.
Take these things down.

Принесите мой багаж.
pr'i-N'I-s'i-t'i moy ba-GASH.
Will you fetch my baggage?

Одно место вы оставили в номере.
ad-NO M'E-stə vɨ a-STA-v'i-l'i vNO-m'i-r'i.
You have left a piece of luggage in the room.

Принесите скорей.
pr'i-n'i-S'I-t'i ska-R'EY.
Fetch it quickly.

Мне нужно такси.
mn'e NUZH-nə tak-S'I.
I want a taxi.

Такси готово?
tak-S'I ga-TO-və?
Is the taxi ready?

Пожалуйста, поскорее.
pa-ZHA-lə-stə pə-ska-R'EY-ə.
Hurry, please.

Лучше быть раньше.
LUCH-shə bɨt' RAN'-shə.
I want to be ahead of time.

Несите этот багаж осторожно.
n'i-S'I-t'i E-tət ba-GASH a-sta-ROZH-nə.
Handle this baggage carefully.

Везите меня на Курский вокзал.
v'i-Z'I-t'i m'i-N'A na KUR-sk'iy vag-ZAL.
Take me to Kursk station.

Скажите шофёру на какой вокзал ехать.
ska-ZHɨ-t'i sha-F'OR-u nə-ka-KOY vag-ZAL YE-ḥət'.
Tell the chauffeur the name of the station.

Поезжайте тише.
pə-yizh'-ZH'AY-t'i T'I-shə.
Do not go so fast.

Поезжайте скорей.
pə-yizh'-ZH'AY-t'i ska-R'EY.
Go more quickly.

MAKING AN APPOINTMENT

Вы свободны сегодня вечером (сегодня днём)?
vɨ sva-BOD-nɨ s'i-VOD'-n'ə V'E-chi-rəm (s'i-VOD'-n'ə DN'OM)?
Do you happen to be free this evening (this afternoon)?

Когда можно вас видеть?
kag-DA MOZH-nə vas V'I-d'it'?
At what time can I see you?

Дайте мне знать, когда освободитесь.
DAY-t'i mn'e ZNAT' kag-DA a-svə-ba-D'I-t'is.
Let me know when you're free.

Я зайду к семи часам.
ya zay-DU k-s'i-M'I chi-SAM.
I'll come around at 7 o'clock.

Я буду здесь около девяти часов.
ya BU-du Z'D'ES' O-kə-lə d'i-v'i-T'I chi-SOF.
I shall be here at 9 o'clock.

Не можете ли прийти в восемь?
n'i MO-zhɨ-t'i-l'i pr'i-T'I vVO-s'im'?
I wish you could come at 8.

Дайте мне ваш адрес.
DAY-t'i mn'e vash A-dr'is.
Give me your address.

Когда мне прийти?
kag-DA mn'e pr'i-T'I?
When shall I call?

DINING OUT

Где хороший ресторан?
GD'E ḥa-RO-shɨy r'i-sta-RAN?
Where is a good restaurant?

Пожалуйста, столик на двоих.
pa-ZHA-lə-stə, STO-l'ik na dva-YIḤ.
I want a table for two.

Пожалуйста, другой стол.
pa-ZHA-lə-stə, dru-GOY STOL.
I want another table.

Пожалуйста, стол около окна.
pa-ZHA-lə-stə, STOL O-kə-lə ak-NA.
I want the table at the window.

Здесь сквозняк.
Z'D'ES' skvaz'-N'AK.
There is a draft here.

Принесите меню.
pr'i-n'i-S'I-t'i m'i-N'U.
Bring me the menu.

Дайте завтрак.
DAY-t'i ZAF-trək.
Serve breakfast.

Дайте обед.
DAY-t'i a-B'ET.
Serve dinner.

Дайте ужин.
DAY-t'i U-zhɨn.
Serve supper.

Принесите карту вин.
pr'i-n'i-S'I-t'i KAR-tu V'IN.
Bring me the wine list.

Принесите бутылку (полбутылки).
pr'i-n'i-S'I-t'i bu-TƗL-ku. (pəl-bu-TƗL-k'i).
Bring me a bottle (a half bottle).

Принесите минеральной воды.
pr'i-n'i-S'I-t'i m'i-n'i-RAL'-nəy va-DƗ.
Bring me some mineral water.

Принесите чайник крепкого чаю.
pr'i-n'i-S'I-t'i CHAY-n'ik KR'EP-kə-və CHA-yu.
Bring me a pot of strong tea.

Принесите чашку черного кофе.
pr'i-n'i-S'I-t'i CHASH-ku CHOR-nə-və KO-f'i.
I want a cup of black coffee.

Пожалуйста, передайте стакан.
pa-ZHA-lə-stə p'i-r'i-DAY-t'i sta-KAN.
Kindly pass the glass.

Принесите острый нож.
pr'i-n'i-S'I-ti O-strɨy NOSH.
Bring me a sharp knife.

Передайте хлеб.
p'i-r'i-DAY-t'i ḤL'EP.
Pass me some bread.

Дайте горячей воды.
DAY-t'i ga-R'A-chəy va-DƗ.
Bring me some hot water.

Дайте воды со льдом.
DAY-t'i va-DƗ sal'-DOM.
Bring me some ice water.

Принесите бутылку со льда.
pr'i-n'i-S'I-t'i bu-TƗL-ku sal'-DA.
Bring me a bottle off the ice.

Вино тёплое, поставьте на лёд.
v'i-NO T'O-plə-yə, pa-STAF'-t'i na L'OT.
This wine is warm; put it on the ice.

Уберите.
u-b'i-R'I-t'i.
Take this away.

Я это не заказывал.
ya E-tə n'i-zə-KA-zɨ-vəl.
I did not order this.

Я заказал другое блюдо.
ya za-ka-ZAL dru-GOY-ə BL'U-də.
I ordered a different dish.

Это холодное.
E-tə ḥa-LOD-nə-yə.
This is cold.

Это не свежее.
E-tə n'i-SV'E-zhɨ-yə.
This is not fresh.

Пережарено.
p'i-r'i-ZHA-r'i-nə.
This is overdone.

Недожарено.
n'i-da-ZHA-r'i-nə.
This is underdone.

Слишком жестко.
SL'ISH-kəm ZHOST-kə.
This is too tough.

Слишком сладко.
SL'ISH-kəm SLAT-kə.
This is too sweet.

Слишком кисло.
SL'ISH-kom K'I-slə.
This is too sour.

Суп пересолен.
SUP p'i-r'i-SO-l'in.
There is too much salt in the soup.

Суп недосолен.
SUP n'i-da-SO-l'in.
There is too little salt in the soup.

Подождите минуту.
pə-dazh-D'I-t'i m'i-NU-tu.
Wait a moment.

Позовите старшего официанта.
pə-za-V'I-t'i STAR-shə-və a-f'itsɨ-AN-tə.
Call the headwaiter.

Не хотите ли кофе?
n'i-ḥa-T'I-t'i-l'i KO-f'i?
Let me help you to a cup of coffee.

Нет, спасибо.
N'ET, spa-S'I-bə.
No, thank you.

Я кончил.
ya KON'-chil.
I have finished.

Дайте мне счёт.
DAY-t'i mn'e SH'CH'OT.
Give me the bill.

Это неправильно.
E-to n'i-PRA-v'il'-nə.
This is not correct.

Правильно.
PRA-v'il'-nə.
All right.

У вас есть сдачи?
u VAS yes't' ZDA-chi?
Have you got change?

Спасибо, суп не нужен.
spa-S'I-bə, sup n'i-NU-zhɨn.
Thank you, no soup.

Подайте пожалуйста поскорей.
pa-DAY-t'i pa-ZHA-lə-stə pə-ska-R'EY.
Serve it more quickly.

Когда здесь обеды?
kag-DA z'd'es' a-B'E-dɨ?
At what time do you serve dinners?

Когда здесь ужины?
kag-DA z'd'es' U-zhɨ-nɨ?
At what time do you serve suppers?

Когда здесь завтраки?
kag-DA z'd'es' ZAF-trə-k'i?
At what time do you serve breakfasts?

Дайте клубники.
DAY-t'i klub-N'I-k'i.
Give me some (garden) strawberries.

Ещё, пожалуйста.
yish'-CHO, pa-ZHA-lə-stə.
Give me some more, please.

Сколько стоит?
SKOL'-kə STOY-it?
How much is it?

Дайте спички.
DAY-t'i SP'ICH-k'i.
Give me some matches.

FOODS

яблоки
YA-blə-k'i
apples

хлеб
ḤL'EP
bread

торт
TORT
cake

вишни
V'ISH-n'i
cherries

кофе
KO-f'i
coffee

фасоль
fa-SOL'
beans

масло
MA-slə
butter

икра
i-KRA
caviar

курица
KU-r'i-tsə
chicken

виноград
v'i-na-GRAT
grapes

борщ
BORSH'ch
beet soup

щи
SH'CHI
cabbage soup

сыр
SɨR
cheese

шоколад
shə-ka-LAT
chocolate

каша
KA-shə
groats

ветчина
v'it-chi-NA
ham

яйца
YAYTsə
eggs

мороженое
ma-RO-zhɨ-nə-yə
ice cream

салат
sa-LAT
lettuce

молоко
mə-la-KO
milk

перец
P'E-r'its
pepper

рис
R'IS
rice

соль
SOL'
salt

суп
SUP
soup

чай
CHAY
tea

сладкое
SLAT-kə-yə
dessert

рыба
Rɨ-bə
fish

квас
KVAS
kvass (a drink)

печёнка
p'i-CHON-kə
liver

горчица
gar-CHITsə
mustard

пирог
p'i-ROK
pie

ростбиф
ROZD'-b'if
roast beef

сандвич
sand-V'ICH
sandwich

бифштекс
b'if-SHTEKS
steak

индейка
in-D'EY-kə
turkey

утка
UT-kə
duck

селедка
s'i-L'OT-kə
herring

лимон
l'i-MON
lemon

мясо
M'A-sə
meat

апельсин
a-p'il'-S'IN
orange

картофель
kar-TO-f'il'
potatoes

салат
sa-LAT
salad

сосиски
sa-S'I-sk'i
sausages

сахар
SA-ḥər
sugar

SIGHTSEEING

Где находится Музей Изящных Искусств?
GD'E na-ḤO-d'it-sə mu-Z'EY i-Z'ASH'-nɨḥ is-KUSTF?
Where is the Museum of Fine Arts?

На какой улице?
nə-ka-KOY U-l'it-sɨ?
What street is it on?

Как туда доехать?
KAK tu-DA da-YE-ḥət'?
How can you get there?

Какой трамвай идёт туда?
ka-KOY tram-VAY i-D'OT tu-DA?
What streetcar goes there?

Какой автобус?
ka-KOY af-TO-bus?
What bus?

В какую сторону?
fka-KU-yu STOR-ə-nu?
In what direction?

Где остановка трамвая (автобуса)?
GD'E a-sta-NOF-kə tram-VA-yə (af-TO-bu-sə)?
Where is the streetcar (bus) stop?

По каким дням он открыт?
pə-ka-K'IM DN'AM on at-KRɨT?
On what days is it open?

От которого часа?
at ka-TOR-ə-və CHA-sə?
From what time?

До которого часа?
də ka-TOR-ə-və CHA-sə?
To what time?

Где касса?
GD'E KAS-sə?
Where do you pay?

Сколько стоит вход?
SKOL'-kə STOY-it fḤOT?
What is the admission?

Где вход?
GD'E fḤOT?
Where is the entrance?

Нужно - ли раздеваться?
NUZH-nə-l'i rəz-d'i-VAT-sə?
Must you take off your things?

Дайте мне номерок.
DAY-t'i mn'e nə-m'i-ROK.
Give me a tag (check), please.

Я хочу получить руководителя.
ya ḥa-CHU pə-lu-CHIT' ru-kə-va-D'I-t'i-l'ə.
I want to get a guide.

Я хочу получить переводчика.
ya ḥa-CHU pə-lu-CHIT' p'i-r'i-VOT'-chi-kə.
I want an interpreter.

Где купить каталог музея?
GD'E ku-P'IT' kə-ta-LOK mu-Z'EY-ə?
Where can you buy the museum catalog?

План музея?
PLAN mu-Z'EY-ə?
A map of the museum?

Хочу купить путеводитель.
ḥa-CHU ku-P'IT' pu-t'i-va-D'I-t'il'.
I want to buy a guidebook.

Когда был основан этот музей?
kag-DA bɨl a-SNO-vən E-tət mu-Z'EY?
When was this museum founded?

Что выставлено на этом этаже?
SHTO Vɨ-stəv-l'i-nə na E-təm i-ta-ZHE?
What is shown on this floor?

Есть-ли скульптура?
YES'T'-l'i skul'p-TU-rə?
Are there any sculptures?

Есть-ли картины?
YES'T'-l'i kar-T'I-nɨ?
Are there any pictures?

Есть-ли документы?
YES'T'-l'i də-ku-M'EN-ti?
Are there any documents?

К какой эпохе это относится?
kka-KOY i-PO-ḥ'i E-tə at-NO-s'it-sə?
What period does this belong to?

Как имя художника?
KAK I-m'ə ḥu-DOZH-n'i-kə?
What is the artist's name?

Имя скульптора?
I-m'ə SKUL'P-tə-rə?
The sculptor's name?

Это современная картина (скульптура, вещь)?
E-tə sə-vr'i-M'EN-nə-yə kar-T'I-nə (skul'p-TU-rə, V'ESHCH)?
Is that a modern picture (piece of sculpture, object)?

К какой школе она относится?
kka-KOY SHKO-l'i a-NA at-NO-s'it-sə?
What school does it belong to?

Это старинная?
E-tə sta-R'IN-nə-yə?
Is this old?

Какого века?
ka-KO-və V'E-kə?
Of what century is it?

Во всех-ли музеях новая экспозиция?
vaf-S'EḤ-l'i mu-Z'EY-əḥ NO-və-yə ik-spa-Z'ITsɨ-yə?
Do they have this new method of exhibition in all museums?

Есть-ли ещё другие залы?
YES'T'-l'i yish'-CH'O dru-G'I-yə ZA-lɨ?
Are there any other (exhibition) rooms?

Есть-ли филиалы этого музея в других городах?
YES'T'-l'i f'i-l'i-A-lɨ E-tə-və mu-Z'EY-ə vdru-G'IX gə-ra-DAḤ?
Are there any branches of this museum in other cities?

Ну, мне пора итти.
NU, MN'E pa-RA i-T'I.
Well, it's time I went.

Хочу купить открытки и альбом музея.
ḥa-CHU ku-P'IT' at-KRɨT-k'i i al'-BOM mu-Z'EY-ə
I want to buy some postcards and an album of the museum.

Где выход?
GD'E Vɨ-ḥət?
Where is the exit?

Когда бывают экскурсии в Кремль
kag-DA bɨ-VA-yut ik-SKUR-s'i-i f KR'EML'?
When are there trips to the Kremlin?

Часто ли бывают туда экскурсии?
CHA-stə-l'i bɨ-VA-yut tu-DA ik-SKUR-s'i-i?
Are there frequent excursions there?

Кто устраивает эти экскурсии?
KTO u-STRA-i-və-it E-t'i ik-SKUR-s'i-i?
Who arranges these excursions?

У кого записаться?
u ka-VO zə-p'i-SAT-sə?
To whom do we give our names?

Я хочу участвовать в этой экскурсии.
YA ḥa-CHU u-CHAST-və-vət' VE-təy ik-SKUR-s'i-i.
I want to go on this excursion.

Могу-ли я получить у вас руководителя (переводчика)?
ma-GU-l'i ya pə-lu-CHIT' u vas ru-kə-va-D'I-t'i-lə (p'i-r'i-VOT'-chi-kə)?
Can I get a guide (interpreter) through you?

Какая плата?
ka-KA-yə PLA-tə?
What must I pay?

Можно-ли осмотреть Кремль?
MOZH-nə-l'i a-sma-TR'ET' KR'EML'?
Can the Kremlin be visited?

Как получить разрешение?
KAK pə-lu-CHIT' rəz-r'i-SHEN'-yə?
How do you get a permit?

Можно-ли снимать?
MOZH-nə-l'i sn'i-MAT'?
Can you take pictures?

Что нельзя снимать?
SHTO n'il'-Z'A sn'i-MAT'?
What mustn't be photographed?

Хочу осмотреть автомобильный завод.
ḥa-CHU a-sma-TR'ET' af-tə-ma-B'IL'-nɨy za-VOD.
I want to visit an automobile factory.

Запишите меня.
zə-p'i-SHƗ-t'i m'i-N'A.
Put my name down, will you?

В котором часу соберётся группа?
fka-TOR-əm chi-SU sə-b'i-R'OT-sə GRU-pə?
At what time does the group meet?

Куда мне притти?
ku-DA mn'e pr'i-T'I?
Where do I have to go?

Куда?
ku-DA?
Where to?

До свидания!
də-sv'i-DAN'-yə!
So long!

SNAPSHOTS FOR REMEMBRANCE

Позвольте мне снять вас.
paz-VOL'-t'i mn'e SN'AT' vas.
Would you mind letting me take your picture?

Продолжайте ваши занятия.
prə-dal-ZHAY-t'i VA-shɨ za-N'A-t'i-yə.
Just continue your work.

Не смотрите в аппарат.
n'i sma-TR'I-t'i və-pa-RAT.
Don't look into the camera.

Повернитесь пожалуйста в эту сторону.
pə-v'ir-N'I-t'is pa-ZHA-lə-stə VE-tu STOR-ə-nu.
Turn this way, please.

Извините за беспокойство.
iz-v'i-N'I-t'i zə b'is-pa-KOYST-və.
Excuse me for having disturbed you.

Мне нужна плёнка.
mn'e nuzh-NA PL'ON-kə.
I need a roll of film.

Есть-ли у вас каталог фотоплёнок?
YEST'-l'i u VAS kə-ta-LOK fo-ta-PL'O-nək?
Do you have a film catalog?

У вас есть цветная плёнка?
u VAS yest' tsv'it-NA-yə PL'ON-kə?
Do you have color film?

Пожалуйста зарядите мне аппарат.
pa-ZHA-lə-stə zə-r'i-D'I-t'i mn'e a-pa-RAT.
Will you load the camera for me, please?

Затвор заел. Поправьте пожалуйста.
za-TVOR za-YEL. pa-PRAF'-t'i pa-ZHA-lə-stə.
The shutter is stuck. Can you fix it?

Почему моя плёнка всегда поцарапана?
pə-chi-MU ma-YA PL'ON-kə fs'ig-DA pət-sa-RA-pə-nə?
Why is my film always scratched?

Думаете-ли вы нужен мне фильтр?
DU-mə-yi-t'i-l'i vɨ NU-zhɨn mn'e F'IL'-tr?
Do you think I should use a filter?

Проявите эту плёнку пожалуйста.
prə-yi-V'I-t'i E-tu PL'ON-ku pa-ZHA-lə-stə.
Please develop this roll.

Сделайте один отпечаток с каждого негатива.
ZD'E-ləy-t'i a-D'IN at-p'i-CHA-tək sKAZH-də-və n'i-ga-T'I-və.
Please make one print of each negative.

Когда они будут готовы?
kag-DA a-N'I BU-dut ga-TO-vɨ?
When will they be ready?

Вы продаёте фотовспышки?
vɨ prə-da-YO-t'i fə-taf-SPɨSH-k'i?
Do you sell flashbulbs?

SHOPPING

Где Универмаг?
GD'E u-n'i-v'ir-MAK?
Where is the department store?

Петровка, дом номер два.
p'i-TROF-kə, DOM NO-m'ir DVA.
On Petrovka No. 2.

Где магазин кустарных изделий?
GD'E mə-ga-Z'IN ku-STAR-nɨḥ iz-D'E-l'iy?
Where is the peasant craft shop?

Леонтьевский переулок, дом семь.
l'i-ONT'-yif-sk'iy p'i-r'i-U-lək, DOM S'EM'.
On Leontievsky No. 7.

Где магазин „Международная Книга"?
GD'E mə-ga-Z'IN m'ezh-du-na-ROD-nə-yə KN'I-gə?
Where is the International Bookshop?

Кузнецкий мост, 18.
kuz-N'ET-sk'iy MOST, və-s'im-NAT-sət'.
At 18 Kuznetsky Most.

Где ближайший рынок?
GD'E bl'i-ZHAY-shɨy Rɨ-nək?
Where is the nearest market?

Проводите меня по этому адресу.
prə-va-D'I-t'i m'i-N'A pa E-tə-mu A-dr'i-su.
Take me to this address.

Дайте мне хороший путеводитель на английском языке.
DAY-t'i mn'e ḥa-RO-shɨy pu-t'i-va-D'I-t'il' nə an-GL'IY-skəm yi-zɨ-K'E
Give me a good guidebook in English.

Дайте мне эту книгу.
DAY-t'i mn'e E-tu KN'I-gu.
Give me that book.

Здесь говорят по английски?
Z'D'ES' gə-va-R'AT pə an-GL'IY-sk'i?
Do they speak English here?

Дайте мне (английские) газеты.
DAY-t'i mn'e (an-GL'IY-sk'i-yə) ga-Z'E-tɨ.
Give me some (English) newspapers.

Сколько всё это стоит?
SKOL'-kə FS'O E-tə STOY-it?
How much will the lot cost?

Хочу купить старые книги.
ḥa-CHU ku-P'IT' STA-rɨ-yə KN'I-g'i.
I'd like to buy some old books.

Хочу купить старые рукописи.
ḥa-CHU ku-P'IT' STA-rɨ-yə RU-kə-p'i-s'i.
I'd like to buy some old manuscripts.

Хочу купить открытки.
ḥa-CHU ku-P'IT' at-KRɨT-k'i.
I'd like to buy some postal cards.

Хочу купить старинные картины.
ḥa-CHU ku-P'IT' sta-R'IN-nɨ-yə kar-T'I-nɨ.
I'd like to buy some old pictures.

Дайте мне англо-русский словарь.
DAY-t'i mn'e an-gla-RU-sk'iy sla-VAR'.
Give me an English-Russian dictionary.

Русско-английский словарь.
ru-skə-an-GL'IY-sk'iy sla-VAR'.
Russian-English dictionary.

Хочу купить безделушки.
ḥa-CHU ku-P'IT' b'iz-d'i-LUSH-k'i.
I want to buy some curios.

Хочу купить старинные вещи.
ḥa-CHU ku-P'IT' sta-R'IN-nɨ-yə V'ESH'-chi.
I'd like to buy old-fashioned things.

Где Антикварный отдел?
GD'E ant-t'i-KVAR-nɨy ad'-D'EL?
Where is the antiques department?

Для чего это?
dl'ə chi-VO E-tə?
What is this used for?

Это солонка.
E-tə sa-LON-kə.
It is a salt box.

Где это сделано?
GD'E E-tə Z'D'E-lə-nə?
Where was it made?

Это выделывается в Сибири.
E-tə vi-D'E-lɨ-və-yit-sə fs'i-B'I-r'i.
It is made in Siberia.

Из какого дерева это сделано?
is ka-KO-və D'E-r'i-və E-tə Z'D'E-lə-nə?
What wood is it made of?

дуб.
dup.
oak.

сосна.
sa-SNA.
pine.

берёза.
b'i-R'O-zə.
birch.

ель.
yel'.
fir.

Дайте этот портсигар.
DAY-t'i E-tət pərt-s'i-GAR.
Give me this cigarette box.

Дайте мне эту шаль.
DAY-t'i mn'e E-tu SHAL'
Give me this shawl.

Дайте мне эту русскую рубашку.
DAY-t'i mn'e E-tu RU-sku-yu ru-BASH-ku.
Give me this Russian blouse.

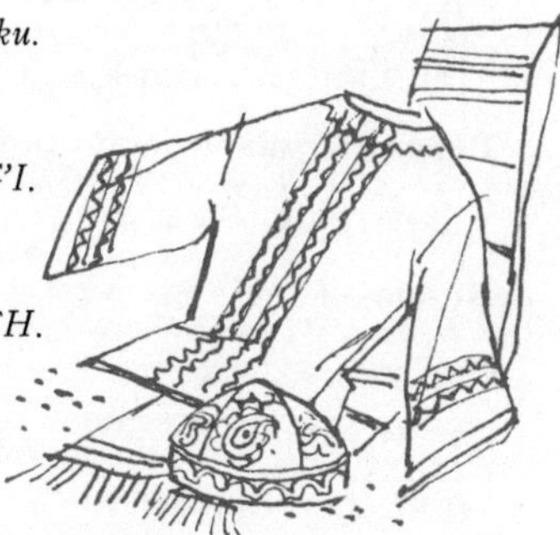

Дайте мне эти татарские сапоги.
DAY-t'i mn'e E-t'i ta-TAR-sk'i-yə sə-pa-G'I.
Give me this pair of Tartar top boots.

Дайте мне эту кавказскую брошь.
DAY-t'i mn'e E-tu kaf-KA-sku-yu BROSH.
Give me this Caucasian brooch.

Это из чистого серебра?
E-tə is CHI-stə-və s'i-r'i-BRA?
Is that made of pure silver?

Покажите мне это украинское платье.
pə-ka-ZHɨ-t'i mn'e E-tə u-kra-IN-skə-yə PLAT'-yə.
Show me this Ukrainian dress.

Покажите мне эту татарскую шапку.
pə-ka-ZHɨ-t'i mn'e E-tu ta-TAR-sku-yu SHAP-ku.
Show me this Tartar cap.

Это ручная вышивка?
E-tə ruch-NA-yə VI-shɨf-kə?
Is it hand embroidered?

Сколько это стоит?
SKOL'-kə E-tə STOY-it?
What is the price?

Какой это размер?
ka-KOY E-tə raz-M'ER?
What size is this?

Слишком узко.
SL'ISH-kəm U-skə.
This is too narrow.

Слишком широко.
SL'ISH-kəm shɨ-ra-KO.
That is too wide.

Слишком дорого.
SL'ISH-kəm DOR-ə-gə.
It is too expensive.

Есть у вас что-нибудь получше?
YES'T' u vas SHTO-n'i-but' pa-LUCH-shə?
Have you anything better?

Есть у вас что-нибудь подешевле?
YES'T' u vas SHTO-n'i-but' pə-d'i-SHEV-l'ə?
Have you any cheaper?

Это все мне не нравится.
E-təf-S'O mn'e n'in-RA-v'it-sə.
I don't care for any of these.

Цена одинаковая?
tsɨ-NA a-d'i-NA-kə-və-yə?
Is the price the same?

Такого же сорта, но большего размера.
ta-KO-və-zhə SOR-tə, nə BOL'-shə-və raz-M'E-rə.
Like this, but larger.

Я куплю это.
ya ku-PL'U E-tə.
I will buy this one.

Что нибудь в этом роде.
SHTO-n'i-but' vE-təm RO-d'i.
I want something like this.

Это не совсем то, что мне нужно.
E-tə n'i saf-S'EM TO, shtə mn'e NUZH-nə.
That is not quite what I want.

Покажите мне что-нибудь другое.
pə-ka-ZHɨ-t'i mn'e SHTO-ni-bud' dru-GOY-ə.
Can you show me anything different?

Нужно-ли чек в кассу?
NUZH-nə-l'i CHEK fKAS-su?
Do I need a check for the cash-desk?

Где касса?
GD'E KAS-sə?
Where is the cash-desk?

Вот там.
VOT TAM.
Over there.

Где выдают покупки?
GD'E vi-da-YUT pa-KUP-k'i?
Where do I get my purchases?

Пожалуйста, запакуйте тщательно.
pa-ZHA-lə-stə, zə-pa-KUY-t'i TSH'CHA-t'il'-nə.
Please pack this carefully.

Пошлите по этому адресу.
pash-L'I-t'i pa E-tə-mu A-dr'i-su.
Send them to this address.

Пошлите это в гостиницу „Метрополь".
pash-L'I-t'i E-tə vga-ST'I-n'itsu m'i-tra-POL'.
Send them to the Metropole Hotel.

Мне это нужно сегодня вечером.
mn'e E-tə NUZH-nə s'i-VOD'-n'ə V'E-chi-rəm.
I must have them tonight.

Я оставлю задаток.
ya a-STAV-l'u za-DA-tək.
I will leave a deposit.

Я возьму это.
ya vaz'-MU E-tə.
I will take it.

Я возьму это с собой.
ya vaz'-MU E-tə ssa-BOY.
I will take them with me.

Будет уплачено при доставке.
BU-d'it u-PLA-chi-nə pr'i da-STAF-k'i.
You will be paid on delivery.

LAUNDRY AND CLEANING

Хочу отдать бельё в стирку.
ḥa-CHU ad-DAT' b'il'-YO fST'IR-ku
I want to have my laundry washed.

Мне это нужно как можно скорее.
mn'e E-tə NUZH-nə kak MOZH-nə ska-R'EY-ə.
I want it as soon as possible.

Когда можно получить обратно?
kag-DA MOZH-nə pə-lu-CHIT' a-BRAT-nə?
When can I have it back?

Просмотрите список.
prə-sma-TR'I-t'i SP'I-sək.
Look over the list.

Верно ли записано?
V'ER-nə-l'i za-P'I-sə-nə?
Is it correct?

Всего десять штук.
fs'i-VO D'E-s'it' SHTUK.
There are 10 pieces altogether.

Это не крахмальте.
E-tə n'i-kraḥ-MAL'-t'i.
Don't put any starch in this.

Это не мое.
E-tə n'i-ma-YO.
This is not mine.

Несколько штук пропало.
N'E-skəl'-kə SHTUK pra-PA-lə.
There are some pieces missing.

Плохо выстирано.
PLO-ḥə Vɨ-st'i-rə-nə.
They are very badly done.

пожалуйста погладьте воротники и рубашки.
pa-ZHA-ə-stə pa-GLAT'-t'i və-rət-n'i-K'I i ru-BASH-k'i.
Please iron my collars and shirts.

Эти воротники и рубашки недостаточно накрахмалены.
E-t'i və-rət-n'i-K'I i ru-BASH-k'i n'i-da-STA-təch-nə nə-kraḥ-MA-l'i-nɨ.
These collars and shirts do not have enough starch in them.

HAIRDRESSER AND BARBER

Где дамский зал (косметический кабинет)?
GD'E DAM-sk'iy ZAL (kəs-m'i-T'I-chi-sk'iy kə-b'i-N'ET)?
Where is the ladies' hairdresser (the beauty parlor)?

Подстригите мне волосы.
pət-str'i-G'I-t'i mn'e VO-lə-sɨ.
I want my hair cut.

Не слишком коротко.
n'i-SL'ISH-kəm KOR-ət-kə.
Not too short.

Завейте мне волосы.
za-V'EY-t'i mn'e VO-lə-sɨ.
I want my hair waved.

Дайте шампунь.
DAY-t'i sham-PUN'.
Give me a shampoo.

Хочу сделать маникюр.
ḥa-CHU Z'D'E-lət' mə-n'i-K'UR.
I want to have a manicure.

Сделайте мне массаж лица.
Z'D'E-ləy-t'i mn'e ma-SASH l'itSA.
I want a face massage.

Дайте немного пудры.
DAY-t'i n'im-NO-gə PU-drɨ.
Bring me a little powder.

Скажите, пожалуйста, где находится парикмахерская?
ska-ZHɨ-t'i, pa-ZHA-lə-stə, GD'E na-ḤO-d'it-sə pə-r'ik-MA-ḥ'ir-skə-yə?
Can you tell me where the barber shop is, please?

Подстригите немного сзади и с боков.
pət-str'i-G'I-t'i n'im-NO-gə ZZA-d'i i zba-KOF.
Just trim round the back and ears.

Снимите немного здесь.
sn'i-M'I-t'i n'im-NO-gə Z'D'ES'.
Take a little off here.

Побрейте меня.
pa-BR'EY-t'i m'i-N'A.
Shave me, please.

Один раз будет достаточно.
a-D’IN RAS BU-d’it da-STA-təch-nə.
Once over will be sufficient.

Подстригите усы.
pət-str’i-G’I-t’i u-Sɨ.
Trim my moustache.

Подстригите бороду.
pət-str’i-G’I-t’i BOR-ə-du.
Trim my beard.

Положите немного крема на волосы.
pə-la-ZHɨ-t’i n’im-NO-gə KR’E-mə na VO-lə-sɨ.
Put on a little hair dressing.

Сделайте мне маникюр.
Z’D’E-ləy-t’i mn’e mə-n’i-K’UR.
Give me a manicure.

Прекрасно!
pr’i-KRA-snə!
Yes, that’s all right.

GOING TO THE THEATER

Где театр Революции?
GD’E t’i-A-tr r’i-va-L’U-tsɨ-i?
Where is the Theater of the Revolution?

Где Художественный театр?
GD’E ḥu-DO-zhist-v’in-nɨy t’i-A-tr?
Where is the Art Theater?

Где оперный театр (балет)?
GD’E O-p’ir-nɨy t’i-A-tr (ba-L’ET)?
Where is the Opera House (ballet)?

Когда начало спектакля?
kag-DA na-CHA-lə sp’ik-TAK-l’ə?
When does the performance begin?

Что идёт сегодня?
SHTO i-D’OT s’i-VOD’-n’ə?
What is on today?

Где вход?
GD’E fḤOT?
Where is the entrance?

Где касса?
GD’E KAS-sə?
Where is the box office?

Сколько стоят билеты?
SKOL’-kə STOY-ət b’i-L’E-tɨ?
What are the prices?

Сколько стоят места в партере?
SKOL’-kə STOY-it m’i-STA fpar-TE-r’i?
What are the prices in the orchestra?

Сколько стоит место в первом ярусе?
SKOL’-kə STOY-it M’E-stə fP’ER-vəm YA-ru-s’i?
What are the prices in the first balcony (dress circle)?

Сколько стоит место на балконе?
SKOL’-kə STOY-it M’E-stə nə-bal-KO-n’i?
What are the prices in the balcony?

Сколько стоит место во втором ярусе?
SKOL'-kə STOY-it M'E-stə vaf-ta-ROM YA-ru-s'i?
What are the prices in the upper circle (second balcony)?

Дайте мне один билет на сегодня.
DAY-t'i mn'e a-D'IN b'i-L'ET nə-s'i-VOD'-n'ə.
Let me have one ticket for tonight's performance.

Два билета.
dva b'i-L'E-tə.
Two tickets.

В десятом ряду.
vd'i-S'A-təm r'i-DU.
In the 10th row.

Где гардероб?
GD'E gər-d'i-ROP?
Where is the cloakroom?

Дайте мне номерок.
DAY-t'i mn'e nə-m'i-ROK.
Give me the cloaktag.

Дайте программу.
DAY-t'i pra-GRAM-mu.
Give me a program.

Где можно достать бинокль?
GD'E MOZH-nə da-STAT' b'i-NO-kl'?
Where can I rent opera glasses?

Пропустите, пожалуйста.
prə-pu-ST'I-t'i, pa-ZHA-lə-stə.
Please allow me to pass.

Извините, это мое место.
iz-v'i-N'I-t'i, E-tə ma-YO M'E-stə.
Pardon me, this is my seat.

Где буфет?
GD'E bu-F'ET?
Where is the refreshment room?

Сколько всего действий?
SKOL'-kə fs'i-VO D'EYST'-v'iy?
How many acts are there?

В котором часу пьеса окончится?
fka-TOR-əm chi-SU p'YE-sə a-KON'-chit-sə?
At what hour is the performance over?

Здесь не курят.
Z'D'ES' n'i-KU-r'ət.
Smoking forbidden.

Запасной выход.
zə-pas-NOY VƗ-ḥət.
Emergency exit.

Где курительная комната?
GD'E ku-R'I-t'il'-nə-yə KOM-nə-tə?
Where is the smoking room?

EXCHANGING MONEY

Где можно обменять американские деньги?
GD'E MOZH-nə ab-m'i-N'AT' a-m'i-r'i-KAN-sk'i-yə D'EN'-g'i?
Where can I get American money changed?

Английские деньги?
an-GL'IY-sk'i-yə D'EN'-g'i?
English money?

Где Государственный банк (Госбанк)?
GD'E gə-su-DARST'-vin-niy BANK (goz-BANK)?
Where is the State Bank?

Где ближайшее отделение Государственного банка?
GD'E bl'i-ZHAY-shə-yə ad'-d'i-L'EN-yə goz-BAN-kə?
Where is the nearest branch of the State Bank?

Можно ли обменять деньги в Интуристе?
MOZH-nə-l'i ab-m'i-N'AT' D'EN'-g'i vin-tu-R'I-st'i?
Can I change money at the Intourist Office?

Можете обменять американские деньги?
MO-zhi-t'i ab-m'i-N'AT' a-m'i-r'i-KAN-sk'i-yə D'EN'-g'i?
Can you change American money?

Каков курс?
ka-KOF KURS?
What is the rate of exchange?

Оплатите этот чек.
a-pla-T'I-t'i E-tət CHEK.
Cash this check.

Дайте мелкие кредитки.
DAY-t'i M'EL-k'i-yə kr'i-D'IT-k'i.
Give me bills of a smaller denomination.

Дайте чек, я должен расписаться.
DAY-t'i CHEK, ya DOL-zhin rə-sp'i-SAT-sə.
Give me the check, I must endorse it.

Вот аккредитив от моего банка.
VOT a-kr'i-d'i-T'IF at mə-yi-VO BAN-kə
Here is the letter of credit from my bank.

Где расписаться?
GD'E rə-sp'i-SAT-sə?
Where should I sign?

COMMUNICATIONS

Mail, Telegrams and Cables

Где ближайшая почта?
GD'E bl'i-ZHAY-shə-yə POCH-tə?
Where is the nearest post office?

Где ближайший телеграф?
GD'E bl'i-ZHAY-shəy t'i-l'i-GRAF?
Where is the nearest telegraph office?

Как туда пройти?
KAK tu-DA pray-T'I?
How do I get there?

Проводите меня до ближайшей почты.
prə-va-D'I-t'i m'i-N'A də-bl'i-ZHAY-shəy POCH-ti.
Take me to the nearest post office.

Каким трамваем нужно туда ехать?
ka-K'IM tram-VA-yim NUZH-nə tu-DA YE-ḥət'
What streetcar should I take to get there?

Как мне итти? Прямо?
KAK mn'e i-T'I? PR'A-mə?
Should I go straight ahead?

Как мне итти? Направо?
KAK mn'e i-T'I? na-PRA-və?
Should I turn to the right?

Как мне итти? Налево?
KAK mn'e i-T'I? na-L'E-və?
Should I turn to the left?

Где получают письма до востребования?
GD'E pə-lu-CHA-yut P'IS'-mə də-vas-TR'E-bə-vən'-yə?
Where is the General Delivery counter?

Моя фамилия Петров.
ma-YA fa-M'IL'-yə p'i-TROF.
My name is Petrov.

Нет ли мне писем?
N'ET-l'i mn'e P'I-s'im?
Are there any letters for me?

Нет ли мне посылки?
N'ET-l'i mn'e pa-SƗL-k'i?
Are there any parcels for me?

Вот мой паспорт.
VOT moy PAS-pərt.
Here is my passport.

Где можно достать марки?
GD'E MOZH-nə da-STAT' MAR-k'i?
Where can I get stamps?

Дайте мне одну марку (марки).
DAY-t'i mn'e ad-NU MAR-ku (MAR-k'i).
Give me a stamp (stamps).

Дайте мне семь конвертов.
DAY-t'i mn'e S'EM' kan-V'ER-təf
Give me seven envelopes.

Дайте мне писчую бумагу.
DAY-t'i mn'e P'ISH'-chu-yu bu-MA-gu.
Give me writing paper.

Какие марки на письмо в Чикаго?
ka-K'I-yə MAR-k'i nə p'is'-MO fchi-KA-gə?
What is the postage for this letter to Chicago?

Пошлите это письмо заказным.
pash-L'I-t'i E-to p'is'-MO zə-kaz-NƗM.
Please register this letter.

Сколько стоят эти открытки?
SKOL'-kə STOY-ət E-t'i at-KRƗT-k'i?
What is the price of these post cards?

Где ближайший почтовый ящик?
GD'E bl'i-ZHAY-shəy pach-TO-viy YASH'-chik.
Where is the nearest mail box?

Дайте мне виды города.
DAY-t'i mn'e V'I-di GOR-ə-də.
I want to have some views of the town.

Хочу послать телеграмму.
ha-CHU pa-SLAT' t'i-l'i-GRA-mu.
I want to send a telegram.

Дайте телеграфный бланк.
DAY-t'i t'i-l'i-GRAF-nɨy BLANK.
Give me a telegraph form.

Сколько стоит слово?
SKOL'kə STOY-it SLO-və?
What is the charge per word?

Сколько нужно платить?
SKOL'-kə NUZH-nə pla-T'IT'?
What is the charge?

Сколько стоит эта телеграмма?
SKOL'-kə STOY-it E-tə t'i-l'i-GRA-mə?
How much will this telegram cost?

Telephoning

Где телефон?
GD'E t'i-l'i-FON?
Where is the phone?

Можно позвонить?
MOZH-nə pəz-va-N'IT'?
May I use your phone?

Дайте телефонную книжку.
DAY-t'i t'i-l'i-FON-nu-yu KN'ISH-ku.
Give me the telephone directory.

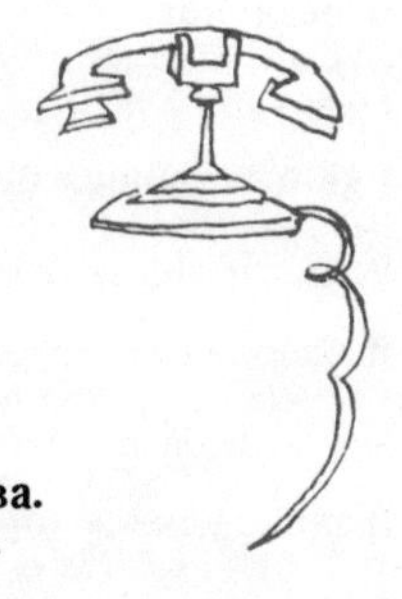

Позвоните по этому номеру.
pəz-va-N'I-t'i pa E-tə-mu NO-m'i-ru.
Please get me this number.

Дайте город (Центральную).
DAY-t'i GOR-ət (tsɨn-TRAL'-nu-yu).
Give me an outside line.

1-64-62, один шестьдесят четыре, шестьдесят два.
a-D'IN shɨz-d'i-S'AT chi-TƗ-r'i shɨz-d'i-S'AD DVA.
1-64-62.

Алло! Это Иван?
a-LO! E-tə i-VAN?
Hello. Is that John?

Попросите его к телефону.
pə-pra-S'I-t'i yi-VO kt'i-l'i-FO-nu.
Ask him to come to the phone.

Говорит Марья.
gə-va-R'IT MAR'-ya.
Mary speaking.

Попросите его позвонить когда вернётся.
pə-pra-S'I-t'i yi-VO pəz-va-N'IT' kag-DA v'ir-N'OT-sə.
Ask him to phone me when he returns.

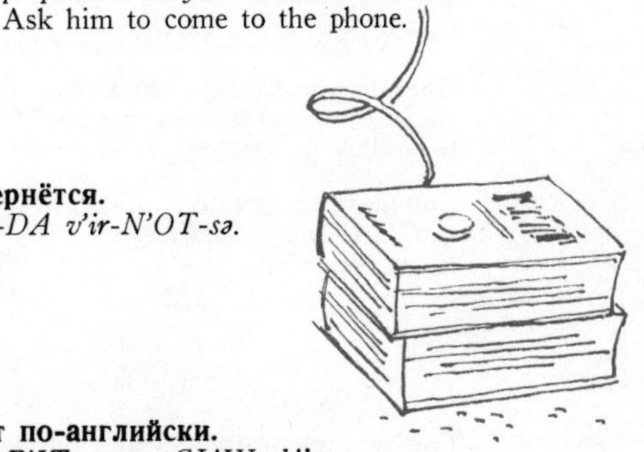

Запишите мой номер.
zə-p'i-SHƗ-t'i moy NO-m'ir.
Take my number.

Позовите кого-нибудь кто говорит по-английски.
pə-za-V'I-t'i ka-VO-n'i-but' kto gə-va-R'IT pə an-GL'IY-sk'i.
Call someone who can speak English.

Не кладите трубку.
n'i kla-D'I-'ti TRUP-ku.
Hold the line.

Говорите громче.
gə-va-R'I-t'i GROM-chə.
Speak louder.

Я позвоню позже.
ya pəz-va-N'U POZH'-zhə.
I'll ring up later.

Алло! Нас разьединили.
a-LO! nas rəz-yi-d'i-N'I-l'i.
Hello. They have cut us off.

Я вас плохо слышу.
ya vas PLO-ḥə SLɨ-shu.
I can't hear you very well.

YOUR HEALTH ABROAD

Проводите меня в аптеку.
prə-va-D'I-t'i m'i-N'A vap-T'E-ku.
Take me to a drugstore.

Я нездоров.
YA n'iz-da-ROF.
I am ill.

Приготовьте это лекарство.
pr'i-ga-TOF'-t'i E-tə l'i-KARST-və.
Make up this medicine.

Пошлите за доктором.
pash-L'I-t'i za DOK-tə-rəm.
Send for the doctor.

Где ближайшая больница?
GD'E bl'i-ZHAY-shə-yə bal'-N'I-tsa?
Where is the nearest hospital?

Здесь болит.
Z'D'ES' ba-L'IT.
I have pain here.

Я заболел (заболела *fem.***) по дороге.**
ya zə-ba-L'EL (zə-ba-L'E-lə) pə-da-RO-g'i.
I was ill on my journey.

Я простудился (простудилась *fem.***).**
YA prə-stu-D'IL-sə (prə-stu-D'I-ləs).
I have caught a cold.

У меня боль в желудке.
u-m'i-N'A BOL' vzhɨ-LUT-k'i.
I've a pain in my stomach.

Пошлите в аптеку; закажите этот рецепт.
pash-L'I-t'i vap-T'E-ku; zə-ka-ZHɨ-t'i E-tət r'it-SEPT.
Send to a drugstore; get this prescription made up.

Сейчас мне лучше.
s'i-CHAS mn'e LUCH-shə.
I feel better now.

VISAS

Где можно продлить выездную визу?
GD'E MOZH-nə prad-L'IT' vɨ-yiz-NU-yu V'I-zu?
Where can I extend my exit visa?

Где можно получить выездную визу?
GD'E MOZH-nə pə-lu-CHIT' vɨ-yiz-NU-yu V'I-zu?
Where does one get the exit visa?

Где Административный Отдел Совета?
GD'E ad-m'i-n'i-stra-T'IV-nɨy ad'-D'EL sa-V'E-tə?
Where is the City Council's Administrative Section?

Где иностранный отдел?
GD'E i-na-STRAN-nɨy ad'-D'EL?
Where is the Foreign Department?

На какой улице?
nə-ka-KOY U-l'itsɨ?
What street is it on?

Здесь иностранный отдел?
Z'D'ES' i-na-STRAN-nɨy ad-D'EL?
Is this the Foreign Department?

Я иностранец.
ya i-na-STRA-n'its.
I am a foreigner (m.).

Я американец.
YA a-m'i-r'i-KA-n'its.
I am an American (m.).

Я англичанин.
YA an-gl'i-CHA-n'in.
I am an Englishman.

Я иностранка.
ya i-na-STRAN-kə.
I am a foreigner (f.).

Я американка.
YA a-m'i-r'i-KAN-kə.
I am an American (f.).

Я англичанка.
YA an-gl'i-CHAN-kə.
I am an Englishwoman.

Я не говорю по-русски.
YA n'i-gə-va-R'U pa-RU-sk'i.
I don't speak Russian.

Кто здесь говорит по-английски?
KTO z'd'es' gə-va-R'IT pə-an-GL'IY-sk'i?
Does anyone here speak English?

Что мне нужно для получения выездной визы?
SHTO mn'e NUZH-nə dl'ə pə-lu-CHEN'-yə vɨ-yiz-NOY V'I-zɨ?
What have I to do to get my exit visa?

Что мне нужно для продления визы?
SHTO mn'e NUHZ-nə dl'ə prad-L'EN'-yə V'I-zɨ?
What must I do to extend my visa?

Я хочу продлить визу на две недели.
ya ha-CHU prad-L'IT' V'I-zu na DV'E n'i-D'E-l'i.
I want to extend my visa for 2 weeks.

Где можно получить анкету для заполнения?
GD'E MOZH-nə pə-lu-CHIT' an-K'E-tu dl'ə zə-pal-N'EN'-yə?
Where do I get a questionnaire?

У вас можно получить анкету?
u VAS MOZH-nə pə-lu-CHIT' an-K'E-tu?
Can we get the questionnaire from you?

Благодарю вас.
blə-gə-da-R'U vas.
Thank you.

Сколько фотографических карточек вам нужно?
SKOL'-kə fə-tə-gra-F'I-chi-sk'iḥ KAR-tə-chik vam NUZH-nə?
How many photographs do you need?

Вот мои фотографические карточки.
VOT ma-YI fə-tə-gra-F'I-chi-sk'iyə KAR-təch-k'i.
Here are my photographs.

Сколько стоит регистрация?
SKOL'-kə STOY-it r'i-g'i-STRATsɨ-yə?
What is the registration fee?

Где я должен подписаться?
GD'E ya DOL-zhɨn pət-p'i-SAT-sə?
Where should I sign?

Когда я могу получить свой паспорт с готовой визой?
kag-DA ya ma-GU pə-lu-CHIT' svəy PAS-pərt zga-TO-vəy V'I-zəy?
When can I get my passport with the visa?

У кого я получу свой паспорт?
u-ka-VO ya pə-lu-CHU svoy PAS-pərt?
Where do I get my passport from?

Когда у вас выходной день?
kag-DA u-VAS vi-ḥad-NOY D'EN'?
When is your day off?

От которого часа вы работаете?
at ka-TOR-ə-və CHA-sə vɨ ra-BO-tə-yi-t'i?
When do you start to work?

До которого часа вы работаете?
də ka-TOR-ə-və CHA-sə vɨ ra-BO-tə-yi-t'i?
When do you stop working?

Как мне проехать в гостиницу „Метрополь"?
KAK mn'e pra-YE-ḥət' vga-ST'I-n'itsu m'i-tra-POL'?
How do I get from here to the Metropole hotel?

Как мне проехать на Киевский вокзал?
KAK mn'e pra-YE-ḥət' na K'I-yif-sk'iy vag-ZAL?
How do I get from here to the Kiev station?

SIGNS

Курить воспрещается
ku-R'IT vəs-pr'ish'-CHA-yit-sə
No smoking allowed

Вход воспрещается
FḤOT vəs-pr'ish'-CHA-yit-sə
No admittance

Тяните
t'i-N'I-t'i
Pull

Толкайте
tal-KAY-t'i
Push

Проезд воспрещен
pra-YEST vəs-pr'ish'-CHON
No thoroughfare

Вход
fḤOT
Entrance

Здесь только выход
Z'D'ES' TOL'-kə Vɨ-ḥət
Exit only

Касса
KAS-sə
Ticket counter (window)

Почта
POCH-tə
Post Office

Камера для хранения багажа
KA-m'i-rə dl'a ḥra-N'EN'-yə bə-ga-ZHA
Baggage room

Буфет
bu-F'ET
Refreshments

Дамская комната
DAM-skə-yə KOM-nə-tə
Ladies waiting room

Курительная
ku-R'I-t'il'-nə-yə
Smoking

Не плевать
n'i pl'i-VAT'
No spitting

Не высовываться
n'i vi-SO-vɨ-vət-sə
Don't lean out

На ходу не сходить
no ḥa-DU n'i s-ḥa-D'IT'
Don't get off while car is moving

Держитесь правой стороны
d'ir-ZHɨ-t'is PRA-vəy stə-ra-Nɨ
Keep to the right

For additional signs, see the Appendix on p. 107.

SPORTS

Tennis

Как мне проехать на теннисные корты?
KAK mn'e pra-YE-ḥət' na TE-n'is-nɨ-yə KOR-tɨ?
How do I get to the tennis courts?

К кому обратиться за разрешением на игру?
kka-MU a-bra-T'IT-sə zə rəz-r'i-SHEN'-yəm nə i-GRU?
From whom do I get permission to play?

Можно тут поиграть в теннис?
MOZH-nə tut pə-i-GRAT' fTE-n'is?
May I play tennis here?

У меня есть своя ракетка.
u m'i-N'A yest' sva-YA ra-K'ET-kə.
I have my own racket.

Мне нужны теннисные мячи; где можно их получить?
mn'e nuzh-Nɨ TE-n'is-nɨ-yə m'i-CHI; GD'E MOZH-nə yiḥ pə-lu-CHIT'?
I need tennis balls; where can I get some?

Soccer Match

Я хотел бы посмотреть настоящий русский футбольный матч.
YA ḥa-T'EL-bɨ pə-sma-TR'ET' nə-sta-YASH'-chiy RU-sk'iy fud-BOL'-nɨy MAT'CH.
I would like to see a real Russian soccer match.

Прекрасно, поедем на Ленинский Стадион.
pr'i-KRAS-nə, pa-YE-d'im na L'E-n'in-sk'iy stə-d'i-ON.
Fine, let's go to Lenin Stadium.

Какие команды играют сегодня?
ka-K'I-yə ka-MAN-dɨ i-GRA-yut s'i-VOD'-n'ə?
Which teams are playing today?

Сколько стоит вход?
SKOL'-kə STOY-it f-ḤOT?
How much is the admission?

Swimming and Bathing

Поедем купаться.
pa-YE-d'im ku-PAT-sə.
Let's go swimming (*lit.*, bathing).

Где пляж? На реке?
GD'E PL'ASH? nə-r'i-K'E?
Where is the beach? On the river?

Да. Не забудьте принести купальный костюм, полотенце и крем для загара.
DA. n'i za-BUT'-t'i pr'i-n'i-ST'I ku-PAL'-nɨy ka-ST'UM, pə-la-T'ENTsə i KR'EM dl'ə za-GA-rə.
Yes. Don't forget to bring your bathing suit, a towel, and sun-tan cream.

Мне крем не нужен, я очень хорошо загораю.
MN'E KR'EM n'i NU-zhɨn. YA O-chin ḥə-ra-SHO zə-ga-RA-yu.
I don't need any cream. I tan very well.

Хотите я принесу одеяло.
ha-T'I-t'i ya pr'i-n'i-SU a-d'i-YA-lə?
Do you want me to bring a blanket?

Нет, не надо. Лучше будем лежать на песке.
N'ET, n'i NA-də. LUCH-shə BU-d'im l'i-ZHAT' nə-p'i-SK'E.
No, that's not necessary. We'll lie on the sand.

Посмотрите какая тихая вода.
pə-sma-TR'I-t'i ka-KA-yə T'I-ḥə-yə va-DA.
Look how still the water is!

Это же река. Если вы хотите большие волны, надо эхать на Чёрное Море.
E-tə-zhə r'i-KA. YE-sl'i vɨ ḥa-T'I-t'i bal'-SHɨ-yə VOL-nɨ, NA-də YE-ḥət' na-CHOR-nə-yə MO-r'ə.
After all, this is a river. If you want big waves, you have to go down to the Black Sea.

О я люблю и море и реку.
O YA l'u-BL'U I MO-r'ə I r'i-KU.
Oh, I like both the sea and the river.

Fishing

Мне нужны удилище, леска, и крючки.
mn'e nuzh-NƗ u-D'I-l'ish'-chə, L'E-skə, i kr'uch-K'I.
I need a rod, line and hooks.

Где можно взять напрокат лодку?
GD'E MOZH-nə vz'at' nə-pra-KAT LOT-ku?
Where can I rent a boat?

Какие рыбы водятся в этой реке (в этом озере)?
ka-K'I-yə RƗ-bɨ VO-d'ət-sə vE-təy r'i-K'E (vE-təm O-z'i-r'i)?
What kind of fish are found in this river (in this lake)?

OUTLINE OF RUSSIAN GRAMMAR

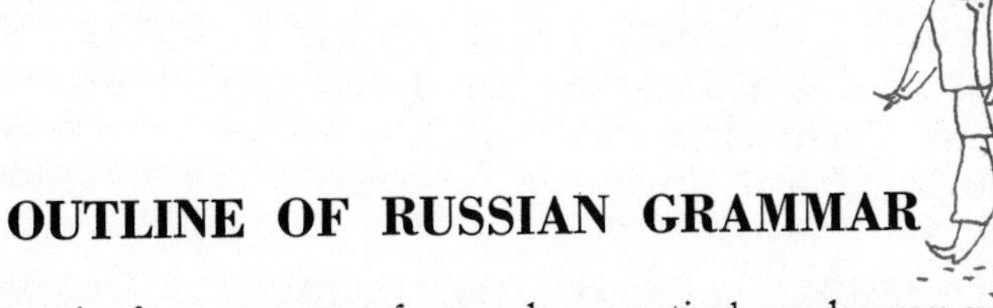

OUTLINE OF RUSSIAN GRAMMAR

Although, for purposes of everyday practical needs, you will be able to get by with some stock of common Russian words and phrases, it is advisable also to have some understanding of the parts of speech and their various forms and uses as well as of the manner in which Russian sentences are constructed. In the following pages we have attempted to present the "highlights" of Russian grammar very concisely, so as to enable you to understand the how and why of the phrases in this book. This survey is of necessity brief, but the main facts for your daily needs have been covered.

1. THE NOUN

1.0. Nouns in Russian are never preceded by a definite or indefinite article because there are no articles in Russian. When translating from Russian into English, *the* and *a* should be supplied to fit the meaning.

1.1. Russian nouns are declined (change endings) for number, gender, and case. There are two numbers (singular and plural) and three genders (masculine, feminine, and neuter). In Russian the gender is grammatical. Although the *meaning* of a word does not usually give a clue to its gender, the gender can generally be determined by the written ending of the *nominative* or first case (see **1.2**) according to the following rules:

Masculine nouns end in a consonant (стол, table); in **й** (чай, tea); and in some cases in **ь** (слова́рь, dictionary).

Feminine nouns end in **а** (газе́та, newspaper) or **я** (дере́вня, village); the majority of nouns ending in **ь** is also feminine (ло́шадь, horse).

Neuter are all words ending in **е** (ко́фе, coffee); in **о** (сло́во, word); and in **мя** (вре́мя, time).

Nouns indicating *animate beings* are generally masculine when they refer to males and feminine when they refer to females. In a few cases, however, nouns with feminine endings are used to refer to male beings and are therefore considered masculine nouns. Thus, дя́дя (uncle) is a masculine noun despite its final -я. Nouns designating *inanimate objects* are masculine, feminine or neuter according to the above rules. See **1.3-6.**

1.2. Russian has six cases. Their basic uses and functions are:

The **nominative** indicates the subject of the sentence.

The **genitive** indicates possession and is usually translated by "of the" or the English possessive case. It is also used with some prepositions, the most common of which are: **без** (without), **для** (for), **до** (up to), **из** (out of), **круго́м** (around), **о́коло** (near, about), **от** (from), **по́сле** (after) and **у** (at, with, by).

It is important to remember that in Russian the meaning of *to have* is idiomatically expressed by the preposition **у** followed by the genitive of a noun or pronoun: у меня́ есть дом is the normal way of saying "I have a house" (literally: With me there is [a] house).

The **dative** is used to indicate the indirect object, so that it usually can be translated with "to the" or "for the." It is also used after the prepositions **к** (to) and **по** (along, according to).

The **accusative** indicates the direct object of the verb and is also used after the prepositions **в** (to, into), **за** (behind), **на** (to, into, on), **под** (under), **про** (about) and **че́рез** (through).

The **instrumental** is used to indicate the agent of action or the instrument (means) with which the action described by the verb is performed. It is usually translated with "by means of," "by (the)" or "with (the)." It is also used after the prepositions **с** or **со** (with), **ме́жду** (between, among), **пе́ред** (in front of), **над** (over), **под** (under) and **за** (behind).

The **prepositional** or **locative** indicates either location or the subject of discourse. It is governed by the prepositions **в** (in), **на** (on), **о, об** or **о́бо** (about, concerning), **при** (in the presence of).

The case to be used with a preposition naturally depends on the meaning of the sentence: в го́роде (*in* the city: prepositional); в го́род (*to* the city: accusative).

1.3. THE FIRST DECLENSION

Nouns ending in **а** or **я** belong to the first declension. These nouns are *feminine*.

Nouns ending in **а**

Nom.	газéта	the newspaper	газéты	the newspapers
Gen.	газéты	of the newspaper	газéт	of the newspapers
Dat.	газéте	to the newspaper	газéтам	to the newspapers
Acc.	газéту	the newspaper	газéты	the newspapers
Instr.	газéтой *	with (by means of) the newspaper	газéтами	with (by means of) the newspapers
Prep.	о газéте	about the newspaper	о газéтах	about the newspapers

Nouns ending in **я**

	Singular		*Plural*	
Nom.	простыня́	the sheet	прóстыни	the sheets
Gen.	простыни́		просты́нь	
Dat.	простыне́		простыня́м	
Acc.	простыню́		прóстыни	
Instr.	простынёй *		простыня́ми	
Prep.	о простыне́		о простыня́х	

Nouns in which the ending **я** is preceded by another vowel are declined as follows:

	Singular		*Plural*
Nom.	теóрия	theory	теóрии
Gen.	теóрии		теори́й
Dat.	теóрии		теóриям
Acc.	теóрию		теóрии
Instr.	теóрией *		теóриями
Prep.	о теóрии		о теóриях

1.4. THE SECOND DECLENSION

Nouns ending in a plain or "hard" consonant or in **й** belong to the second declension. They are always masculine. To the same declension belong some of the masculine nouns which end in **ь**.

Nouns ending in **о** or **е** also belong to the second declension. The gender of these nouns is *neuter*.

---

* Feminine instrumental forms in -ою or -ёю are not used in normal speech, but constitute literary and poetic usage.

Nouns ending in hard consonants

	Singular		*Plural*
Nom.	стол	table	столы́
Gen.	стола́		столо́в
Dat.	столу́		стола́м
Acc.	стол		столы́
Instr.	столо́м		стола́ми
Prep.	о столе́		о стола́х

Nouns ending in **ь**

	Singular		*Plural*
Nom.	слова́рь	dictionary	словари́
Gen.	словаря́		словаре́й
Dat.	словарю́		словаря́м
Acc.	слова́рь		словари́
Instr.	словарём		словаря́ми
Prep.	о словаре́		о словаря́х

Nouns ending in **й**

	Singular		*Plural*
Nom.	слу́чай	case, occasion	слу́чаи
Gen.	слу́чая		слу́чаев
Dat.	слу́чаю		слу́чаям
Acc.	слу́чай		слу́чаи
Instr.	слу́чаем		слу́чаями
Prep.	о слу́чае		о спу́чаях

Nouns ending in **о**

	Singular		*Plural*
Nom.	сло́во	word	слова́
Gen.	сло́ва		слов
Dat.	сло́ву		слова́м
Acc.	сло́во		слова́
Instr.	сло́вом		слова́ми
Prep.	о сло́ве		о слова́х

Nouns ending in **е**

	Singular		*Plural*
Nom.	по́ле	field	поля́
Gen.	по́ля		поле́й
Dat.	по́лю		поля́м
Acc.	по́ле		поля́
Instr.	по́лем		поля́ми
Prep.	о по́ле		о поля́х

1.5. THE THIRD DECLENSION

Feminine nouns ending in **ь** belong to the third declension.

	Singular		*Plural*
Nom.	дверь	door	две́ри
Gen.	две́ри		двере́й
Dat.	две́ри		дверя́м
Acc.	дверь		две́ри
Instr.	две́рью		дверя́ми
Prep.	о две́ри		о дверя́х

1.6. Masculine nouns in both singular and plural, and feminine nouns in the plural only, have identical endings in the nominative and accusative when they designate *inanimate* objects, and in the genitive and accusative when they designate *animate* beings. Examples: Nominative and accusative singular заво́д (factory), nom. and acc. pl. заво́ды; nom. singular оте́ц (father), gen. and acc. singular отца́, nom. pl. отцы́, gen. and acc. pl. отцо́в.

1.7. Contrary to the general rule, the final **а** or **я** of the *genitive singular* of some masculine nouns is often replaced by **у**, especially in a partitive sense: ча́шка ча́**ю** (a cup of tea), са́хар**у** (some sugar), фунт табак**у́** (a pound of tobacco).

Also, the *prepositional singular* of some monosyllabic masculine nouns ends in stressed **у** (instead of **е**), but only after в (in) and на (on): в сад**у́** (in the garden), в снег**у́** (in the snow), на пол**у́** (on the floor).

The *nominative plural* of a number of masculine nouns ending in a consonant terminates in stressed **а** (instead of **ы** or **и**): дом**а́** (houses), город**а́** (cities), глаз**а́** (eyes), лес**а́** (forests). A few nouns of foreign origin also have this irregular case ending: доктор**а́** (doctors), профессор**а́** (professors).

1.8. Russian names and patronymics. In Russian it is common practice to address adult persons by their first name and the patronymic:

Никола́й Ива́нович	Nikolai, son of Ivan
Ви́ктор Никола́евич	Victor, son of Nikolai
Мари́я Ива́новна	Maria, daughter of Ivan
Ве́ра Никола́евна	Vera, daughter of Nikolai

The patronymic is derived from the first name of the father. Whenever that name ends in a hard consonant, the suffix -ович (for persons of the male sex) or the suffix -овна́ (for persons of the female sex) is added:

Ива́н { + ович = Ива́нович (*m.*)
+ овна = Ива́новна (*f.*) }

In all other cases, the suffixes **-евич** (for males) and **-евна** (for females) are used:

Никола́й { + евич = Никола́евич (*m.*)
+ евна = Никола́евна (*f.*) }

2. THE ADJECTIVE

2.0. In Russian, the adjectives agree with the noun they modify in number, gender and case. This includes the cases where the masculine genitive singular and the feminine genitive plural are used as accusative forms of animate beings (see **1.6**).

2.1. *Hard* adjectives, in the nominative singular, end in **ый** or **ой** when they govern masculine nouns; in **ая** when they govern feminine nouns; and in **ое** when they govern neuter nouns. Examples: большо́й дом (a large house); твёрдый каранда́ш (a hard pencil); больша́я ко́мната (a large room); большо́е окно́ (a large window).

2.2. *Soft* adjectives, in the nominative singular, end in **ий** when they govern masculine nouns; in **яя** when they govern feminine nouns; and in **ее** when they govern neuter nouns. Examples: си́ний каранда́ш (a blue pencil); си́няя кни́га (a blue book); си́нее стекло́ (a blue glass).

2.3. DECLENSION OF ADJECTIVES

Hard, ending in **ый, ая, ое**

Singular

	Masculine		*Feminine*	*Neuter*
Nom.	но́вый	new	но́вая	но́вое
Gen.	но́вого		но́вой	но́вого
Dat.	но́вому		но́вой	но́вому
Acc.	но́вый		но́вую	но́вое
Instr.	но́вым		но́вой	но́вым
Prep.	о но́вом		о но́вой	о но́вом

Plural

Nom.	но́вые	но́вые	но́вые
Gen.	но́вых	но́вых	но́вых
Dat.	но́вым	но́вым	но́вым
Acc.	но́вые	но́вые	но́вые
Instr.	но́выми	но́выми	но́выми
Prep.	о но́вых	о но́вых	о но́вых

Hard, ending in **ой, ая, ое**

Nom.	густóй	thick	густáя	густóе
Gen.	густóго		густóй	густóго
Dat.	густóму		густóй	густóму
Acc.	густóй		густýю	густóе
Instr.	густы́м		густóй	густы́м
Prep.	о густóм		о густóй	о густóм

The plural of hard adjectives ending in **ой, ая, ое** is formed like that of the other hard adjectives.

Hard adjectives, when used predicatively, are sometimes shortened: дом нóвый or дом нов (the house [is] new). The shortened forms are more common in literature than in conversational speech. However, there are some adjectives which are always short in predicative position: он бóлен (he is sick), онá больнá (she is sick); это нýжно (this is necessary). The "long" forms of these two adjectives are больнóй and нýжный.

Soft, ending in **ий, яя, ее**

Singular

	Masc.		*Fem.*	*Neut.*
Nom.	си́ний	blue	си́няя	си́нее
Gen.	си́него		си́ней	си́него
Dat.	си́нему		си́ней	си́нему
Acc.	си́ний		си́нюю	си́нее
Instr.	си́ним		си́ней	си́ним
Prep.	о си́нем		о си́ней	о си́нем

Plural

Nom.	си́ние	си́ние	си́ние
Gen.	си́них	си́них	си́них
Dat.	си́ним	си́ним	си́ним
Acc.	си́ние	си́ние	си́ние
Instr.	си́ними	си́ними	си́ними
Prep.	о си́них	о си́них	о си́них

Adjectives having a stem in **ж, ц, ш, щ**

Singular

	Masc.		*Fem.*	*Neut.*
Nom.	свéжий	fresh	свéжая	свéжее
Gen.	свéжего		свéжей	свéжего
Dat.	свéжему		свéжей	свéжему

Acc.	свéжий	свежую	свéжее
Instr.	свéжим	свéжей	свéжим
Prep.	о свéжем	о свéжей	о свéжем

The plural is formed like синий, above.

2.4. THE COMPARATIVE DEGREE

The comparative degree in many cases is formed by placing the word **бóлее** (more) before the adjective: интерéсный (interesting), бóлее интерéсный (more interesting); дорогóй (expensive or dear), более дорогóй (more expensive or dearer). There is another form of the comparative degree which has the same meaning and is produced by adding **е** or **ее** to the stem of the adjective: интерéсн(ый) (interesting), интерéснее (more interesting).

2.4.1. The comparative degree of some important adjectives is formed irregularly:

хорóший	good	лýчше	better
плохóй	bad	хýже	worse
ширóкий	wide	шúре	wider
ýзкий	narrow, tight	ýже	narrower, tighter
высóкий	high	вы́ше	higher
нúзкий	low	нúже	lower
дорогóй	expensive	дорóже	more expensive
дешёвый	cheap	дешéвле	cheaper

2.5. THE SUPERLATIVE DEGREE

The superlative degree is formed by placing the word **сáмый, -ая, -ое,** which is declined like an adjective, before the adjective:

плохóй	bad (m.)	сáмый плохóй	the worst
плохáя	bad (f.)	сáмая плохáя	the worst
плохóе	bad (n.)	сáмое плохóе	the worst

The endings **-áйший** and **-éйший** are sometimes used to form superlatives. Examples: ближáйший, nearest (from блúзкий, near); новéйший, latest, newest (from нóвый, new).

2.6. Many adverbs are derived from adjectives by adding the letter **о** to the stem of the adjective: хорóш(ий) (good), хорошó (well); плох(óй) (bad), плóхо (badly).

2.7. Adverbs of time, like ле́том (in summer), зимо́й (in winter), у́тром (in the morning), днём (during the daytime), ра́но (early) and пото́м (then, later), denote the time when an action is performed or takes place. These forms actually are the instrumentals of the respective nouns (see **1.2**). Compare:

Nouns		*Adverbs*	
у́тро	morning	у́тром	in the morning
день	day	днём	in the daytime
ве́чер	evening	ве́чером	in the evening
ночь	night	но́чью	at night, in the night

3. THE NUMERALS

3.0. The cardinal numbers are listed on page 36.

3.1. The numeral оди́н (one) agrees in gender and case with the noun it qualifies: оди́н стул (one chair), одна́ ко́мната (one room), одно́ окно́ (one window). Оди́н is declined as follows:

	Singular			*Plural*
	Masc.	*Fem.*	*Neut.*	(*all genders*)
Nom.	оди́н	одна́	одно́	одни́
Gen.	одного́	одно́й	одного́	одни́х
Dat.	одному́	одно́й	одному́	одни́м
Acc.	оди́н or одного́	одну́	одно́	одни́
Instr.	одни́м	одно́й	одни́м	одни́ми
Prep.	об одно́м	об одно́й	об одно́м	об одни́х

The plural form is used with nouns which have no singular form: одни́ часы́ (one watch) and одни́ но́жницы (one pair of scissors).

3.2. The numbers 2, 3 and 4 are followed by the genitive singular of the noun they qualify when they are in the nominative or accusative. All other numbers are followed by the genitive plural when they are in the nominative or accusative: два, три, четы́ре окна́ (two, three, four windows); пять, шесть око́н (five, six windows), etc.

Два (two) and о́ба (both) are masculine and neuter forms. Their feminine counterparts are две and о́бе. The other numerals make no such differentiation between genders.

	Masc. & neut.	*Fem.*	*All genders*
Nom.	два (2)	две (2)	три (3)
Gen.	двух	двух	трёх
Dat.	двум	двум	трём
Acc.	два	две	три
Instr.	двумя́	двумя́	тремя́
Prep.	о двух	о двух	о трёх
	All genders	*Masc. & neut.*	*Fem.*
Nom.	четы́ре (4)	о́ба (both)	о́бе (both)
Gen.	четырёх	обо́их	обе́их
Dat.	четырём	обо́им	обе́им
Acc.	четы́ре	о́ба	о́бе
Instr.	четырьмя́	обо́ими	обе́ими
Prep.	о четырёх	об обо́их	об обе́их

3.3. The numbers from 5 to 20 and the number 30 are declined like feminine nouns in **-ь**. The declensions of the cardinal numbers from 5 to 10 are given below:

Nom.	пять (5)	шесть (6)	семь (7)
Gen.	пяти́	шести́	семи́
Dat.	пяти́	шести́	семи́
Acc.	пять	шесть	семь
Instr.	пятью́	шестью́	семью́
Prep.	о пяти́	о шести́	о семи́
Nom.	во́семь (8)	де́вять (9)	де́сять (10)
Gen.	восьми́	девяти́	десяти́
Dat.	восьми́	девяти́	десяти́
Acc.	во́семь	де́вять	де́сять
Instr.	восемью́	девятью́	десятью́
Prep.	о восьми́	о девяти́	о десяти́

3.4. The numbers 40, 90 and 100 have only two declensional forms, one for the nominative and accusative and one for all the other cases. They are: со́рок, сорока́; девяно́сто, девяно́ста; сто, ста.

Both parts of the compound numerals 50, 60, 70, 80 and the number for hundreds from 200 to 900 are declined.

3.5. The ordinal numbers are listed on page 37. They are declined like regular adjectives.

3.6. Ordinal numerals used in dates appear in the neuter gender: деся́тое февраля́ (February 10th), деся́того февраля́ (*on* February 10th).

3.7. In fractions, a cardinal number is used for the numerator and an ordinal for the denominator in the genitive plural: три восьмы́х (three eighths).

4. THE PRONOUN

4.1. The **personal pronouns** are:

Singular

	1st person	*2nd person*
Nom.	я (I)	ты (you)
Gen.	меня́ (of me)	тебя́
Dat.	мне (to me)	тебе́
Acc.	меня́ (me)	тебя́
Instr.	мной (by me)	тобо́й
Prep.	обо мне́ (about me)	о тебе́

3rd person

	Masc.	*Fem.*	*Neut.*
Nom.	он (he)	она́ (she)	оно́ (it)
Gen.	(н)его́	(н)её	(н)его́
Dat.	(н)ему́	(н)ей	(н)ему́
Acc.	(н)его́	(н)её	(н)его́
Instr.	(н)им	(н)ей	(н)им
Prep.	о нём	о ней	о нём

Plural

Nom.	мы (we)	вы (you)	они́ (they)
Gen.	нас (of us)	вас (of you)	(н)их (of them)
Dat.	нам (to us)	вам (to you)	(н)им (to them)
Acc.	нас (us)	вас (you)	(н)их (them)
Instr.	на́ми (by us)	ва́ми (by you)	(н)и́ми (by them)
Prep.	о нас (about us)	о вас (about you)	о них (about them)

The two forms of the third person (его́ and него́; её and неё, etc.) are not interchangeable. The forms with н- are used when the pronoun is governed by a preposition.

Note that "you" can be expressed in two ways in Russian:

a) The familiar or ты-form, which is used in addressing close friends, relatives, children and pets.

b) The polite or вы-form, which is used in addressing mere acquaintances, strangers, older persons and superiors.

Ты and вы correspond in form and usage to French *tu* and *vous*.

4.2. The **reflexive pronouns** are себя́ and сам.

Себя́ (self) may refer to any person in the singular or plural, and corresponds to the English pronouns myself, yourself, himself, herself, itself, ourselves, yourselves, themselves. It has no nominative. The form себя́ is used for the genitive and accusative; себе for the dative; собо́й for the instrumental; and о себе́ for the prepositional. This word is used when no special emphasis is desired: он ду́мает о себе́ (he thinks about himself).

Сам, which is used to express the idea of myself, yourself, himself, etc., in an emphatical manner, follows the pronoun immediately, but generally precedes the noun: он сам (he himself); сам дире́ктор (the manager himself). The declension of сам is as follows:

	Singular			*Plural*
	Masc.	*Fem.*	*Neut.*	*All genders*
Nom.	сам	сама́	само́	сами́
Gen.	самого́	само́й	самого́	сами́х
Dat.	самому́	само́й	самому́	сами́м
Acc.	самого́	самоё	само́	сами́х
Instr.	сами́м	само́й	сами́м	сами́ми
Prep.	о само́м	о само́й	о само́м	о сами́х

4.3. The **possessive adjectives** and **pronouns** are:

		Singular		
		Masc.	*Fem.*	*Neut.*
1st person		мой (my)	моя́	моё
2nd person		твой (your)	твоя́	твоё
3rd person	*masc.*	его́ (his)	его́	его́
	fem.	её (her)	её	её
	neut.	его́ (its)	его́	его́

Plural

1st person	наш (our)	на́ша	на́ше
2nd person	ваш (your)	ва́ша	ва́ше
3rd person	их (their)	их	их

The possessive pronouns of the third person plural do not change for gender, number, and case. They have only one form.

Мой (my), твой (your, sing.), свой (one's own, their own) are declined in the same way, as follows:

	Singular			*Plural*
	Masc.	*Fem.*	*Neut.*	*All genders*
Nom.	мой	моя́	моё	мои́
Gen.	моего́	мое́й	моего́	мои́х
Dat.	моему́	мое́й	моему́	мои́м
Acc.	мой	мою́	моё	мои́
Instr.	мои́м	мое́й	мои́м	мои́ми
Prep.	о моём	о мое́й	о моём	о мои́х

The declensions of наш (our) and ваш (your: plural and/or polite) are identical, so that any declined form of ваш can be determined simply by substituting в for н.

	Singular			*Plural*
	Masc.	*Fem.*	*Neut.*	*All genders*
Nom.	наш	на́ша	наше	на́ши
Gen.	на́шего	на́шей	на́шего	на́ших
Dat.	на́шему	на́шей	на́шему	на́ших
Acc.	наш	на́шу	наш	на́ши
Instr.	на́шим	на́шей	на́шим	на́шими
Prep.	о на́шем	о на́шей	о на́шем	о на́ших

The possessive pronouns мой, твой, наш, ваш agree in gender, number, and case with the noun they qualify: моё письмо́ (my letter), твоего́ словаря́ (of your dictionary), на́ши кни́ги (our books).

As explained in **1.6**, when two forms are shown for the accusative, the fact whether an inanimate object or an animate being is designated determines if the accusative has the form of the nominative or of the genitive.

4.4. The most common **demonstrative adjectives** and **pronouns** in Russian are э́тот (this *or* that) and тот (that, contrasting with *this*). They are declined as follows:

	Singular					
	Masc.	*Fem.*	*Neut.*	*Masc.*	*Fem.*	*Neut.*
Nom.	э́тот	э́та	э́то	тот	та	то
Gen.	э́того	э́той	э́того	того́	той	того́
Dat.	э́тому	э́той	э́тому	тому́	той	тому́
Acc.	э́тот	э́ту	э́то	тот	ту	то
Instr.	э́тим	э́той	э́тим	тем	той	тем
Prep.	об э́том	об э́той	об э́том	о то́м	о той	о то́м

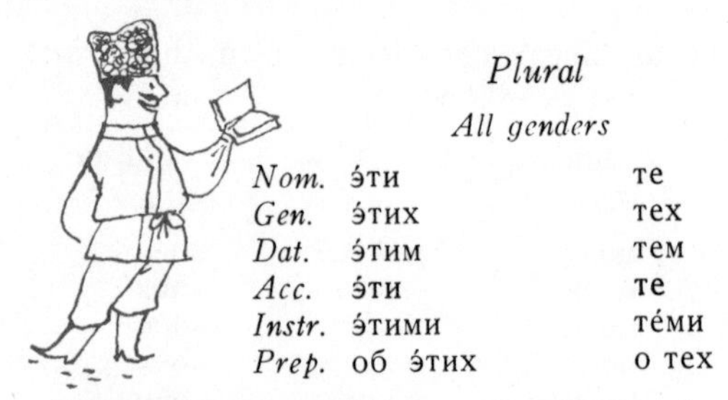

Plural

All genders

Nom.	э́ти	те
Gen.	э́тих	тех
Dat.	э́тим	тем
Acc.	э́ти	те
Instr.	э́тими	те́ми
Prep.	об э́тих	о тех

4.5. The **interrogative adjectives** and **pronouns** are:

Кото́рый, -ая, -ое, -ые (who *or* which; *also* that *when used as a relative pronoun*).

Какой, -ая, -ое, -ые (what kind of).

Both кото́рый and како́й are declined as regular adjectives.

Чей, чья, чьё, чьи (whose), which has the same declension as мой.

Кто (who) and **что** (what, which), which are also used as relative pronouns. They are declined as follows:

Nom.	кто	(who)	что	(what)
Gen.	кого́	(of whom)	чего́	(of what, which)
Dat.	кому́	(to whom)	чему́	(to what, which)
Acc.	кого́	(whom)	что	(what, which)
Instr.	кем	(by whom)	чем	(by what, which)
Prep.	о ком	(about whom)	о чём	(about what, which)

4.6. The **indefinite pronouns** and **adjectives**, declined as regular adjectives, are:

Masc.		*Fem.*	*Neut.*	*Plur.*
вся́кий	(any)	вся́кая	вся́кое	вся́кие
любо́й	(anyone)	люба́я	любо́е	любы́е
ка́ждый	(every, each)	ка́ждая	ка́ждое	ка́ждые
друго́й	(other)	друга́я	друго́е	други́е
тако́й	(such)	така́я	тако́е	таки́е

The particles **-то** and **-нибу́дь** are added to кто, что and other interrogative words to form compounds of *any* and *some*: кто́-то (someone); кто́-нибу́дь (anyone); что́-то (something); что́-нибу́дь (anything); где́-то (somewhere); где́-нибу́дь (anywhere).

The adjective and pronoun **весь** (all) is declined as follows:

	Singular			Plural
	Masc.	*Fem.*	*Neut.*	*All genders*
Nom.	весь	вся	всё	все
Gen.	всегó	всей	всегó	всех
Dat.	всемý	всей	всемý	всем
Acc.	весь	всю	всё	все
Instr.	всем	всéй	всем	всéми
Prep.	обо всём	обо всéй	обо всём	обо всéх

5. THE CONJUNCTION

5.1. *Coordinating* conjunctions join sentences, clauses, phrases, and words of equal rank. The most common ones are: **и** (and), **а** (and, but), **но** (but), **и . . . и** (both . . . and), **и́ли** (or), **и́ли . . . и́ли** (either . . . or), **ни . . . ни** (neither . . . nor).

5.2. *Subordinating* conjunctions introduce dependent clauses. The most common ones are: **éсли** (if), **когдá** (when), **как** (as), **потомý что** (because).

6. THE VERB

6.1. The verb быть (to be) has no forms for the present tense. The words *am, is* and *are,* therefore, are implied, not expressed: я инженéр (I am an engineer); он студéнт (he [is a] student); мы друзья́ (we [are] friends); они́ коммерсáнты (they [are] businessmen).

The future of быть is: я бýду, ты бýдешь, он (онá, онó) бýдет, мы бýдем, вы бýдете, они́ бýдут (I shall *or* will be, you will be, etc.).

The past of быть has the following forms: был (1st, 2nd and 3rd person masc. sing.), былá (1st, 2nd and 3rd person fem. sing.), бы́ло (1st, 2nd and 3rd person neut. sing.), бы́ли (1st, 2nd and 3rd person plural for all three genders).

The word есть, which is the third person singular of быть, is most generally used in the meaning of *there is* or *there are*. In combination with у меня́, у тебé, у негó, у неё, у нас, у вас and у них, it forms the common Russian idiom for *I have, you have,* etc. (lit.: "with me, you, etc., there is"): У вас есть карандáш? (have you [got] a pencil?); у меня́ есть два билéта (I have two tickets); есть у негó дéньги? (does he have [any] money?). The negative form requires the use of the genitive: у меня́ нет кни́ги (I do not have the book *or* I have no book).

6.2. ASPECTS

Most Russian verbs have two kinds of forms which are called "aspects" because they have to do with two ways of expressing actions or processes.

The *imperfective* aspect is used to describe an action in progress or one which is repeated or habitual without reference to the completion of the action.

The *perfective* aspect, on the other hand, is used to express the fact of the completion of the action. Consequently, there can be no present tense in this aspect.

Examples:

Я хочу́ чита́ть	I want to read (in general).
Я хочу́ писа́ть	I want to write (in general).
Я хочу́ прочита́ть э́ту кни́гу	I want to read this book through.
Я хочу́ написа́ть э́то письмо́	I want to write this letter (and finish it).

The infinitive of the perfective aspect is derived from the infinitive of the imperfective in various manners:

a) By prefixing prepositions to the infinitive of the imperfective:

чита́ть to read	прочита́ть to read through
писа́ть to write	написа́ть to write (and finish writing)

b) By changing the vowel which connects the stem with the infinitive ending **-ть**:

получа́ть to get (in general)	получи́ть to get (one particular thing)

c) By using a verb of a different stem:

говори́ть to speak	сказа́ть to say

6.3. CONJUGATIONS

The Russian verb is changed according to person, number and tense. This change is known as conjugation. There are two conjugations in Russian. The *first conjugation* is characterized by the vowel **е** which is predominant in the personal endings of the present tense. The *second conjugation* is characterized by the vowel **и** which predominates the personal endings of the present tense.

6.4. THE IMPERFECTIVE ASPECT

Infinitive

читáть to read — строи́ть to build

Present

FIRST CONJUGATION

Singular		*Plural*	
Я читáю	I read	мы читáем	we read
ты читáешь	you read	вы читáете	you read
он / онá } читáет	he / she } reads	они́ читáют	they read

Imperative

читáй! read! (familiar) — читáйте! read! (plural or polite)

SECOND CONJUGATION

Singular		*Plural*	
я стрóю	I build	мы стрóим	we build
ты стрóишь	you build	вы стрóите	you build
он / онá } стрóит	he / she } builds	они́ стрóят	they build

Imperative

стрóй! build! (familiar) — стрóйте! build! (plural or polite)

Future

The future is formed by adding the future of the verb быть (to be) to the infinitive:

я бýду читáть	I shall be reading
ты бýдешь читáть	you will be reading
он / онá / онó } бýдет читáть	he / she / it } will be reading
мы бýдем читáть	we shall be reading
вы бýдете читáть	you will be reading
они́ бýдут читáть	they will be reading

The imperfective future is generally used to express future meaning with no prediction as to the end of the contemplated action.

Past

The past tense is formed by changing the ending -ть of the infinitive into л, ла, ло:

Singular			*Plural*	
я	чита́л (*masc.*)	I read	мы чита́ли	we read
я	чита́ла (*fem.*)	I read	вы чита́ли	you read
ты	чита́л (*m.*)	you read	они́ чита́ли	they read
ты	чита́ла (*f.*)	you read		
он	чита́л (*m.*)	he read		
она́	чита́ла (*f.*)	she read		
оно́	чита́ло (*n.*)	it read		

The imperfective past may describe a number of repeated actions or it may describe a single past action or process. In all such cases, this form is used to express interest in the action itself without taking into account its possible completion.

6.5. THE PERFECTIVE ASPECT

Infinitive

прочита́ть	to read through
постро́ить	to build something (and finish it)

Present

The verbs belonging to the perfective aspect have no present tense.

Future

FIRST CONJUGATION

я прочита́ю I shall read (through)	мы прочита́ем we shall read (through)
ты прочита́ешь you will read	вы прочита́ете you will read
он прочита́ет he will read	они прочита́ют they will read

SECOND CONJUGATION

Я постро́ю I shall build (and finish it)	мы постро́им we shall build
ты постро́ишь you will build	вы постро́ите you will build.
он постро́ит he will build	они постро́ят they will build

The perfective future expresses future meaning with the expectation that the contemplated action will be completed.

Past

The past tense is formed by changing the ending **-ть** of the infinitive into **л, ла, ло.**

Singular		*Plural*
я прочита́л (*m.*)	I read through I have read I have read through	мы прочита́ли вы прочита́ли они́ прочита́ли
я прочита́ла (*f.*)		
ты прочита́л (*m.*)		
ты прочита́ла (*f.*)		
он прочита́л (*m.*)		
она́ прочита́ла (*f.*)		
оно́ прочита́ло (*n.*)		

The perfective past is used to describe a past action or a series of past actions which have been completed. Я прочита́л э́ту кни́гу (I read the book through, I have read the book *or* I have read the book through).

The **conditional** is formed by adding the particle **бы** after the imperfective past: я чита́л бы (I would read *or* I would have read).

6.6. The passive voice is frequently expressed by attaching the particle **-ся (-сь** after a vowel sound) to all the forms of a transitive verb: стро́ит дом (he builds a house); дом стро́ится (a house is built).

6.6.1. The particle -ся is also used with reflexive verbs: она́ одева́ется (she dresses herself *or* she is dressing). Она́ одева́ет means *she dresses* (*someone*); it requires an object to complete its sense.

6.7. A number of verbs are classified as irregular by most grammarians. Actually, they constitute an additional conjugation and share the same endings, which are characterized by the vowel **ё** in the present tense. The most important of these verbs are: **брать** (to take), **вести́** (to lead), **дава́ть** (to give), **идти́** (to go), **жить** (to live), **звать** (to call), **нести́** (to carry).

Singular	*Plural*	*Singular*	*Plural*
я беру́ I take	мы берём	я даю I give	мы даём
ты берёшь	вы берёте	ты даёшь	вы даёте
он берёт	они́ беру́т	он даёт	они дают

6.8. VERBS OF MOTION

There are two main groups of verbs of motion in Russian:

I. ходи́ть	е́здить	бега́ть	лета́ть	вози́ть	носи́ть
II. идти́	е́хать	бежа́ть	лете́ть	везти́	нести́
to go, to walk	to ride	to run	to fly	to drive	to carry

Each verb of group I has a corresponding verb in group II. In English both the verb of group I and its corresponding verb in group II are rendered by the same verb.

The verbs of group I denote an action of movement that has taken place repeatedly or during an indefinite period of time. Those of the second group indicate an action of movement that takes place at a definite time and in a definite direction: Ива́н ходи́т в шко́лу (John goes to school [usually or in general]); Ива́н идёт в шко́лу (John is going to school [at this moment]).

In the Dictionary section, verbs of group I are labeled *indefinite* (*ind.*) and those of group II are labeled *definite* (*def.*).

6.9. Russian **participles** usually have the following endings:

a) Present active participle, in **-щий**: чита́ющий he who reads
b) Past active participle, in **-вший**: чита́вший he who read
c) Present passive participle, in **-мый**: чита́емый he that is read
d) Past passive participle, in **-нный**: чи́танный he that was read

There are two **gerunds** in Russian:

a) Present gerund, in **-я**: чита́я when reading
b) Past gerund, in **-в** or **-вши**: чита́вши when having read

7. WORD ORDER

7.1. Word order is not so strict in Russian as it is in English since there is little possibility of misinterpreting the function of a word, regardless of its position. Since each function is characterized by specific word endings, the normal word order often is not different from that of English, but transpositions of subject and verb for stylistic effect are very common. This phenomenon is amply illustrated by the conversational sentences in this book.

7.2. The double negative is required in Russian: я ничего́ не зна́ю or я не зна́ю ничего́ (I don't know anything [*lit.*: "not nothing"]); он никогда́ не идёт or он не идёт никогда́ (he doesn't go anywhere [*lit.*: "not nowhere"]).

APPENDICES

IMPORTANT SIGNS

Биле́тная ка́сса	Ticket window
Внима́ние	Attention
Вокза́л	Railroad station
Вска́кивать и соска́кивать на ходу́ стро́го воспреща́ется	Getting on or off while car is in motion is strictly forbidden
Вход	Entrance
Вход воспреща́ется	No admittance, keep out
Вы́ход	Exit
Грунтова́я доро́га	Dirt road
Да́мская ко́мната	Ladies' room
Держа́ться пра́вой (ле́вой) стороны́	Keep to the right (left)
Для же́нщин	Women
Для мужчи́н	Men
Доро́га в плохо́м состоя́нии	Road in bad condition
Доро́га ремонти́руется	Road under repair
Железнодоро́жный перее́зд	Railroad crossing
Закры́то	Closed
Заме́длить ход	Slow down
Круто́й поворо́т	Sharp curve
Круто́й спуск	Sharp slope
Кури́ть воспреща́ется	No smoking
Ме́дленная езда́	Drive slowly
Мост	Bridge
Му́жская ко́мната	Men's room
Объе́зд	Detour
Опа́сно	Danger
Остано́вка ваго́нов	Streetcar stop
Осторо́жно	Caution
Отделе́ние мили́ции	Police station
Откры́то	Open
Перекрёсток	Street crossing, intersection
Пересече́ние доро́г	Road crossing
Переходи́те у́лицу то́лько на перекрёстках	Cross the street at corners only
Плева́ть воспреща́ется	No spitting
Пожа́рная ле́стница	Fire escape
Почто́вое отделе́ние	Post office

Преде́льная ско́рость 50 км. в час	Speed limit 50 km. per hour	**Стой! (стоп!)**	Stop!
Прое́зд в одну́ сто́рону	One-way traffic	**Стоя́нка воспреща́ется**	No parking
Прое́зд закры́т	Road closed	**Телегра́ф**	Telegraph office
Путь свобо́ден	Road open	**Ток высо́кого напряже́ния**	High tension line
Разгова́ривать с вагоново-жа́тым стро́го воспреща́ется	Talking to conductor prohibited	**Тупи́к**	Dead end
Сквозно́й прое́зд закры́т	No thoroughfare	**Убо́рная**	Toilet, washroom
Спра́вки	Information bureau	**Ходи́ть и е́здить по путя́м стро́го воспреща́ется**	All persons are forbidden to enter or cross the tracks
Ста́нция ско́рой по́мощи	First aid station	**Ходи́ть по траве́ воспреща́ется**	Keep off the grass
		Ша́гом	Go slow
		Шоссе́	Paved road

A few more signs will be found on page 81.

COUNTRIES AND PEOPLES

This list, which also contains the names of continents, gives the names of the countries in the first column and the English equivalent in the second column. The third and fourth columns give the corresponding words for the adjectives and inhabitants, respectively. Example: **Фра́нция** (France), **францу́зский** (French), **францу́з** (Frenchman). Note that the adjectives and the words for the inhabitants are not spelled with an initial capital letter.

Name of Country	*English Equivalent*	*Adjective*	*Inhabitant*
Австра́лия	Australia	австрали́йский	австрали́ец
А́встрия	Austria	австри́йский	австри́ец
А́зия	Asia	азиа́тский	азиа́т
Аля́ска	Alaska	аля́скский	—
Аме́рика	America	америка́нский	америка́нец
А́нглия	England	англи́йский	англича́нин
Ара́вия	Arabia	ара́бский	ара́б
Аргенти́на	Argentina	аргенти́нский	аргенти́нец
Афганиста́н	Afghanistan	афга́нский	афга́нец
А́фрика	Africa	африка́нский	африка́нец
Бе́льгия	Belgium	бельги́йский	бельги́ец

Name of Country	*English Equivalent*	*Adjective*	*Inhabitant*
Би́рма	Burma	бирма́нский	бирма́нец
Болга́рия	Bulgaria	болга́рский	болга́рин
Боли́вия	Bolivia	боливи́йский	боливи́ец
Брази́лия	Brazil	брази́льский	бразилья́нец
Беликобри-та́ния	Great Britain	брита́нский	брита́нец
Ве́нгрия	Hungary	венге́рский	венге́рец
Венецуэ́ла	Venezuela	венецуэ́льский	венецуэ́лец
Герма́ния	Germany	неме́цкий	не́мец
Голла́ндия	Holland	голла́ндский	голла́ндец
Гре́ция	Greece	гре́ческий	грек
Да́ния	Denmark	да́тский	датча́нин
Евро́па	Europe	европе́йский	европе́ец
Еги́пет	Egypt	еги́петский	египтя́нин
Изра́иль	Israel	изра́ильский	изра́илец
Ира́к	Iraq	—	—
Ира́н	Iran, Persia	ира́нский, перси́дский	ира́нец, перс
Ирла́ндия	Ireland	ирла́ндский	ирла́ндец
Исла́ндия	Iceland	исла́ндский	исла́ндец
Испа́ния	Spain	испа́нский	испа́нец
Ита́лия	Italy	италья́нский	италья́нец
Кана́да	Canada	кана́дский	кана́дец
Китай	China	кита́йский	кита́ец
Колу́мбия	Colombia	колумби́йский	колумби́ец
Люксембу́рг	Luxemburg	люксембу́рг-ский	люксембу́ржец
Манчжу́рия	Manchuria	манчжу́рский	манчжу́р
Ме́ксика	Mexico	мексика́нский	мексика́нец
Монго́лия	Mongolia	монго́льский	монго́л
Норве́гия	Norway	норве́жский	норве́жец
Пана́ма	Panama	пана́мский	пана́мец
Парагва́й	Paraguay	парагва́йский	парагва́ец
По́льша	Poland	по́льский	поля́к
Португа́лия	Portugal	португа́льский	португа́лец
Росси́я (СССР)	Russia (USSR)	ру́сский	ру́сский
Румы́ния	Rumania	румы́нский	румы́н
Се́верная Аме́рика	North America	се́веро-амери-ка́нский	—

Name of Country	*English Equivalent*	*Adjective*	*Inhabitant*
Соединённые Шта́ты Аме́рики (США)	United States of America (USA)	америка́нский	америка́нец
Ту́рция	Turkey	туре́цкии	ту́рок
Уругва́й	Uruguay	уругва́йский	уругва́ец
Финля́ндия	Finland	финля́ндский, фи́нский	финля́ндец, финн
Фра́нция	France	францу́зский	францу́з
Центра́льная Аме́рика	Central America	—	—
Чехослова́кия	Czechoslovakia	чехослова́цкий, че́шский	чех
Чи́ли	Chile	чили́йский	чили́ец
Швейца́рия	Switzerland	швейца́рский	швейца́рец
Шве́ция	Sweden	шве́дский	швед
Эквадо́р	Ecuador	эквадо́рский	эквадо́рец
Югосла́вия	Yugoslavia	югосла́вский	—
Ю́жная Аме́рика	South America	ю́жно-америка́нский	—
Япо́ния	Japan	япо́нский	япо́нец

GIVEN NAMES

Male

Full Names	*Diminutives*	*Full Names*	*Diminutives*
Апекса́ндр	Са́ша, Шу́ра, Са́ня	Константи́н	Ко́стя
Алексе́й	Алёша	Лев	Лёва
Андре́й	Андрю́ша	Макси́м	—
Бори́с	Бо́ря	Михаи́л	Ми́ша
Васи́лий	Ва́ся	Никола́й	Ко́ля
Влади́мир	Воло́дя, Во́ва	О́сип	О́ся
Григо́рий	Гри́ша	Па́вел	Па́ша, Па́влик
Дми́трий	Ми́тя, Ди́ма	Пётр	Пе́тя
Евге́ний	Же́ня	Семён	Се́ня
Его́р	Его́рушка	Серге́й	Серёжа
Ива́н	Ва́ня	Степа́н	Стёпа
Игорь	Го́ря	Фёдор	Фе́дя
Илья́	Илью́ша	Юрий	Юра
Ио́сиф	О́ся	Яков	Яша

Female

Full Names	*Diminutives*	*Full Names*	*Diminutives*
Алекса́ндра	Са́ша, Шу́ра	Коения	Ксюша
Анаста́сия	На́стя	Ли́дия	Ли́да
А́нна	А́ня, А́нюта, А́ннушка	Любо́вь	Люба
		Людми́ла	Лю́да, Ми́ла
Валенти́на	Ва́ля	Мари́я	Ма́ша, Ма́ня
Варва́ра	Ва́ря	Ма́рфа	Марфу́ша
Ве́ра	—	Наде́жда	На́дя
Гали́на	Га́ля	Ната́лья	Ната́ша, На́та
Да́рья	Да́ша	Ни́на	—
Екатери́на	Ка́тя	О́льга	О́ля
Еле́на	Ле́на, Лёля	Со́фья	Со́ня
Елизаве́та	Ли́за	Тама́ра	—
Ири́на	Ира	Татья́на	Та́ня
Зинаи́да	Зи́на, Ида		

RUSSIAN MONEY

черво́нец	chervonets (monetary unit of the USSR)
бума́жный черво́нец	paper chervonets (2-dollar bill*)
рубль	ruble (1/10 chervonets)
копе́йка	kopek (1/100 ruble)

Nickel-bronze Coins

копе́йка	(1-kopek piece)	kopek
две копе́йки	(2-kopek piece)	
три копе́йки	(3-kopek piece)	
пятачо́к, пыта́к	(5-kopek piece)	piatachok

Silver Coins

гри́венник	(10-kopek piece)	grivennik
пятна́дцать копе́ек	(15-kopek piece)	
два́дцать копе́ек	(20-kopek piece)	
полти́нник	(50-kopek piece)	poltinnik
рубль	(1-ruble piece)	ruble

Gold Coin

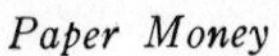
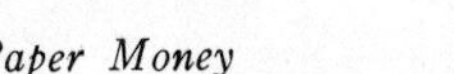

черво́нец	(1-chervonets piece)	chervonets

Paper Money

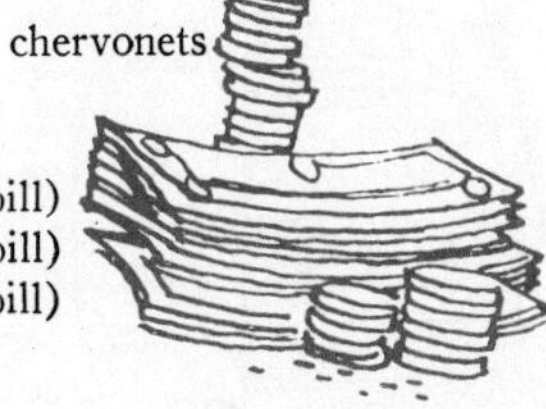

рублёвая бума́жка	(1-ruble bill)
трёхрублёвка	(3-ruble bill)
пятирублёвка	(5-ruble bill)

---
* U.S. equivalent.

десятирублёвка	(10-ruble bill)
червóнец	(1-chervonets bill)
бумáжка в два червóнца	(2-chervonets bill)
бумáжка в три червóнца	(3-chervonets bill)
бумáжка в пять червóнцев	(5-chervonets bill)
бумáжка в дéсять червóнцев	(10-chervonets bill)
бумáжка в двáдцать пять червóнцев	(25-chervonets bill)
бумáжка в пятьдеся́т червóнцев	(50-chervonets bill)

RUSSIAN MEASURES

Length

	Metric system		*Old measures still in use*
метр	meter (39.37 inches)	верстá	verst (0.66 mile)
сантимéтр	centimeter (0.39 inch)	сáжень	sazhen (7 feet)
миллимéтр	millimeter (0.04 inch)	арши́н	arshin (28 inches)
киломéтр	kilometer (0.62 mile)	вершóк	vershok (1.75 inches)
		фут	fut (1 foot)
		дюйм	dyuim (1 inch)

Area

	Metric system		*Old measure still in use*
гектáр	hectare (2.47 acres)	десяти́на	desyatina (2.7 acres)

Weight

	Metric system		*Old measures still in use*
килогрáмм	kilogram (2.2 pounds)	фунт	funt (0.9 pound)
грамм	gram (0.04 ounce)	пуд	pud (36.07 pounds)
тóнна	ton (2,204 pounds)		

Liquid

литр liter (1.05 liquid quarts)

RUSSIAN-ENGLISH
AND
ENGLISH-RUSSIAN DICTIONARY

ABBREVIATIONS USED IN THE DICTIONARY SECTION

acc. accusative
adj. adjective
adv. adverb
conj. conjunction
dat. dative
def. definite
f. feminine
gen. genitive
imp. imperfective
indecl. indeclinable
indef. indefinite
loc. locative (= prepositional)
m. masculine
n. neuter
perf. perfective
pl. plural
prep. preposition
pron. pronoun
rel. relative

RUSSIAN-ENGLISH DICTIONARY

In the Russian-English Dictionary, the following points should be noted:

Nouns are always given with their gender, so that their pattern of declension can be easily located in the Outline of Grammar (**1.3-5**).

Adjectives are listed in their masculine nominative singular form. (For the declension of adjectives, see **2.3** in the Grammar section.) When English words used both as nouns and adjectives function as adjectives, they are marked with (adj.) following the English word.

Verbs: The imperfective and the perfective infinitives are listed as separate entries (when both exist), marked *imp.* and *perf.,* respectively. Those not marked are imperfective in form and/or function, and do not have a perfective counterpart. For verbs of motion, both the indefinite and definite infinitives (see Grammar, **6.8**) are given, marked *indef.* and *def.,* respectively. When the reflexive has the same meaning as the non-reflexive form of the verb, it is marked with (**ся**) or (**сь**) attached to the infinitive of the verb, but when the reflexive has a different meaning it is given as a separate entry.

А

а but; and
абзáц *m.* paragraph
абрикóс *m.* apricot
áвгуст *m.* August
автóбус *m.* bus
автомоби́ль *m.* automobile
áвтор *m.* author
áгент *m.* agent
агóния *f.* agony
агрéссия *f.* aggression
ад *m.* hell
адвокáт *m.* lawyer
администрáтор *m.* administrator
администрати́вный administrative
áдрес *m.* address
аккредити́в *m.* letter of credit
актёр *m.* actor
актри́са *f.* actress
алкогóль *m.* alcohol
альбóм *m.* album
аллó! hello! (on telephone)
Амéрика *f.* America
америкáнский American (adj.)
америкáнец American (masc.)
америкáнка American (fem.)
анáлиз *m.* analysis
англи́йский English
англичáнин *m.* Englishman
англичáнка *f.* Englishwoman
Англия *f.* England
анкéта *f.* questionnaire
антиквáрный antiquarian
аппарáт *m.* apparatus
апрéль *m.* April
аптéка *f.* drugstore
арбу́з *m.* watermelon
аргумéнт *m.* argument
арéст *m.* arrest
арифмéтика *f.* arithmetic
áрмия *f.* army
архитéктор *m.* architect
атáка *f.* attack
атлéт *m.* athlete

áтом *m.* atom
афи́ша *f.* bill, poster
ах! ah!
аэродро́м *m.* airport
аэропла́н *m.* airplane

Б

ба́ба *f.* peasant woman
ба́бочка *f.* butterfly
ба́бушка *f.* grandmother
бага́ж *m.* baggage
ба́за *f.* base, basis
база́р *m.* market
баклажа́н *m.* eggplant
бал *m.* ball, dance
бала́нс *f.* balance
бале́т *m.* ballet
балко́н *m.* balcony
балова́ть *imp.* to spoil, to indulge
бана́н *m.* banana
банк *m.* bank
ба́нка *f.* jar
бара́нина *f.* mutton
бастова́ть *imp.* to (go on) strike
башма́к *m.* shoe
бе́гать *indef.* to run
беда́ *f.* trouble, mishap
бе́лный poor
бежа́ть *def.* to run; to escape
без without
безделу́шка *f.* curio, trifle
бе́лый white
бельё *n.* linen; laundry
бе́рег *m.* shore; coast; bank (of a river)
берёза *f.* birch
бесе́да *f.* conversation, talk
беспереса́дочный express (train)
беспоко́йство *n.* disturbance
беспоко́ить *imp.* to disturb
беспоко́иться *imp.* to worry
биле́т *m.* ticket
бино́кль *m.* binoculars
бискви́т *m.* sponge cake
бить *imp.* to beat; to hit; to strike
бифште́кс *m.* steak
благодари́ть *imp.* to thank
благода́рный thankful, grateful
благодаря́ thanks to
благоро́дный noble
бланк *m.* form
бле́дный pale
блесте́ть *imp.* to glitter; to shine
блестя́щий brilliant
бли́зкий near
бли́зко near
ближа́йший nearest, closest
бли́же nearer, closer
блонди́н *m.* blonde
блонди́нка *f.* blonde
блу́зка *f.* blouse
блю́до *n.* dish
Бог *m.* God
бога́тый rich, wealthy
бо́дрый cheerful
бой *m.* fight, conflict
бо́йкий smart, sharp; glib
бок *m.* side
бо́лее more
боле́знь *f.* illness, sickness
боле́ть *imp.* to hurt, to be sick
болта́ть *imp.* to chatter
боль *f.* pain
бо́льно painful
больно́й sick, ill
бо́льше more, bigger
большинство́ *n.* majority
большо́й big, large, great
борода́ *f.* beard
боро́ться *imp.* to struggle; to wrestle
борщ *m.* borsht, beet soup
борьба́ *f.* fight, struggle
боя́ться *imp.* to be afraid
брат *m.* brother
брать *imp.* to take
брить (ся) *imp.* to shave (oneself)
бровь *f.* eyebrow
броса́ть *imp.* to throw; to give up
бро́сить *perf.* to throw; to give up
брошь *f.* brooch
буди́ть *imp.* to awaken, to wake up
бу́дто as if, as though
бу́дущее *n.* the future
бу́дущий future, next
бульо́н *m.* bouillon, broth
бума́га *f.* paper
буты́лка *f.* bottle
буфе́т *m.* refreshment room
бы *conditional particle*
быва́ть *iter.* to take place
бы́стро fast, quickly
бы́стрый fast, quick
быть to be

В

в in
вагóн *m.* railroad car
вагóн-ресторáн *m.* dining car
вáжный important
вам *dat.* of вы
вáнна *f.* bath
вáнная *f.* bathroom
варúть *imp.* to cook
вас *gen.* and *loc.* of вы
ваш your (*plural and polite form*)
вверх up, upward
ввестú *perf.* to introduce; to lead in
вдоль along, by
вдруг suddenly
ведь well; after all
вездé everywhere
везтú *def.* to convey, to transport
век *m.* century
велéть *imp.* to order, to command
велúкий great
великолéпный splendid
вéна *f.* vein
венчáть *imp.* to marry
вéра *f.* belief, faith
верёвка *f.* cord, rope, string
вéрить *imp.* to believe, to trust
вéрно true, right
вернýть, *perf.* to bring back; to return
вернýться to return
вéрный true, faithful
вероя́тно probably, likely
вертéться *imp.* to turn; to revolve
верх *m.* upper part, top
вéрхний upper
вершúна *f.* top, peak, summit
вес *m.* weight; influence
вéсело gaily, merrily
весёлый gay, cheerful
вéсить *imp.* to weigh
веснá *f.* spring
вестú *def.* to lead
весь all
весьмá very much, exceedingly
вéтер *m.* wind
вéчер *m.* evening
вéчером in the evening
вéчный eternal
вещь *f.* thing
взгляд *m.* glance; view
взгля́дывать *imp.* to throw a glance (at)
взглянýть *perf.* to throw a glance at
вздор *m.* nonsense
вздохнýть *perf.* to sigh
вздыхáть *imp.* to sigh
взимáть to levy (taxes, duties, etc.)
взять *perf.* to take
вид *m.* view
видáть *iter.* to see (now and then)
вúдеть *imp.* to see
вúдимо apparently, evidently
вúдно evidently, apparently
вúдный visible; prominent
вúза *f.* visa
вúлка *f.* fork
винá *f.* fault, guilt
винó *n.* wine
виновáтый guilty; sorry
висéть *imp.* to hang
вúшня *f.* cherry
включáть *imp.* to include
включúть *perf.* to include
вкус *m.* taste
вкýсный tasty
владéть *imp.* to own, to possess; to control
власть *f.* power; authority, rule
влия́ние *n.* influence
влюбúться *perf.* to fall in love
влюбля́ться *imp.* to fall in love
вмéсте together
вмéсто instead of
вначáле in the beginning, at first
вне outside
внезáпно suddenly
внéшний external
вниз downwards
внизý downstairs; below
внимáние *n.* attention
внимáтельно attentively
вновь anew, over again
внýк *m.* grandson
внýтренний inner, internal
внутрú inside, within
во врéмя during
вó-время on time
вóвсе completely, altogether
...нет not at all
во-вторы́х secondly
водá *f.* water

води́ть *indef.* to lead
води́ться to live, to inhabit
во́дка *f.* vodka
водоро́д *m.* hydrogen
вое́нный military
возвраща́ть *imp.* to bring back; to return
возвраща́ться to come back, to return
во́здух *m.* air
возду́шный air-
во́зле near; beside
возмо́жно possible
возмо́жность *f.* possibility; chance
возмо́жный possible
возника́ть *imp.* to arise
возни́кнуть *perf.* to arise
во́зраст *m.* age
война́ *f.* war
во́йско *n.* troops, army
войти́ *perf.* to go in
вокза́л *m.* railroad station
вокру́г around, about
волна́ *f.* wave
волне́ние *n.* agitation, disturbance
во́лос *m.* hair
во́льность *f.* freedom, liberty
во́ля *f.* will; freedom
вон there (is); yonder
вообще́ generally, in general
во-пе́рвых in the first place
вопро́с *m.* question
воро́та *f., pl.* gate, gateway
воротни́к *m.* collar
восемна́дцать eighteen
во́семь eight
во́семьдесят eighty
восемьсо́т eight hundred
воскли́кнуть *perf.* to exclaim
восклица́ть *imp.* to exclaim
воскресе́нье *n.* Sunday
воспита́ние *n.* upbringing; education
воспомина́ние *n.* recollection, reminiscence
воспрети́ть *perf.* to forbid, to prohibit
воспреща́ть *imp.* to forbid, to prohibit
восто́к *m.* east
восто́рг *m.* delight
востре́бование *n.* claiming
до востре́бования general delivery (at post office)
восхити́тельный delightful
восьмо́й eighth
вот here is, are
впервы́е the first time
вперёд ahead; forward
впереди́ ahead (of); in front (of); before
впечатле́ние *n.* impression
вполне́ completely, entirely, quite
враг *m.* enemy
врать *imp.* to lie, to tell lies
врач *m.* physician
вре́дно harmful
вре́мя *n.* time
всегда́ always
всё everything
всё-таки nevertheless, still
вско́ре shortly, soon (after)
вска́кивать *imp.* to jump up
вскочи́ть *perf.* to jump up
вслух aloud
вспомина́ть *imp.* to remember, to recall
вспо́мнить *perf.* to remember, to recall
вспы́шка *f.* outburst; flash bulb
встава́ть *imp.* to get up, to stand up, to rise
встать *perf.* to get up, to stand up, to rise
встре́тить *perf.* to meet
встре́ча *f.* meeting
встре́чать *imp.* to meet
вступа́ть *imp.* to enter; to join
вступи́ть *perf.* to enter; to join
всю́ду everywhere
вся́кий any, every
вто́рник *m.* Tuesday
второ́й second
вход *m.* entrance
входи́ть *imp.* to go in
вчера́ yesterday
вчера́шний yesterday's
вы you (*plural and polite*)
выбира́ть *imp.* to choose; to elect
вы́бор *m.* choice
вы́брать *perf.* choose; to elect
вы́вести *perf.* to lead out; to conclude

выводи́ть *imp.* to lead out; to conclude
вы́глядеть to look like
выдава́ть *imp.* to distribute; to betray
вы́дать *perf.* to distribute; to betray
вы́держать *perf.* to bear, to stand, to endure
выде́рживать *imp.* to bear, to stand, to endure
вы́езд *n.* departure
выездно́й exit-
выезжа́ть *imp.* to leave, to depart
вы́ехать *perf.* to leave, to depart
вызвать *perf.* to call out; to challenge; to provoke
вызыва́ть *imp.* to call out; to challenge; to provoke
вы́йти *perf.* to go out, to get out
вы́нести *perf.* to carry out, to take out
вынима́ть *imp.* to take out, to remove
выноси́ть *imp.* to carry out, to take out
вы́нуть *perf.* to take out, to remove
вы́пить *perf.* to drink up
выпуска́ть *imp.* to let out, to release
вы́пустить *perf.* to let out, to release
выража́ть(ся) *imp.* to express (oneself)
выраже́ние *n.* expression
вы́разить(ся) *perf.* to express (oneself)
выраста́ть *imp.* to grow (up)
вы́расти *perf.* to grow (up)
выставля́ть *imp.* to stick out, to put out
высо́вываться *imp.* to lean out
высо́кий high, tall
высоко́ high
вы́ставить *perf.* to put out, to display
выставля́ть *imp.* to put out, to display
вы́ставка *f.* exhibition
вы́стирать *perf.* to launder, to wash
выступа́ть *imp.* to come forward; to perform
вы́ступить *perf.* to step forward; to break out
вы́шивка *f.* embroidery
вы́ход *m.* exit
выходи́ть *perf.* to go out, to get off

выходно́й день day off

Г

газе́та *f* newspaper
галере́я *f.* gallery
гало́ша *f.* rubbers
га́лстук *m.* necktie
гара́ж *m.* garage
гаранти́ровать *imp.* to guarantee
гара́нтия *f.* guarantee
гардеро́б *m.* wardrobe
гармо́ния *f.* harmony
где where
где-то somewhere
генера́л *m.* general
ге́ний *m.* genius
геогра́фия *f.* geography
геоме́трия *f.* geometry
геро́й *m.* hero
гибнуть *imp.* to perish
гита́ра *f.* guitar
глава́ *f.* head, chief; chapter
гла́вный main, chief
глаго́л *m.* verb
гла́дить *imp.* to iron
глаз *m.* eye
глота́ть *imp.* to swallow
глубина́ *f.* depth
глубо́кий deep
глубоко́ deeply, profoundly
глу́пый stupid, silly, foolish
глухо́й deaf
гляде́ть *imp.* to look
гнев *m.* anger
гнездо́ *n.* nest
говори́ть *imp.* to speak
говя́дина *f.* beef
год *m.* year
годи́ться *imp.,* to be valid
голова́ *f.* head
го́лод *m.* hunger
голо́дный hungry
го́лос *m.* voice
голу́бка *f.* darling
голубо́й light-blue, sky-blue

голу́бчик *m.* dear
го́лый bare, naked
гора́ *f.* mountain
гора́здо by far; much
горди́ться *imp.* to be proud of
го́рдость *f.* pride
го́рдый proud
го́ре *n.* grief; misfortune
горе́ть *imp.* to burn; to glow
го́рло *n.* throat
го́род *m.* city
городско́й urban, municipal
го́рький bitter
горя́чий hot
го́спиталь *m.* hospital
господи́н *m.* mister, gentleman
госпожа́ *f.* Mrs., lady
гости́ная *f.* living room
гости́ница *f.* hotel
гость *m.* guest
госуда́рственный state-, government-
госуда́рство n. state, government
гото́вить *imp.* to prepare, to cook
гото́виться to prepare (oneself)
гото́вый ready
гра́дус *m.* degree
граждани́н *m.* citizen
гражда́нка *f.* citizeness
грани́ца *f.* border
грех *m.* sin
грибы́ *m. pl.* mushrooms
гроза́ *f.* thunderstorm
грози́ть *imp.* to threaten
грома́дный huge, vast
гро́мкий loud
гро́мко aloud, loudly
гро́мче louder
гру́бый crude, rough, coarse
грудь *f.* breast, chest, bosom
гру́ппа *f.* group
гру́стный sad
гру́ша *f.* pear
гря́зный dirty, muddy, filthy
грязь *f.* dirt, mud, filth
губа́ *f.* lip
гуля́ть *imp.* to take a walk
густо́й thick, dense

Д

да yes
дава́ть *imp.* to give
давно́ long ago
да́же even
да́лее farther, further
далеко́ far
далёкий far; remote
дальне́йший further
да́льний distant
да́льше farther away
да́ма *f.* lady; queen (cards)
да́мский ladies'
дать perf. to give
да́ча *f.* country house, cottage
два two
два́дцать twenty
двена́дцать twelve
дверь *f.* door
две́сти two hundred
дви́гатель *m.* motor
дви́гаться *imp.,* to move, to stir
дви́нуться *perf.* to move, to advance
движе́ние *n.* movement, traffic
двое two
двойно́й double
двор *m.* back yard, courtyard
де́вочка *f.* little girl
де́вушка *f.* young lady, girl
девятна́дцать nineteen
девяно́сто ninety
девя́тый ninth
де́вять nine
девятьсо́т nine hundred
де́душка *m.* grandfather
де́йствие *n.* act (of a play), action
действи́тельно really, actually
действи́тельность *f.* reality; validity
действи́тельный actual, real, valid
де́йствовать *imp.* to act; to function, to work
дека́брь *m.* December
де́лать *imp.* to make, to do
де́латься to become
деле́ние *f.* division
дели́ть *imp.* to divide
де́ло *n.* affair, matter, business
день *m.* day
де́ньги *f. pl.* money
дере́вня *f.* village; country
де́рево *n.* tree
деревя́нный wooden

держáть *imp.* to hold; to keep
дéрзкий impudent, insolent
десéрт *m.* dessert
десяток *m.* ten
дéсять ten
десятый tenth
детáль *f.* detail
дéти *n. pl.* children
дéтский children's, childish
дéтство *n.* childhood
дешéвле cheaper
дёшево cheaply
дешёвый cheap
дéятельность *f.* activity
дивáн *m.* divan, sofa
дúкий wild; savage
дирéктор *m.* director
дитя *n.* child
длúнный long
для for
дно *n.* bottom
до until, up to, as far as
добивáться *imp.* to strive (for), to seek
добúться *perf.* to get, to obtain
дóбрый good, kind
довóльно enough; rather
довóльный pleased, satisfied
доезжáть *imp.* to ride up to, to reach
дождевúк *m.* raincoat
дождь *m.* rain
дойтú *perf.* to reach, to get to
доказáть *perf.* to prove
докáзывать *imp.* to prove
дóктор *m.* doctor
докумéнт *m.* document
долг *m.* debt; duty
дóлгий long, prolonged
дóлго for a long time
дóлжен must, have to, ought to
дóлжный due, proper
дóллар *m.* dollar
дóля *f.* share; lot, fate
дом *m.* house, home
дóма at home
домáшний domestic
домóй home
допускáть *imp.* to admit, to allow
допустúть *perf.* to admit, to allow
дорóга *f.* road, way
дорогóй dear, expensive
доскá *f.* board; plank
доставáть *imp.* to get; to fetch
достáвить *perf.* to deliver
доставлять *imp.* to deliver
достáточно enough
достáточный sufficient
достáть *perf.* to get; to reach
достижéние *n.* achievement
достóинство *n.* dignity; quality
достóйный deserving, worthy
дохóд *m.* profit
доходúть *imp.* to reach, to get to
дóчка *f.* daughter
дочь *f.* daughter
дрáма *f.* drama
дрáться *imp.* to fight
дрéвний ancient
дрожáть *imp.* to tremble; to shiver
друг *m.* friend
другóй other
дуб *m.* oak
дрýжба *f.* friendship
дýмать *imp.* to think
дýра *f.* fool
дурáк *m.* fool
дурнóй bad, nasty
дуть *imp.* to blow
дух *m.* spirit
духóвный spiritual
душá *f.* soul
душéвный sincere; mental
дýшный stuffy
дым *m.* smoke
дыня *f.* melon
дырá *f.* hole
дышáть *imp.* to breathe
дыхáние *n.* breathing, respiration
дюжина *f.* dozen
дядя *m.* uncle

Е

егó his; its
едá *f.* food
едвá hardly, scarcely
едúнственный only
едúный single; united
ездá *f.* drive, ride
éздить *indef.* to go (by vehicle), to ride
ель *f.* fir tree
éсли if

есте́ственный natural
есть *imp.* to eat
есть there is, are
е́хать *def.* to go (by vehicle), to ride
ещё still, yet

Ж

жа́дный greedy
жале́ть *imp.* to feel sorry, to regret
жа́лкий miserable, pitiful
жа́лоба *f.* complaint
жа́ловаться *imp.* to complain
жаль *impers.* pity, be sorry
жар *m.* heat; fever
жара́ *m.* heat; hot weather
жа́рить *imp.* to fry, to roast
жа́ркий hot
ждать *imp.* to wait
же *emphatic particle*
жела́ние *n.* wish, desire
жела́ть *imp.* to wish
желе́за *f.* iron
желе́зный iron, ferrous
жёлтый yellow
желу́док *m.* stomach
жена́ *f.* wife
жени́ться *imp. & perf.*, to marry; to get married
же́нский female, feminine
же́нщина *f.* woman
же́ртва *f.* victim
жёсткий stiff, hard
жесто́кий cruel; severe
жи́во lively
живо́й alive; lively
живо́т *m.* abdomen, belly
жизнь *f.* life
жир *m.* fat, grease
жи́рный fat
жить *imp.* to live
журна́л *m.* journal, magazine
журнали́ст *m.* journalist

З

за after, behind
заблуди́ться *perf.* to lose one's way
заблужда́ться *imp.* to lose one's way
забыва́ть *imp.* to forget
забы́ть *perf.* to forget
заве́дующий *m.* manager
завести́ *perf.* to acquire; to start (a motor); to wind up (a watch)
завива́ть *imp.* to wave (hair)
зави́ть *perf.* to wave (hair)
заво́д *m.* factory, plant
за́втра tomorrow
за́втрак *m.* breakfast
за́втракать *imp.* to have breakfast
зага́дка *f.* riddle
зага́р *m.* suntan
за́говор *m.* plot, conspiracy
загля́дывать *imp.* to peep in, to drop in
загляну́ть *perf.* to peep in, to drop in
заговори́ть *perf.* begin to speak
загора́ть *imp.* to tan
загоре́ть *perf.* to tan
зада́ча *f.* problem
зада́ток *m.* deposit, down payment
за́дний back-
заду́маться *perf.* to become thoughtful, pensive
заду́мываться *imp.* to become thoughtful
зае́дать *imp.* to jam, to get stuck
зае́сть *perf.* to jam, to get stuck
зайти́ *perf.* to drop by
зака́з *m.* order
заказа́ть *perf.* to order
заказно́й registered (letter)
зака́зывать *imp.* to order
заключе́ние *n.* conclusion; imprisonment
зако́н *m.* law
закрича́ть *perf.* to cry out, to scream, to yell
закрыва́ть *imp.* to close, to shut
закры́ть *perf.* to close, to shut
зал *m.* hall, salon
заме́на *f.* replacement, substitution
замени́ть *perf.* to substitute, to replace
заменя́ть *imp.* to substitute, to replace
замерза́ть *imp.* to freeze
замёрзнуть *perf.* to freeze
замести́тель *m.* substitute
заме́тить *perf.* to notice; to remark

замéтно noticeably
замечáтельный remarkable
замечáть *imp.* to notice
замóк *m.* lock
занимáть *imp.* to occupy
занятие *n.* occupation; activity
занять *perf.* to occupy; to borrow
зáнятый busy
зáпад *m.* west
зáпадный western
запаковáть *perf.* to pack; to wrap
запакóвывать *imp.* to pack; to wrap
запáс *m.* fund; supply
запаснóй emergency (door, exit)
зáпах *m.* smell, scent, odor
заперéть *perf.* to lock
запирáть *imp.* to lock
записáть *perf.* to write down
запúска *f.* note
запúсывать *imp.* to write down
заплáкать *perf.* to start crying
заполнéние *n.* filling out
запóлнить *perf.* to fill out
заполнять *imp.* to fill out
запретúть *perf.* to forbid
запрещáть *imp.* to forbid
зарядúть *perf.* to load (a camera)
заряжáть *imp.* to load (a camera)
засмеяться *perf.* to begin to laugh
заснýть *perf.* to fall asleep
заставáть *imp.* to find in
застáвить *perf.* to compel, to force
заставлять *imp.* to compel, to force
застáть *perf.* to find in
засыпáть *imp.* to fall asleep
затвóр *m.* shutter (camera)
затéм thereupon, subsequently
затó whereas; on the other hand
затруднéние *n.* trouble, difficulty
захватúть *perf.* to seize, to capture
захвáтывать *imp.* to seize, to capture
заходúть *imp.* to drop by
захотéть *perf.* to want, to feel like
зачéм why, what for
защúта *f.* defense; protection
заявúть *perf.* to declare
заявлять *imp.* to declare
звать *imp.* to call
звездá *f.* star
зверь *m.* beast
звонúть *imp.* to call, to ring, to telephone
звук *m.* sound
здáние *n.* building
здесь here
здорóвый well, healthy
здорóвье *n.* health
зелёный green
зéлень *f.* greens, vegetables
землЯ́ *f.* earth, land
земнóй earthly
зéркало *n.* mirror
зимá *f.* winter
зло *n.* evil; harm
злóба *f.* malice, wickedness
злой evil, wicked
знак *m.* sign; mark; symbol
знакóмить *imp.* to acquaint; to introduce
знакóмиться *imp.* to become acquainted with
знакóмство *n.* acquaintance
знакóмый familiar
знаменúтый famous
знáние *n.* knowledge
знатóк *m.* expert
знать *imp.* to know
значéние *n.* meaning; significance
знáчить *imp.* to mean
зóлото *n.* gold
золотóй golden
зрéние *n.* (eye)sight, vision
зуб *m.* tooth

И

и and
и . . . и both . . . and
игóлка *f.* needle
игрá *f.* playing, game
игрáть *imp.* to play
игрýшка *f.* toy
идéя *f.* idea
идтú *def.* to go, to walk
из out of, from
извéстный well-known
извинúть *perf.* to excuse
извинúться to apologize
извинять *imp.* to excuse
извиняться to apologize
издéлие *n.* manufactured article, ware

из-за from behind; from; because of
изли́шек *m.* excess
из-под from under
изю́м *m.* raisins
изя́щный elegant, refined
икра́ *f.* caviar
и́ли or
и́ли . . . и́ли either . . . or
и́менно just, exactly; namely
име́ть to have (used in a very few expressions)
и́мя *n.* first name
ина́че otherwise; else
иногда́ sometimes
иностра́нец *m.* foreigner
иностра́нка *f.* foreigner
иностра́нный foreign
интере́с *m.* interest
интере́сный interesting
интересова́ть *imp.* to interest
интересова́ться to be interested in
инти́мность *f.* intimacy
инти́мный intimate
Интури́ст *m.* intourist
иро́ния *f.* irony
иска́ть *imp.* to look for, to seek
исключе́ние *n.* exception; expulsion
и́скренний sincere
иску́сство *n.* art
испыта́ть *perf.* to try out, to test
испы́тывать *imp.* to try out, to test
исполне́ние *n.* performance; fulfilment
истори́ческий historic(al)
исто́рия *f.* history; story, tale
исчеза́ть *imp.* to disappear
исче́знуть *perf.* to disappear
итти́ or **идти́** *def.* to go (on foot)
их their
ию́ль *m.* July
ию́нь *m.* June

К

к to, toward
кабине́т *m.* study; private office
каблу́к *m.* heel
кавка́зкий Caucasian
ка́ждый each, every
каза́ться *imp.* to seem; to look like
как how, as
как-бу́дто as if, it seems
как-то somehow
како́в how, what, which
како́й what kind, which
како́й-нибудь some; any (kind)
како́й-то some kind of, any
ка́менный stone, of stone
ка́мень *m.* stone
ка́мера *f.* chamber, room
. . . хране́ния cloak room, luggage room
капита́л *m.* capital
капита́н *m.* captain
ка́пля *f.* drop
капу́ста *f.* cabbage
каранда́ш *m.* pencil
карма́н *m.* pocket
ка́рта *f.* map
карти́на *f.* picture
ка́рточка *f.* card
карто́шка *f.* potato
ка́сса *f.* ticket window, booking office, cashier's window
катало́г *m.* catalog
ка́чество *n.* quality
ка́шель *m.* cough
ка́шлять *imp.* to cough
каю́та *f.* cabin
кварти́ра *f.* apartment
квита́нция *f.* receipt
кино́ *n.* movies
кипяти́ть *imp.* to boil
кислоро́д *m.* oxygen
ки́слый sour
класс *m.* class
класть *imp.* to put
клуб *m.* club
клубни́ка *f.* strawberries
ключ *m.* key
кни́га *f.* book
кни́жка *f.* book(let)
кни́жный book-, bookish
князь *m.* prince
ковёр *m.* rug, carpet
когда́ when
когда́-нибу́дь ever; sometime or other
когда́-то once, formerly
ко́е-что something
ко́жа *f.* skin, leather
колбаса́ *f.* sausage
коле́но *n.* knee

колесó *n.* wheel
колúчество *n.* quantity; amount
кóлокол *m.* bell
колхóз *m.* collective farm
колхóзник *m.* collective farmer
колыбéль *f.* cradle
кольцó *n.* ring
комáнда *f.* team
комéдия *f.* comedy
кóмната *f.* room
конвéрт *m.* envelope
кондýктор *m.* conductor
конéц *m.* end
конéчно of course
конéчный final, last
контóра *f.* office
кончáть(ся) *imp.* to finish, to end
кóнчить(ся) *perf.* to finish, to end
коньяк *m.* cognac
копейка *f.* kopek
кóрень *m.* root
коридóр *m.* corridor
кормúть *imp.* to feed
корóбка *f.* box
корóва *f.* cow
корóткий short
кóротко briefly
корт *m.* court (tennis)
кость *f.* bone
костюм *m.* suit
котлéта *f.* cutlet, chop
котóрый which
кóфе *n.* coffee
крáйний extreme, utmost
красúвый pretty, handsome
крáска *f.* paint, dye
крáсный red
красотá *f.* beauty
крахмáлить *imp.* to starch
кредúтка *f.* money bill, banknote
крем *m.* cream
крéпкий strong
крéпко solidly, strongly, firmly
крéсло *n.* armchair, easy chair
крест *m.* cross
крестьянин *m.* peasant
крик *m.* cry, shout
крúкнуть *perf.* to shout, to cry out
кричáть *imp.* to shout, to scream
кровáть *f.* bed
кровь *f.* blood
крóме except
круг *m.* circle
крýглый round; complete
кругóм around
крýпный large, big
крылó *n.* wing, fender
крыльцó *n.* doorstep
крыша *f.* roof
крючóк *m.* hook
кто who
ктó-то someone
ктó-нибýдь anyone
кудá where (whereto)
кулáк *m.* fist; rich peasant
купáльный bathing (adj.)
купáть(ся) *imp.* to bathe
купé *n.* railroad compartment
купúть *imp.* to buy
курúтельная *f.* smoking car
курúть *imp.* to smoke
кýрица *f.* chicken
курс *m.* course, rate of exchange
курящий *m.* smoker
кусóк *m.* piece, bit
куст *m.* bush
кустáрный handicraft (adj.)
кýхня *f.* kitchen
кýча *f.* heap, lot

Л

лáдно all right, okay
ладóнь *f.* palm
дáзать, лáзить *indef.* to climb
лáска *f.* caress
ласкáть *imp.* to caress
лáсково kindly
лáсковый affectionate
лáять *imp.* to bark
лев *m.* lion
лéвый left
лёгкий light, easy
легкó lightly, easily
лёд *m.* ice
лежáть *imp.* to lie
лезть *def.* to climb
лекáрство *n.* medicine
лéкция *f.* lecture
ленúвый lazy
лентяй *m.* lazy person
лентяйка *f.* lazy person
лес *m.* forest; wood
лéска *f.* fishing line

ле́стница *f.* ladder, steps
ле́стничка *f.* little ladder
лета́ть *indef.* to fly
лете́ть *def.* to fly
ле́тний summer-
ле́то *n.* summer
ли *interrogative particle*
лимо́н *m.* lemon
ли́ния *f.* line
лист *m.* leaf, sheet (of paper)
лите́йный заво́д *m.* foundry
литерату́ра *f.* literature
лифт *m.* elevator, lift
ли́фчик *m.* brassiere
лицо́ *n.* face, person
ли́чно personally, in person
ли́чность *f.* personality
ли́чный personal, individual
ли́шний superfluous; unnecessary; spare
лоб *m.* forehead; brow
ло́дка *f.* boat
ложи́ться *imp.* to lie down, to go to bed
ло́жка *f.* spoon
ложь *f.* lie
ло́коть *m.* elbow
лома́ть *imp.* to break
лососи́на *f.* salmon
ло́шадь *f.* horse
луг *m.* meadow
лу́жа *f.* puddle, pool
лужа́йка *f.* lawn
лук *m.* onion
луна́ *f.* moon
луч *m.* ray, beam
лу́чше better
лу́чший better
любе́зный kind, polite
люби́ть *imp.* to love
любо́вь *f.* love
любо́й any, every
любопы́тство *n.* curiosity
любопы́тный curious
лю́ди *m. pl.* people

М

магази́н *m.* store
май *m.* May
ма́ленький small, little
ма́ло little, few
ма́лый small, little
ма́льчик *m.* boy
ма́ма *f.* mama
ма́никюр *m.* manicure
ма́рка *f.* stamp
март *m.* March
ма́сло *n.* butter; oil
ма́сса *f.* mass, heap, lot
масса́ж *m.* massage
ма́стер *m.* craftsman; skilled worker; foreman
матема́тика *f.* mathematics
материа́л *m.* material, cloth
матч *m.* match (sports)
мать *f.* mother
маха́ть *imp.* to wave; to wag
махну́ть *perf.* to wave; to wag
маши́на *f.* machine, engine
ме́бель *f.* furniture
мёд *m.* honey
медве́дь *m.* bear
ме́дленно slowly
медсестра́ *f.* nurse
медь *f.* copper
ме́жду between, among
междунаро́дный international
мел *m.* chalk
ме́лкий shallow; fine
ме́лочь *f.* detail, trifle; (small) change
ме́нее less
ме́ньше less
меню́ *n.* menu
меня́ *acc. & gen. of* **я**
у . . . I have
меня́ть *imp.* to change
ме́ра *f.* measure
ме́стный local
ме́сто *n.* place; seat; piece of luggage
ме́сяц *m* month
мета́лл *m.* metal
метла́ *f.* broom
ме́тод *m.* method
метр *m.* meter
метро́ *n.* subway
меха́ник *m.* mechanic
мечта́ *f.* daydream; ambition
мечта́ть *imp.* to daydream
меша́ть *imp.* to hinder; to disturb
мешо́к *m.* sack, bag
мёртвый dead

миг *m.* instant, moment
миллиа́рд *m.* billion
миллио́н *m.* million
ми́лость *f.* favor, mercy
ми́лый nice, sweet; dear
ми́ля *f.* mile
ми́мо by, past
минда́ль *m.* almond
минера́льный mineral
мину́та *f.* minute
мир *m.* world; peace
мирово́й world-wide, world
мне *dat., loc. of* **я**
мне́ние *n.* opinion
мно́гий many a, numerous (*used mostly in plural*)
мно́го much, many
моги́ла *f.* grave
мо́да *f.* fashion, vogue
мо́жно possible, permissible
мой my
молодёжь *f.* youth, young people
молодо́й young
мо́лодость *f.* youth
молоко́ *n.* milk
молото́к *m.* hammer
мо́лча silently, in silence
молча́ние *n.* silence
молча́ть *imp.* to be silent, to keep quiet
моме́нт *m.* moment
мо́ре *n.* sea
морко́вь *f.* carrot(s)
мост *m.* bridge
мочь to be able
мра́чный dark, gloomy
муж *m.* husband
мужи́к *m.* peasant
мужчи́на *m.* man
музе́й *m.* museum
му́зыка *f.* music
му́ка *f.* torment, torture
мука́ *f.* flour
мураве́й *m.* ant
му́скул *m.* muscle
му́ха *f.* fly
мы we
мы́ло *n.* soap
мысль *f.* thought, idea
мы́ть(ся) *imp.* to wash (oneself)
мышь *f.* mouse
мя́гкий soft; mild
мя́со *n.* meat
мяч *m.* ball (sports)

Н

на on
наблюда́ть to watch, to observe
наве́рно probably; surely
наверху́ upstairs
навести́ть *perf.* to visit
навеща́ть *imp.* to visit
навсегда́ forever, for good
навстре́чу towards
над over, above
надева́ть *imp.* to put on
наде́жда *f.* hope
наде́ть *perf.* to put on
наде́яться *imp.* to hope
на́до it is necessary
надоеда́ть *imp.* to bore, annoy
надое́сть *perf.,* to bore, to annoy
наза́д back; ago
назва́ть *perf.* to call, to name
назнача́ть *imp.* to set; to appoint; to assign
назна́чить *perf.* to set; to appoint; to assign
называ́емый called, named
называ́ть *imp.* to call, to name
называ́тся to be called, to be named
наибо́лее the most
наилу́чший the best
найти́ *perf.* to find
найти́сь to be found, to be located
наконе́ц finally, at last
нале́во to the left
налива́ть *imp.* to pour
нали́ть *perf.* to pour
нало́г *m.* tax
наме́рение *n.* intention, purpose
нанима́ть *imp.* to hire
наня́ть *perf.* to hire
наоборо́т *adv.* on the contrary, just the opposite
написа́ть *perf.* to write
напомина́ть *imp.* to remind
напо́мнить *perf.* to remind
направле́ние *n.* direction; way
напра́во to the right
напра́сно in vain
наприме́р for example, for instance
напрока́т for hire

напро́тив *prep.* across, opposite
наро́д *m.* people; nation
наро́дный national, people's
наро́чно purposely, on purpose
настоя́щий real, genuine
настрое́ние *n.* mood
насчёт about, concerning
нау́ка *f.* science; scholarship
нау́чный scientific; scholarly
находи́ть *imp.* to find
находи́ться to be found, to be located
на́ция *f.* nation
нача́ло *n.* beginning
нача́льник *m.* chief, boss
нача́ть *perf.* to begin, to start
нача́ть(ся) to start, to begin
начина́ть(ся) *imp.* to begin, to start
наш our
нашёл found (masc.)
не not
не́бо *n.* sky; heaven
невозмо́жно impossible
нево́льно involuntarily
негати́в *m.* negative (photography)
неда́вно recently, lately
неде́ля *f.* week
недожа́реный insufficiently fried, roasted (= rare)
недоса́ливать *imp.* not to salt enough
недосоли́ть *perf.* not to salt enough
недоста́точно not enough, insufficiently
не́жный tender; affectionate; delicate
незаме́тно unnoticed
нездоро́виться not to feel well
нездоро́вый not well, sick, ill
незнако́мый unfamiliar, unknown
некото́рый some, certain
нельзя́ impossible, not permitted
неме́дленно immediately
не́мец *m.* German
не́мка *f.* German
неме́цкий German
немно́го a little, a while
немно́жко a little bit
не́нависть *f.* hatred
необходи́мость *f.* necessity
необходи́мый necessary
необыкнове́нный unusual
неожи́данно unexpectedly; suddenly
неожи́данный unexpected
непоня́тный incomprehensible
непра́вильный not right, incorrect
непреме́нно without fail, certainly
неприя́тный unpleasant
не́сколько several, a few
несмотря́ in spite of
нести́ *def.* to carry
нести́сь to rush (about)
несча́стный unhappy, unfortunate
несча́стье *n.* misfortune; disaster
нет no, there is (are) not
неуже́ли really? indeed?
неча́янно accidentally
не́что something
ни not
нигде́ nowhere
ни́зкий low
ни́зко low, down
ни́жний lower
ника́к by no means
никогда́ never
никто́ nobody
никуда́ nowhere
ниско́лько not a bit, not at all
ни́тка *f.* thread
ничего́ nothing
ничто́ nothing
но but
но́вость *f.* news
но́вый new
нога́ *f.* foot; leg
нож *m.* knife
но́жницы *f. pl.* scissors
но́мер *m.* number, room (in hotel)
номеро́к *m.* tag (with number), check
но́рма *f.* norm, standard
норма́льно normally
норма́льный normal
нос *m.* nose
носи́льщик *m.* porter
носи́ть *iter.* to carry
носи́ться to wear
носки́ *m. pl.* socks
ночь *f.* night
ночно́й night, nocturnal
но́чью at night
ноя́брь *m.* November
нрав *m.* disposition, temper

нра́виться *imp.* to please
нра́вственный moral
нра́вы *m. pl.* customs; morals
ну well (*exclamation*)
нужда́ *f.* want, need
ну́жно necessary; must
ну́жный necessary
ны́не nowadays
ны́нешний present, modern

О

о about; against
о́ба *m.* both
обе́д *m.* dinner
обе́дать *imp.* to dine; to have dinner
обезья́на *m.* monkey
оберну́ть *perf.* to wrap up
оберну́ться to turn around
обёртывать *imp.* to wrap up
обеща́ть *imp. & perf.* to promise
оби́да *f.* insult; offense
оби́деть(ся) *perf.* to offend
обижа́ть(ся) *imp.* to offend
о́блако *n.* cloud
о́бласть *f.* district, province; domain, field
обме́нивать *imp.* to exchange
обмени́ть or **обменя́ть** *perf.* to exchange
обмени́ться to switch
обора́чивать *imp.* to wrap up
обора́чиваться to turn around
о́браз *m.* image; form; icon
образова́ние *n.* education
образо́ванный (well)-educated
обрати́ть *perf.* to direct; to convert
обрати́ться to apply to; to turn to
обра́тно back (adv.)
обра́тный reverse
обраща́ть *imp.* to direct; to change
обраща́ться to turn to, to apply or appeal to
обстано́вка *f.* furnishings; conditions, atmosphere
обстоя́тельство *n.* circumstance
обще́ственный public, social
о́бщество *n.* society
о́бщий common; general
объяви́ть *perf.* to announce
объясне́ние *n.* explanation
объявля́ть *imp.* to announce
объясни́ть *perf.* to explain
объясня́ть *imp.* to explain
обыкнове́нно usually; generally
обыкнове́нный ordinary
обы́чный usual, ordinary
обя́занность *f.* duty, responsibility
обя́занный obligated, indebted
обяза́тельно obligatory
овладева́ть *imp.* to take possession; to master
овладе́ть *perf.* to take possession; to master
огля́дываться *imp.* to look back (around)
огляну́ться *perf.* to look back (around)
ого́нь *m.* fire
огро́мный huge; tremendous
ограни́чивать *imp.* to limit
ограни́чить *perf.* to limit, to restrict
огуре́ц *m.* cucumber
оде́жда *f.* clothing, clothes
одева́ть(ся) *imp.* to dress (oneself)
оде́тый dressed, clothed
оде́ть(ся) *perf.* to dress (oneself)
одея́ло *n.* blanket
оди́н one
одина́ковый identical
оди́ннадцать eleven
одино́кий lonely; single
одна́жды once
одна́ко however; but
ожере́лье *n.* necklace
ожида́ние *n.* expectation
ожида́ть to expect
о́зеро *n.* lake
оказа́ть *perf.* to render
оказа́ться to happen to be; to find oneself
ока́зывать *imp.* to render
ока́зываться to happen to be, to happen, to turn out to be; to find oneself
ока́нчивать(ся) *imp.* to end
око́нчить(ся) *perf.* to end
окно́ *n.* window
о́коло near; about
оконча́тельно absolutely

октя́брь *m.* October
ома́р *m.* lobster
омле́т *m.* omelette
он he
она́ she
они́ they
оно́ it
опа́здывать *imp.* to be late
опа́сность *f.* danger
опа́сный dangerous
о́пера *f.* opera
опера́ция *f.* operation
о́перный opera (adj.)
описа́ние *n.* description
описа́ть *perf.* to describe
опи́сывать *imp.* to describe
опла́та *f.* payment
оплати́ть *perf.* to pay
опла́чивать *imp.* to pay
опозда́ние *n.* delay
опозда́ть *perf.* to be late
определённый definite, certain
определи́ть *perf.* to define, to determine
определя́ть *imp.* to define
опуска́ть *imp.* to lower
опусти́ть *perf.* to lower; to omit
о́пыт *m.* experiment; experience
опя́ть again
организа́ция *f.* organization
орёл *m.* eagle
оре́х *m.* nut
ору́дие *n.* equipment, tool; gun
ору́жие *n.* weapon, arms
освободи́ть *perf.* to liberate; to release
освободи́ться to become vacant
освобожда́ть *imp.* to liberate; to release
освобожда́ться to become vacant
осёл *m.* donkey, ass
о́сень *f.* autumn, fall
осмотре́ть *perf.* to examine, to inspect
осма́тривать *imp.* to examine, to inspect
осмо́тр *m.* inspection; examination
осно́ва *f.* basis
основа́ние *n.* basis, foundation
основа́ть *perf.* to found
основно́й basic, main
осно́вывать *imp.* to found
осо́бенно especially
осо́бенность *f.* peculiarity, feature
осо́бенный particular, peculiar
осо́бый special, extra
остава́ться *imp.* to stay, to remain
оста́вить *perf.* to leave; to abandon
оставля́ть *imp.* to leave
остально́й remaining
останови́ть(ся) *perf.* to stop; to stay
остано́вка *f.* stop
остана́вливать(ся) *imp.* to stop; to stay
оста́ться *perf.* to stay, to remain
осторо́жно carefully
осторо́жный careful
о́стрый sharp
от away from, from
отве́т *m.* answer, reply
отве́тить *perf.* to answer, to reply
отвеча́ть *imp.* to answer; to be responsible
отдава́ть *imp.* to give up; to give back
отда́ть *perf.* to give up; to give back
отде́л *m.* section, department
отделе́ние *n.* department, branch
отде́льный separate
о́тдых *m.* rest, relaxation
оте́ц *m.* father
отказа́ться *perf.* to refuse
отка́зываться *imp.* to refuse
открыва́ть *imp.* to open
откры́тка *f.* postcard
откры́ть *perf.* to open
откры́тый open, outspoken
отку́да whence, where from
отлича́ть *imp.* to distinguish, to tell from
отлича́ться to be different, to stand out
отличи́ть *perf.* to distinguish, to tell from
отличи́ться to distinguish oneself, to excel
отнести́ *perf.* to take or carry to (someone)
отнести́сь to treat
относи́ть *imp.* to take or carry to (someone)
относи́ться to refer; to treat

отноше́ние *n.* attitude, relation
отойти́ *perf.* to go away, to depart
отпеча́ток *m.* print (photography)
отпра́вить *perf.* to send off, to forward (mail), to dispatch
отпра́виться to betake oneself, to start out
отправля́ть *imp.* to send off, to forward (mail), to dispatch
отправля́тся to betake oneself, to start out
отря́д *m.* outfit, detachment
отсу́тствие *n.* absence
отсю́да from here
оттого́ therefore
отту́да from there
отча́яние *n.* despair
отчего́ why, wherefore
отхо́д *m.* departure
отходи́ть *imp.* to go away, to depart
офице́р *m.* officer
официа́нт *m.* waiter
ох oh! ah!
охо́та *f.* hunt; inclination
очеви́дно obviously, apparently
о́чень very
о́чередь *f.* line, queue; turn
оши́бка *f.* mistake
ощуще́ние *n.* sensation

П

па́дать *imp.* to fall, to drop
па́лец *m.* finger
па́лка *f.* stick, cane
па́луба *f.* deck
пальто́ *n.* coat
па́мять *f.* memory
па́ра *f.* pair, couple
па́рень *m.* fellow, chap
парикма́хер *m.* barber
парохо́д *m.* steamship
парте́р *m.* orchestra (in theater)
па́ртия *f.* party (political)
па́спорт *m.* passport
па́хнуть to smell (of)
пе́рвый first
перебива́ть *imp.* to interrupt
переби́ть *perf.* to interrupt
перевести́ *perf.* to translate
перево́д *m.* translation
переводи́ть *imp.* to translate
перево́дчик *m.* interpreter
пе́ред in front of, before
передава́ть *imp.* to pass, to hand, to transmit
переда́ть *perf.* to pass; to hand
пере́дний front (adj.)
пере́дник *m.* apron
перейти́ *perf.* to get over; to cross
пережа́ренный overfried, overroasted
переме́на *f.* change, alteration
перемени́ть *perf.* to change
переменя́ть *imp.* to change
переса́дка *f.* change (of train, station)
переса́ливать *imp.* to oversalt
пересоли́ть *perf.* to oversalt
перестава́ть *imp.* to stop
переста́ть *perf.* to stop
переу́лок *m.* alley, lane
переходи́ть *imp.* to get over; to cross
пери́од *m.* period, phase
перо́ *n.* pen
пе́рсик *m.* peach
пе́сня *f.* song
песо́к *m.* sand
петь *imp.* to sing
печа́льный sad, mournful
печа́ть *m.* seal
пи́во *n.* beer
пиро́жное *n.* pastry
писа́тель *m.* writer
писа́ть *imp.* to write
письмо́ *n.* letter
пи́счий writing-
пи́счая бума́га *f.* writing paper
пить *imp.* to drink
питьё *n.* drinking, drink
пла́вать *indef.* to swim
пла́кать *imp.* to weep, to cry
план *m.* plan, chart
пла́та *f.* pay
плати́ть *imp.* to pay
плато́к *m.* handkerchief; shawl
платфо́рма *f.* platform
пла́тье *n.* dress
плова́ть *imp.* to spit
плечо́ *n.* shoulder
плёнка *f.* film, roll of film
пло́хо badly, poorly

плохо́й bad
площа́дка *f.* platform
пло́щадь *f.* square
пляж *m.* beach
по along, according to, in (a language)
побе́да *f.* victory
побежа́ть *perf.* to run
побере́жье *n.* shore, coast
пове́рить *perf.* to believe
поверну́ть(ся) *perf.* to turn
по-ви́димому evidently
по́вод *m.* cause, reason
повора́чивать(ся) *imp.* to turn (around)
поворо́т *m.* turn
повтори́ть *perf.* to repeat
повторя́ть *imp.* to repeat
погиба́ть *imp.* to perish
поги́бнуть *perf.* to perish
поговори́ть *perf.* to talk (over), to chat
под under, below, underneath
подава́ть *imp.* to give, to hand; to serve; to submit
пода́ть *perf.* to give, to hand; to serve; to submit
поддержа́ть *perf.* to support, to maintain
подде́рживать *imp.* to support, to maintain
подлежа́ть *imp.* to be subject to
поднима́ть *imp.* to lift, to raise
поднима́ться to go up, to come up
подня́ть *perf.* to lift, to raise
подня́ться to go up, to come up
подо́бный similar
подожда́ть *perf.* to wait for
подойти́ *perf.* to approach
подписа́ться *perf.* to sign, to subscribe
подпи́сываться *imp.* to sign, to subscribe
подро́бность *f.* detail
подстрига́ть *imp.* to cut, to trim (hair)
подстри́чь *perf.* to cut, to trim (hair)
поду́мать *perf.* to think (a little, for a while)
поду́шка *f.* pillow, cushion
подходи́ть *imp.* to approach; to fit
по́езд *m.* train
пое́здка *f.* journey, trip
пое́хать *perf.* to depart
пожа́луйста please
пожа́луй perhaps, maybe, possibly
пожива́ть to get along, to live
позва́ть *perf.* to call
позво́лить *imp.* to permit, to allow
позволя́ть *perf.* to permit, to allow
по́здно late
по́зже later
пойти́ *perf.* to go
пока́ while; for the time being; so long!
пока́ . . . не until
показа́ть *perf.* to show
показа́ться to seem, to appear; to show off
пока́зывать *imp.* to show
пока́зываться to show off
поко́й *m.* rest
поко́йный calm, restful
покрыва́ть *imp.* to cover
покры́ть *perf.* to cover
покупа́ть *imp.* to buy
пол *m.* floor; sex
полага́ть *imp.* to suppose, to deem
полбуты́лка *f.* half a bottle
по́ле *n.* field
поле́зный useful; healthful
полёт *m.* flight
поли́тика *f.* politics; policy
полити́ческий political
полк *m.* regiment
по́лка *f.* shelf
по́лный full, complete; stout
полови́на *f.* half
положе́ние *n.* situation, condition
положи́ть *perf.* to put; to suppose
полоса́ *f.* stripe, strip; zone
полоте́нце *n.* towel
получа́ть *imp.* to receive
получе́ние *n.* receiving
получи́ть *perf.* to receive
по́льза *f.* profit; benefit; use
по́льзоваться *imp.* to use
по́мнить *imp.* to remember
помога́ть *imp.* to help
помо́чь *perf.* to help
по́мощь *f.* aid, help
понеде́льник *m.* Monday
понима́ть *imp.* to understand

поня́тие *n.* idea, notion
поня́тный understandable, clear
поня́ть *perf.* to understand
попада́ть *imp.* to hit, to strike; to get (into or to something)
попа́сть *perf.* to hit, to strike; to get (into or to something)
попра́вить *perf.* to correct, to fix
поправля́ть *imp.* to correct, to fix
попре́жнему as before, as usual
попро́бовать *perf.* to try, to taste
попроси́ть *perf.* to ask
попы́тка *f.* attempt
пора́ *f.* time, season
поража́ть *imp.* to amaze
порази́ть *perf.* to amaze
порт *m.* port
портни́ха *f.* dressmaker
портно́й *m.* tailor
портре́т *m.* portrait
портфе́ль *m.* briefcase
портсига́р *m.* cigarette case
поря́док *m.* order
посади́ть *perf.* to seat; to plant; to imprison
поскоре́е (more) quickly, hurry it up!
посла́ть *perf.* to send
по́сле after
после́дний last; latest
послеза́втра the day after tomorrow
послу́шать *perf.* to listen
посмотре́ть *perf.* to look, to take a look
поста́вить *perf.* to put, to stand
посте́ль *f.* bed
постоя́нно constantly, always
постоя́нный steady, constant
постоя́ть *perf.* to stand; to wait
поступа́ть *imp.* to act; to enroll
поступи́ть *perf.* to act; to enroll
посту́пок *m.* action
посыла́ть *imp.* to send
посы́лка *f.* package, parcel
пот *m.* sweat, perspiration
потеря́ть *perf.* to lose
пото́м afterwards, then
потому́ что because
поторопи́ть(ся) *perf.* to hurry
похо́жий like, resembling
поцелова́ть *perf.* to kiss
почему́ why
по́чта *f.* post office, mail
почти́ almost, nearly
почто́вый postal
почу́вствовать *perf.* to feel
по́шлина *f.* duty, customs
поэ́т *m.* poet
поэ́тому therefore, so
появи́ться *perf.* to appear, to show up
появля́ться *imp.* to appear, to show up
по́яс *m.* belt
пра́вда *f.* truth
пра́вильно correctly, right
пра́вильный right, correct, regular
прави́тельство *n.* government
пра́во *n.* right
пра́вый right (adj.)
пра́здник *m.* holiday
предлага́ть *imp.* to suggest; to propose
предложи́ть *perf.* to suggest, to propose
предме́т *m.* object; subject, topic
председа́тель *m.* chairman, president
представи́тель *m.* representative, delegate
предста́вить *perf.* to represent
предста́виться to occur, to present itself
представле́ние *n.* performance
представля́ть *imp.* to represent; to imagine
представля́ться to occur, to present itself
пре́жде before, formerly
пре́жний former
прекра́сный excellent, fine
при at, near
приба́вить *perf.* to add
прибавля́ть *imp.* to add
прибыва́ть *imp.* to arrive
прибы́ть *perf.* to arrive
прибы́тие *n.* arrival
привести́ *perf.* to bring (along, over, into)
приводи́ть *imp.* to bring (along, over, into)
привыка́ть *imp.* to get used to
привы́кнуть *perf.* to get used to

привы́чка *f.* habit
пригото́вить *perf.* to prepare
приготовля́ть *imp.* to prepare
придава́ть *imp.* to give; to add; to attach
прида́ть *perf.* to give; to add; to attach
приезжа́ть *imp.* to arrive, to come
прие́хать *perf.* to arrive, to come
признава́ть *imp.* to acknowledge, to recognize
признава́ться to admit; to confess
при́знак *m.* sign
призна́ть *perf.* to acknowledge, to recognize
призна́ться to admit; to confess
приём *m.* reception
прийти́ (придти́ or **притти́)** *perf.* to come
прийти́сь to have to
прика́з *m.* order, command
приказа́ть *perf.* to order
прика́зывать *imp.* to order
приме́р *m.* example
принадлежа́ть to belong
принести́ *perf.* to bring, to fetch
принима́ть to accept, to take, to receive
приноси́ть *imp.* to bring, to fetch
при́нятый accepted, adopted
приня́ть *perf.* to accept, to take, to receive
приро́да *f.* nature
присла́ть *perf.* to send (over)
присыла́ть *imp.* to send (over)
прису́тствие *n.* presence
приходи́ть *imp.* to come
приходи́ться to have to
причи́на *f.* cause, reason
прия́тно pleasantly, pleasant
прия́тный pleasant, nice
про about
про́бка *f.* cork
пробле́ма *f.* problem
про́бовать *imp.* to try, to taste
про́бочник *m.* corkscrew
провести́ *perf.* to spend (time)
про́вод *m.* wire
проводи́ть *imp.* to spend (time)
проводи́ть *perf.* to accompany; to see off
проводни́к *m.* porter (on train)
провожа́ть *imp.* to accompany; to see off
програ́мма *f.* program
прогу́ливаться *imp.* to go for a walk
прогу́лка *f.* walk
прогуля́ться *perf.* to go for a walk
продава́ть *imp.* to sell
продаве́ц *m.* salesman
продавщи́ца *f.* salesgirl
прода́жа *f.* sale
прода́ть *perf.* to sell
продле́ние *n.* prolongation, extension
продли́ть *perf.* to prolong, to extend
продолжа́ть *imp.* to continue, to go on
продо́лжить *perf.* to continue, to go on
прое́зд *m.* passage
проезжа́ть *imp.* to pass (in a vehicle)
прое́хать *perf.* to pass (in a vehicle)
произвести́ *perf.* to produce
производи́ть *imp.* to produce
произнести́ *perf.* to pronounce
произноси́ть *imp.* to pronounce
произойти́ *perf.* to take place
происходи́ть *imp.* to take place
пройти́ *perf.* to pass (on foot)
пропада́ть *imp.* to get lost, to vanish
пропа́сть *perf.* to get lost, to vanish
про́пуск *m.* pass, permit
пропуска́ть *imp.* to let pass
пропусти́ть *perf.* to let pass
проси́ть *imp.* to ask, to request
просма́тривать *imp.* to look over, to glance through
просмотре́ть *perf.* to look over, to glance through
просну́ться *perf.* to wake up
прости́ть *perf.* to forgive
про́сто simply
просто́й simple
простуди́ться *perf.* to catch cold
простужа́ться *imp.* to catch cold
про́сьба *f.* request
просыпа́ться *imp.* to wake up

про́тив against
проти́вник *m.* opponent
проти́вный nasty; contrary
протя́гивать *imp.* to stretch; to extend
протяну́ть *perf.* to stretch; to extend
профе́ссор *m.* professor
проходи́ть *imp.* to pass (on foot)
проце́нт *m.* per cent, percentage
проце́сс *m.* process
проче́сть *perf.* to read, to peruse
про́чий other
прочита́ть *perf.* to read, to peruse
про́шлый past, last
проща́ть *imp.* to forgive
прояви́ть *perf.* to develop (film); to display
проявля́ть *imp.* to develop; to display
пря́мо straight ahead
прямо́й straight, upright
пти́ца *f.* bird
пу́блика *f.* public, audience
пу́дра *f.* powder
пуска́ть *imp.* to let, to allow
пусти́ть *perf.* to let, to allow
пусто́й empty
пусть let (*imperative*)
пустя́к *m.* trifle
путеводи́тель *m.* guide book, itinerary
путь *m.* path, road, way
пчела́ *f.* bee
пылесо́с *m.* vacuum cleaner
пыль *f.* dust
пыта́ться *imp.* to try, to endeavor
пье́са *f.* play (drama)
пья́ный drunk
пятна́дцать fifteen
пя́тница *f.* Friday
пятно́ *n.* spot, blot, stain
пя́тый fifth
пять five
пятьдеся́т fifty
пятьсо́т five hundred
пя́тый fifth

Р

рабо́та *f.* work; job
рабо́тать *imp.* to work
рабо́тник *m.* worker
рабо́чий workers'
ра́венство *n.* equality
равно́ equally
ра́вный equal
рад glad
ра́ди for the sake of
ра́дио *indecl. n.* radio
ра́доваться *imp.* to rejoice, to be happy
ра́достно joyfully, happily
ра́достный happy, joyful
ра́дость *f.* joy, gladness
раз time, one time, once
разбива́ть *imp.* to break, to smash
разби́ть *perf.* to break, to smash
разбуди́ть *perf.* to awaken, to wake up
ра́зве ——? is that so?; really, perhaps
разгова́ривать *imp.* to converse
разгово́р *m.* conversation, talk
раздева́лка *f.* dressing room
раздева́ть(ся) *imp.* to undress
разде́ть(ся) *perf.* to undress
разли́чный different
разме́р *m.* size, dimension
ра́зница *f.* difference
ра́зный different, various
разреша́ть *imp.* to permit; to solve
разреше́ние *n.* permission; solution
разреши́ть *perf.* to permit; to solve
разуме́ется of course (*lit.,* it is understood)
разъединя́ть *imp.* to separate; to disconnect
разъедини́ть *perf.* to separate; to disconnect
рак *m.* crawfish, lobster; cancer
ра́нний early
ра́но early
ра́ньше earlier, ahead of time
расписа́ние *n.* timetable, schedule
расписа́ть(ся) *perf.* to sign, to endorse
распи́ска *f.* receipt
распи́сывать(ся) *imp.* to sign, to endorse
расска́з *m.* story, tale
рассказа́ть *perf.* to tell, to relate

расска́зывать *imp.* to tell, to relate
рассма́тривать *imp.* to look at; to consider
рассмотре́ть *perf.* to look at; to consider
расти́ *imp.* to grow
расхо́д *m.* expense
расчёт *m.* calculation
рвать *imp.* to tear
ребёнок *m.* child
ребя́та *pl.* fellows, guys
револю́ция *f.* revolution
регистра́ция *f.* registration
ре́дкий rare; sparse; uncommon
ре́дко seldom, rarely
ре́зать *imp.* to cut
рези́на *f.* rubber; elastic
ре́зкий harsh; sharp; biting
ре́зко sharply, harshly
результа́т *m.* result
река́ *f.* river
рекомендова́ть to recommend
рестора́н *m.* restaurant
реце́пт *m.* prescription; recipe
речь *f.* speech
реша́ть *imp.* to decide
реше́ние *n.* decision
реши́тельно definitely, absolutely
реши́ть *perf.* to decide
ро́вно equally; exactly
ро́вный even, equal
род *m.* kind, species
ро́дина *f.* native country
роди́ть *perf.* to give birth (to)
роди́ться to be born
родно́й kindred, own, native
рожа́ть *imp.* to give birth (to)
рожда́ться *imp.* to be born
ро́за *f.* rose
ро́зовый pink
роль *f.* part, role
рома́н *m.* novel; love affair
рост *m.* growth; height
ро́стбиф *m.* roastbeef
рот *m.* mouth
руба́шка *f.* shirt
рубль *m.* ruble
рука́ *f.* hand
рука́в *m.* sleeve
руководи́тель *m.* leader, guide
ру́копись *f.* manuscript
ру́сский Russian
ручно́й by hand, manual
ры́ба *f.* fish
ры́нок *m.* market
ряд *m.* row
ря́дом beside, side by side

С

с with
сад *m.* garden, orchard
сади́ть *imp.* to seat; to plant
сади́ться to sit down
сажа́ть *imp.* to seat; to plant
сала́т *m.* salad; lettuce
салфе́тка *f.* napkin
сам self; myself, yourself, himself, etc.
самолёт *m.* airplane
са́мый *pron.* same, most; *adj., adv.* very
сапо́г *m.* boot
са́хар *m.* sugar
све́дение *n.* information
све́жий fresh
све́рху from above, on top
свет *m.* light; world
све́тлый bright; light
свёкла *f.* beet
сверх above, beyond
свида́ние *n.* meeting, rendez-vous, date
свобо́дно freely, easily, fluently
свобо́дный free
свобо́да *f.* freedom
свой one's own
свя́занный tied (up), bound
связа́ть *perf.* to tie, to bind; to knit
связь *f.* connection, contact; tie, bond
свя́зывать *imp.* to tie, to bind; to knit
свято́й holy
сдава́ть to give up, to check (baggage)
сда́ча *f.* small change (money)
сде́лать *perf.* to make, to do
сде́латься to become
себя́ oneself
сего́дня today
седо́й grey
седьмо́й seventh

сейча́с now, immediately
секрета́рь *m.* secretary
село́ *n.* village
семе́йный domestic, family-
семна́дцать seventeen
семь seven
се́мьдесят seventy
семья́ *f.* family
сентя́брь *m.* September
серди́то angrily
серди́ться *imp.* to be angry, to get angry
се́рдце *n.* heart
серебро́ *n.* silver
сере́бряный silver-
се́рый grey
серьёзно seriously
серьёзный serious, earnest
сестра́ *f.* sister
сесть *perf.* to sit down
се́ять to sow
сза́ди from behind
сиде́ть *imp.* to sit
си́ла *f.* force, power, strength
си́льно powerfully, greatly
си́льный strong, powerful
си́ний dark-blue
систе́ма *f.* system
сказа́ть *perf.* to say, to tell
сквозня́к *m.* draft, current of air
сквозь through
скла́дывать *imp.* to fold, to arrange
ско́лько how much
скоре́е quickly, sooner
ско́ро quickly, rapidly
ско́рый quick, rapid
скро́мный modest
скрыва́ть *imp.* to hide, to conceal
скрыть *perf.* to hide, to conceal
ску́льптор *m.* sculptor
скульпту́ра *f.* sculpture
скуча́ть *imp.* to be bored; to be lonely (for); to miss
сла́бость *f.* weakness
сла́бый weak, feeble
сла́ва *f.* fame, glory
сла́вный famous, renowned
сла́дкий sweet
слегка́ slightly
след *m.* trace, footprint
следи́ть *imp.* to follow, to spy, to watch
сле́довать *imp.* to follow
сле́дующий next, following
слеза́ *f.* tear
слеза́ть *imp.* to alight, to get out
слезть *perf.* to alight, to get out
слепо́й blind
сли́шком too
слова́рь *m.* dictionary
сло́вно as if, as though
сло́во *n.* word
сло́жный complicated
сложи́ть *perf.* to fold, to arrange
слома́ть *perf.* to break
слу́жба *f.* service; job, work
служи́ть *imp.* to serve
слух *m.* hearing; rumor
слу́чай *m.* chance; case; accident
случа́йно by chance, accidentally
случа́ться *imp.* to happen
случи́ться *perf.* to happen
слу́шать *imp.* to listen
слы́шать *imp.* to hear
слы́шный audible
сме́лый daring, bold
смерть *f.* death
сметь *imp.* to dare
смешно́й funny, comical
смех *m.* laughter
смея́ться *imp.* to laugh
смотре́ть *imp.* to look (at)
смысл *m.* sense, meaning
снача́ла (at) first
снег *m.* snow
сни́зу from below
снима́ть *imp.* to take off; to snap (pictures)
сно́ва again
снять *perf.* to take off; to snap (pictures)
соба́ка *f.* dog
собира́ть(ся) *imp.* to gather; to get ready
собра́ние *n.* meeting, gathering
собра́ть(ся) *perf.* to gather; to get ready
со́бственно properly
со́бственный own (adj.)
собы́тие *n.* event.
соверше́нно entirely, completely
со́весть *f.* conscience
сове́т *m.* council; counsel, advice
сове́тский Soviet (adj.)

совре́менный modern
совсе́м entirely, completely
согласи́ться *perf.* to agree, to consent
соглаша́ться *imp.* to agree, to consent
содержа́ние *n.* contents; maintenance
содержа́ть *imp.* to contain; to support; to maintain
Соединённые Шта́ты United States
сожале́ние *n.* regret; pity
к сожале́нию unfortunately
созда́ние *n.* creation; creature
создава́ть *imp.* to create
созда́ть *perf.* to create
созна́ние *n.* realization; consciousness
сойти́ *perf.* to get off, to alight
солда́т *m.* soldier
со́лнечный sunny; solar
со́лнце *n.* sun
соло́нка *f.* salt shaker
соль *f.* salt
сомнева́ться *imp.* to doubt
сомне́ние *n.* doubt
сон *m.* sleep; dream
сообща́ть *imp.* to inform, to notify, to communicate
сообще́ние *n.* communication, message
сообщи́ть *perf.* to communicate, to notify, to inform
со́рок forty
сорт *m.* sort, kind
сосе́д *m.* neighbor
сосе́дка *f.* neighbor
сосе́дний neighboring, adjoining
соску́читься *perf.* to be bored; to be lonely (for), to miss
сосна́ *f.* pinetree
соста́вить(ся) *perf.* to compose, to compile
составля́ть(ся) *imp.* to compose, to compile
состоя́ние *n.* condition, state; fortune
состоя́ть *imp.* to be made up, to consist of
сосчита́ть *perf.* to count
со́тня *f.* hundred
сохрани́ть(ся) *perf.* to keep, to preserve
сохраня́ть(ся) *imp.* to keep, to preserve
сою́з *m.* union, alliance
спа́льный sleeping-
спа́льня *f.* bedroom
спа́ржа, *f.* asparagus
спаса́ть *imp.* to save, to rescue
спаси́бо thank you
спасти́ *perf.* to save, to rescue
спать *imp.* to sleep
спекта́кль *m.* performance, production
спеши́ть *perf.* to hurry
спина́ *f.* back
спи́сок *m.* list
спи́чка *f.* match
споко́йно calmly
споко́йный quiet, peaceful
споко́йствие *n.* peacefulness
спор *m.* argument; debate
спо́рить *imp.* to argue, to debate
спорт *m.* sport
спо́соб *m.* way, method
спосо́бность *f.* ability; faculty
спосо́бный capable, gifted
справедли́вый just, fair
спра́вка *f.* information
спра́вочный information (adj.)
спра́шивать *imp.* to ask, to inquire
спроси́ть *perf.* to ask, to inquire
спустя́ after, later
сравне́ние *n.* comparison
сра́внивать *imp.* to compare
сравни́тельный comparative
сравни́ть *perf.* to compare
сра́зу all at once, immediately
среда́ *f.* Wednesday
среди́ in the middle of, among
сре́дний middle; average
сре́дство *n.* means
срок *m.* term, period of time
ста́вить *imp.* to put; to stand
стадио́н *m.* stadium
стака́н *m.* glass, tumbler
сталь *f.* steel
станда́рт *m.* standard
станови́ться *imp.* to stand, to become
ста́нция *f.* station
стара́ться *imp.* to try, to endeavor

стари́к *m.* old man
стари́нный ancient, antique
ста́рший senior, chief
ста́рый old
стару́ха *f.* old woman
стать *perf.* to stand, to become; to begin
статья́ *f.* article
стекло́ *n.* glass
стена́ *f.* wall
степень *f.* degree; grade; extent
степь *f.* steppe, prairie
стира́ть *imp.* to wash, to launder
сти́рка *f.* laundering
стих *m.* verse
сто hundred
сто́ить *imp.* to cost
стол *m.* table
столб *m.* pole
столе́тие *n.* century
сто́лик *m.* small table
столова́ться *imp.* to board, to eat out
сто́лько so much, so many
сторона́ *f.* side
стоя́нка *f.* stand
стоя́ть *imp.* to stand
страда́ние *n.* suffering
страда́ть *imp.* to suffer
страна́ *f.* country, land
страни́ца *f.* page
стра́нно strangely, oddly
стра́нный strange
стра́стный passionate
страсть *f.* passion, temper
страх *m.* fright, fear, scare
стра́шно terribly
стра́шный terrible
стреля́ть *imp.* to shoot
стреми́ться *imp.* to aim, to be anxious
стро́гий strict
стро́го strictly
стро́ить *imp.* to build, construct
стро́й *m.* ranks, arrangement, order
стро́йка *f.* construction
стул *m.* chair
ступа́ть *imp.* to step
ступи́ть *perf.* to step
стуча́ть *imp.* to knock
суббо́та *f.* Saturday
суд *m.* court
суди́ть *imp.* to judge, to try
судьба́ *f.* fate
суме́ть *perf.* to be able
суп *m.* soup
суро́вый strict, stern, severe
сухо́й dry; stale
суши́ть *imp.* to dry
существо́ *n.* being, creature
существова́ние *n.* existence
существова́ть *imp.* to exist
су́щность *f.* essence
схвати́ть *perf.* to catch
схва́тывать *imp.* to catch (on)
сходи́ть *imp.* to get off, to alight
сце́на *f.* stage, scene
счастли́вый happy, lucky
сча́стье *n.* happiness, luck
счесть *perf.* to count
счёт *m.* bill
счита́ть *imp.* to count; to consider
счита́ться to be considered; to take into consideration
сын *m.* son
сыр *m.* cheese
сыро́й damp; raw
сюда́ here (= to here)

Т

таба́к *m.* tobacco
та́йна *f.* mystery; secret
та́йный mysterious; secret
так so, thus
та́кже also, too
тако́й such
такси́ *indecl. n.* taxi
тала́нт *m.* talent
та́лия *f.* waist
там there
тамо́жня *f.* custom house
таре́лка *f.* plate
тата́рский Tartar-
твёрдый hard
твой thy, thine; your, yours
теа́тр *m.* theater
тебя́ *gen., acc. of* ты
телегра́мма *f.* telegram
телегра́ф *m.* telegraph
телефо́н *m.* telephone
телефо́нный telephone (adj.)
те́ло *n.* body
те́ма *f.* theme, subject, topic

темнота́ *f.* darkness
тёмный dark, obscure
те́ннис *m.* tennis
те́ннисный tennis (adj.)
тень *f.* shade, shadow
тео́рия *f.* theory
тепе́рь now
тепло́ warmly, warm
тёплый warm, cordial
терпели́вость *f.* patience
терпели́вый patient
терпе́ть *imp.* to endure, to stand, to suffer
торже́ственный solemn; gala
теря́ть *imp.* to lose
те́сный tight
тётя *f.* aunt
тече́ние *n.* current, stream
ти́хий quiet
ти́хо quietly, slowly
ти́ше more quiet, more slowly
тишина́ *f.* silence
то *pron.* that; *adv.* then
това́рищ *m.* comrade, close friend
тогда́ then, at that time
то́-есть that is; namely
то́же also, too
толка́ть *imp.* to push
толпа́ *f.* crowd
то́лстый thick; stout, fat
то́лько only
том *m.* volume
тому́ наза́д ago
тон *m.* tone
то́нкий thin, slender; delicate
торопли́во hastily, hurriedly
торопи́ть(ся) *imp.* to hurry, to hasten
торт *m.* cake
торча́ть *imp.* to stick out, protrude
тоска́ *f.* longing, distress, anguish
тот that (one)
то́тчас at once
то́чка *f.* dot, period, point
то́чно exactly
трава́ *f.* grass
трамва́й *m.* tram, street car, trolley
трамва́йный street car, trolley (adj.)
тра́тить *imp.* to spend
тре́бование *n.* claim, demand, request
тре́бовать *imp.* to demand, to request
трево́га *f.* alarm, anxiety
трево́жный anxious, alarming
тре́тий third
три three
три́дцать thirty
трина́дцать thirteen
три́ста three hundred
тро́е three
труба́ *f.* pipe; chimney; trumpet
тру́бка *f.* pipe; tube; telephone receiver
труд *m.* labor; difficulty
тру́дно difficult
тру́дный difficult, hard
тури́ст *m.* tourist
тури́стка *f.* tourist
туда́ there (to there)
тума́н *m.* fog, mist
тут here
ту́ча *f.* cloud
ту́фля *f.* slipper, shoe
тща́тельно thoroughly, with great care
тща́тельный careful, painstaking
ты thou; you
ты́сяча thousand
тюрьма́ *f.* prison
тяжело́ hard, difficult, heavy
тя́жесть *f.* weight, gravity
тяжёлый heavy, hard, difficult
тяну́ть *imp.* to pull, to drag
тяну́ться to stretch, to extend

У

у at, by
убега́ть *imp.* to run away
убеди́ть *perf.* to convince, to persuade
убеди́ться to become convinced (of)
убежа́ть *perf.* to run away
убежда́ть *imp.* to convince, to persuade
убежда́ться to become convinced (of)
убежде́ние *n.* conviction, persuasion
убива́ть *imp.* to kill

убийство *n.* murder
убийца *m. & f.* killer
убира́ть *imp.* to take away; to clean up
уби́ть *perf.* to kill
убо́рная *f.* toilet
убра́ть *perf.* to take away; to clean up
уважа́ть *imp.* to respect, to esteem
уваже́ние *n.* respect, esteem
уве́ренный sure, confident
уверя́ть *imp.* to assure
уве́рить *perf.* to assure
уви́деть *perf.* to see, to catch sight of
увы́! alas!
у́гол *m.* corner; angle
у́голь *m.* coal
угости́ть *perf.* to treat, to entertain
угоща́ть *imp.* to treat, to entertain
удава́ться *imp.* to succeed, to be successful
уда́р *m.* blow
уда́рить *perf.* to hit, to strike
ударя́ть *imp.* to hit, to strike
уда́ться *perf.* to succeed, to be successful
уда́ча *f.* good luck; success
уда́чный successful
удиви́тельный surprising, astonishing
удиви́ть *perf.* to surprise, to astonish
удиви́ть(ся) to be astonished, to be amazed
удивле́ние *n.* surprise, astonishment
удивля́ть *imp.* to surprise, to astonish
удивля́ться to be astonished, to be amazed
уди́лище *n.* fishing rod
удо́бный comfortable, convenient
удово́льствие *n.* pleasure
уезжа́ть *imp.* to go away, to ride away
уе́хать *perf.* to go away, to ride away
у́жас *m.* horror, terror
ужа́сно awfully, terribly
ужа́сный awful, terrible
уже́ already
у́жин *m.* supper
у́жинать *imp.* to have supper
у́зкий narrow
узлово́й main, nodal
  узлова́я ста́нция junction
узнава́ть *imp.* to recognize
узна́ть *perf.* to recognize, to find out
уйти́ *perf.* to go away, to leave
указа́ть *perf.* to point out, to indicate
ука́зывать *imp.* to point out, to indicate
украинский Ukrainian
у́ксус *m.* vinegar
у́лица *f.* street
улыба́ться *imp.* to smile
улы́бка *f.* smile
улыбну́ться *perf.* to smile
ум *m.* mind
умере́ть *perf.* to die
уме́ть *imp.* to know how, to be able
умира́ть *imp.* to die
у́мный clever, intelligent
универма́г (= **универса́льный магази́н**) department store
универса́льный universal
университе́т *m.* university
упа́сть *perf.* to fall, to drop
уплати́ть *perf.* to pay (off)
упла́чивать *imp.* to pay (off)
употребле́ние *n.* use
употреби́ть *perf.* to use
употребля́ть *imp.* to use
управля́ющий *m.* manager, head
усилие *n.* effort
усло́вие *n.* condition
усла́вливаться *imp.* to agree, to reach an agreement
усло́виться *perf.* to agree, to reach an agreement
услу́га *f.* service, good turn
услы́шать *perf.* to hear
успева́ть *imp.* to have time, to manage
успе́ть *perf.* to have time, to manage
успе́х *m.* success
  успе́хи progress
успока́ивать(ся) *imp.* to calm; to soothe

успоко́ить(ся) *perf.* to calm; to soothe
устава́ть *imp.* to get tired
уста́лый tired
уста́ть *perf.* to get tired
устра́ивать *imp.* to arrange
устро́ить *perf.* to arrange
усы́ *m. pl.* moustache
у́тка *f.* duck
у́тро *n.* morning
у́тром in the morning
утю́г *m.* (pressing) iron
у́хо *n.* ear
уходи́ть *imp.* to go away, to leave
уча́ствовать *imp.* to participate
уча́стие *n.* participation
уча́сток *m.* ,plot (of land), lot; police station
учени́к *m.* student
учени́ца *f.* student
учёный *m.* learned (person); scholar; scientist
учи́тель *m.* teacher
учи́тельница *f.* teacher
учи́ть *imp.* to teach; to learn
учи́ться *imp.* to study, to learn
учрежде́ние *n.* institution

Ф

фа́брика *f.* factory
факт *m.* fact
фами́лия *f.* family name, surname
фасо́ль *f.* beans
февра́ль *m.* February
фигу́ра *f.* figure
филиа́л branch (of an institution, store, etc.)
флаг *m.* flag
флиртова́ть *imp.* to flirt
фло́т *m.* fleet, navy
фо́кус *m.* trick; focus
фона́рь *m.* lantern; flashlight; headlight
фо́рма *f.* form, shape; uniform
фото- photographic
фра́за phrase, sentence
францу́зский French
фронт *m.* front
фунт *m.* pound
футбо́л *m.* soccer
футбо́льный soccer-

Х

хара́ктер *m.* character; disposition
хвали́ть *imp.* to praise
хва́стать(ся) *imp.* to brag
хвата́ть *imp.* to seize, to snatch; to suffice
хвати́ть *perf.* to suffice, to be enough
хвост *m.* tail; line
хи́трый cunning, sly
хлеб *m.* bread
ход *m.* movement, motion
  на ходу́ in motion
ходи́ть *imp.* to go, to walk
хозя́ин *m.* landlord, host, master, owner
хозя́йка *f.* landlady, hostess, housekeeper
хозя́йство *n.* economy; housekeeping
хо́лод *m.* cold
холо́дный cold
хоро́ший good
хорошо́ very well! all right! nice, good
хоте́ть *imp.* to want
хоте́ться to want, to feel, like (impersonal)
хоть even; though; at least
хотя́ although, though
хране́ние *n.* storage
храни́ть *imp.* to keep, to store
худо́жественный artistic
худо́жество *n.* art
худо́жник *m.* artist
худо́й lean, thin; bad
ху́же worse

Ц

ца́рство *n.* kingdom, empire
царь *m.* czar
цвет *m.* color
цветно́й colored
цвето́к *m.* flower
це́лый whole, entire, intact
цель *f.* aim; target; purpose
цена́ *f.* price, value
це́нный valuable
центр *m.* center
центра́льный central
цепь *f.* chain, bonds

церко́вный ecclesiastical, church-
це́рковь *f.* church

Ч

чай *m.* tea
ча́йка *f.* seagull
ча́йник *m.* teapot
час *m.* hour
ча́сто often, frequently
часть *f.* part
часы́ *m. pl.* watch, clock
ча́шка *f.* cup
ча́ще more often
чей whose
чек *m.* check
челове́к *m.* human being, person
челове́чество *n.* humanity, mankind
челове́ческий human
чем than
чемода́н *m.* suitcase
чепуха́ *f.* nonsense
че́рез through, over, across
черни́ла *n. pl.* ink
чёрный black
черта́ *f.* line, trait
че́стный honest
честь *f.* honor
четве́рг *m.* Thursday
че́тверть *f.* quarter
четвёртый fourth
четы́ре four
четы́реста four hundred
четы́рнадцать fourteen
число́ *n.* number; date
чи́стить *imp.* to clean
чи́сто clean, neatly
чи́стый pure, clean, neat
чита́тель *m.* reader
чита́ть *imp.* to read
чиха́ть *imp.* to sneeze
чихну́ть *perf.* to sneeze
чи́ще cleaner
член *m.* member
чорт *m.* devil
чрезвыча́йно extremely, most
что what, that (*rel. pron.*)
что́бы in order to, so that
что за what kind of
что́-нибудь something; anything
что-то something
чу́вство *n.* feeling; sense
чу́вствовать *imp.* to feel, to sense
чуде́сный wonderful, miraculous
чу́дный wonderful, marvelous
чу́до *n.* miracle, wonder
чужо́й someone else's; foreign
чуть hardly
чуть . . . не almost

Ш

шаг *m.* step; pace
шали́ть *imp.* to be naughty
шаль *f.* shawl
шампа́нское *n.* champagne
шампу́нь *f.* shampoo
шанс *m.* chance
ша́пка *f.* cap
шар *m.* ball; globe; sphere
ша́хматы *m. pl.* chess
шёл was going
шёлк *m.* silk
шёлковый silken
шепну́ть *perf.* whisper
шепта́ть *imp.* to whisper
шерсть *f.* wool
шерстяно́й woolen
шесто́й sixth
шесть six
шестьдеся́т sixty
ше́я *f.* neck
ши́на *f.* tire
широ́кий wide, broad
шко́ла *f.* school
шку́ра *f.* skin, hide
шля́па *f.* hat
шокола́д *m.* chocolate
шофёр *m.* chauffeur
шпина́т *m.* spinach
што́пор *m.* corkscrew
шту́ка *f.* piece, item
шум *m.* noise
шути́ть *imp.* to joke
шу́тка *f.* joke

Щ

щека́ *f.* cheek
щи *m. pl.* cabbage soup

Э

экспози́ция *f.* exposition
экску́рсия *f.* excursion, guided tour
эне́ргия *f.* energy

эпо́ха *f.* epoch
эта́ж *m.* floor, story
э́тика *f.* ethics
э́то *n. nom. & acc. of* that, this
э́тот this, that
эх! eh! oh!

Ю

юбиле́й *m.* anniversary, jubilee
ю́бка *f.* skirt
юг *m.* south
ю́жный southern
ю́мор *m.* humor
ю́ность *f.* youth
ю́ноша *m.* young fellow
юри́ст *m.* lawyer

Я

я I
я́блоко *n.* apple

яви́ться *perf.* to appear, to show up
явле́ние *n.* appearance
явля́ться *imp.* to appear, to show up
яд *m.* poison
ядови́тый poisonous, toxic
я́зва *f.* ulcer, sore
язы́к *m.* language, tongue
яйцо́ *n.* egg
янва́рь *m.* January
я́ркий bright, brilliant
я́рко brightly, colorfully
я́рус *m.* balcony, tier (theatr.)
я́сно clearly
я́сный clear, distinct
я́щик *m.* drawer, box

ENGLISH-RUSSIAN DICTIONARY

In the English-Russian Dictionary, the following points should be noted:

Nouns are always given with their gender, so that their pattern of declension can be easily located in the Outline of Grammar (**1.3-5**).

Adjectives are given only in the masculine nominative singular form. (For the declension of adjectives, see **2.3** in the Grammar section.) English words which can function both as nouns and as adjectives are marked *adj.* when used as adjectives.

Verbs: The English entry is given in the infinitive form; the corresponding Russian verb is given first in the imperfective and then in the perfective infinitive (the two forms are separated by a comma).

In phraseologic examples the entry is replaced by a mark of repetition (~).

A hyphen in Russian words indicates that a part of the preceding word is repeated, e.g.: открыва́ть, -кры́ть (i.e. откры́ть); впуска́ть, -сти́ть (i.e. впусти́ть).

When the form of the perfective is identical with that of the imperfective except that it is preceded by a prefix, the perfective is indicated by this prefix followed by a hyphen. E.g.: ду́мать, по- (i.e. поду́мать).

A

ability спосо́бность *f.*
able, to be мочь, с-; быть в состоя́нии; уме́ть, с-
about о, насчёт; о́коло; вокру́г
to be ~ собира́ться, -бра́ться
above над; (с)вы́ше
from ~ све́рху
abroad за грани́цей
absence отсу́тствие *n.*
absolutely совсе́м; соверше́нно
accept, to принима́ть, -ня́ть
accidentally случа́йно, нечая́нно
accompany, to сопровожда́ть, -води́ть
according to согла́сно
account счёт *m.*
achievement достиже́ние *n.*
acid ки́слый
acknowledge, to признава́ть, -зна́ть
acquaint, to знако́мить, по-
to become ~ed with знако́миться, по-
acquaintance знако́мство *n.*
across че́рез, сквозь
act акт *m.*; де́йствие *n.*
act, to де́йствовать, по-
action посту́пок *m.*, де́йствие *n.*
activity де́ятельность *f.*
actor актёр *m.*
actress актри́са *f.*
actual действи́тельный
actually на са́мом де́ле
add, to прибавля́ть, -ба́вить

address а́дрес *m.*
adjust, to ула́живать, ула́дить
admire, to восхища́ться, -хити́ться
admit, to допуска́ть, -сти́ть
advance, to продвига́ть(ся), -дви́нуть(ся)
adventure приключе́ние *n.*
advertisement объявле́ние *n.*
advice сове́т *m.*
advise, to сове́товать, по-
affair де́ло *n.*
affectionate ла́сковый, не́жный
afraid, to be боя́ться *imp.*
after *prep.* по́сле, за; *adv.* пото́м, зате́м; *conj.* по́сле того́ как
afterwards пото́м
again опя́ть, сно́ва
against про́тив
age во́зраст *m.*; век *m.*
agent а́гент *m.*
aggression агре́ссия *f.*
agitation волне́ние *n.*
ago тому́ наза́д
agony аго́ния *f.*
agree, to соглаша́ться, -аси́ться
ahead впереди́; вперёд
aid по́мощь *f.*
aim цель *f.*
aim, to стреми́ться *imp.*
air во́здух *m.*; *adj.* возду́шный
air mail авиапо́чта
airplane самолёт *m.*
airport аэропо́рт *m.*
alarm трево́га *f.*
alarm clock буди́льник *m.*
alas увы́
album альбо́м *m.*
alcohol алкого́ль *m.*, спирт *m.*
alight, to сходи́ть, сойти́; спуска́ться, -сти́ться
alive живо́й
all весь; всё; вся́кий
alley переу́лок *m.*
alliance сою́з *m.*
allow, to позволя́ть, -зво́лить; допуска́ть, -сти́ть
all right ла́дно, хорошо́
almond минда́ль *m.*
almost почти́
alone оди́н, одино́кий
along вдоль, по
aloud вслух, гро́мко
already уже́
also та́кже, то́же
alteration переме́на *f.*
although хотя́
always всегда́
amaze, to поража́ть, -рази́ть
to be ∼d удивля́ться, -ви́ться
ambassador посо́л *m.*
ambulance каре́та ско́рой по́мощи
America Аме́рика *f.*
American америка́нец *m.*, -нка *f.*; *adj.* америка́нский
among ме́жду
amount коли́чество *n.*, су́мма *f.*
amuse, to забавля́ть, -ба́вить
amusement заба́ва *f.*
amusing заба́вный, смешно́й
analysis ана́лиз *m.*
ancient дре́вний, стари́нный
and и; а
angel а́нгел *m.*
anger гнев *m.*
angle у́гол *m.*
angry серди́тый
to be (get) ∼ серди́ться, рас-
animal живо́тное *n.*
anniversary юбиле́й *m.*, годовщи́на *f.*
announce, to объявля́ть, -ви́ть
annoy, to надоеда́ть, -е́сть
annual годово́й, ежего́дный
another друго́й
answer отве́т *m.*
answer, to отвеча́ть, -ве́тить
ant мураве́й *m.*
antique дре́вний, анти́чный
anxiety трево́га *f.*, забо́та *f.*
anxious озабо́ченный
any како́й-нибудь, любо́й
anyone кто́-нибудь; вся́кий
anything что́-нибудь, что уго́дно
apartment кварти́ра *f.*
apologize, to извиня́ться, -ни́ться
apparatus аппара́т *m.*, прибо́р *m.*
apparently очеви́дно, повиди́мому
appeal to, to обраща́ться, -ати́ться
appear, to появля́ться, -ви́ться

appearance появле́ние *n.*; нару́жность *f.*
apple я́блоко *n.*
apple-tree я́блоня *f.*
apply to, to обраща́ться, -ати́ться
appoint, to назнача́ть, -а́чить
appointment назначе́ние *n.*; свида́ние *n.*
approach, to приближа́ться, -и́зиться; подходи́ть, подойти́
approximately приблизи́тельно
apricot абрико́с *m.*
April апре́ль *m.*
architect архите́ктор *m.*
argue, to спо́рить, по-
argument аргуме́нт *m.*
arise, to возника́ть, -ни́кнуть
arithmetic арифме́тика *f.*
arm рука́ *f.*
armchair кре́сло *n.*
arms ору́жие *n.*
army а́рмия *f.*, во́йско *n.*
around круго́м, вокру́г
arrange, to устра́ивать, -ро́ить
arrest аре́ст *m.*
arrival прибы́тие *n.*
arrive, to прибыва́ть, -бы́ть
art иску́сство *n.*
article статья́ *f.*
artist худо́жник *m.*
artistic худо́жественный
as как; так; так как; когда́
 ~ if как бу́дто
 ~ to что каса́ется
ask, to спра́шивать, спроси́ть
 to ~ for проси́ть, по-
asleep, to fall засыпа́ть, -сну́ть
ass осёл *m.*
assume, to предполага́ть, -ложи́ть
assure, to уверя́ть, уве́рить
astonished, to be удивля́ться, -ви́ться
astonishment удивле́ние *n.*
at в, на; при, у; о́коло, по
at all вообще́
athlete атле́т *m.*
atom а́том *m.*
attach, to придава́ть, -да́ть
attack нападе́ние *n.*
attempt попы́тка *f.*
attend, to прису́тствовать *imp.*
attention внима́ние *n.*
attentive внима́тельный
attitude отноше́ние *n.*
audience пу́блика *f.*
August а́вгуст *m.*
aunt тётя *f.*
author а́втор *m.*
authority власть *f.*
automobile автомоби́ль *m.*
autumn о́сень *f.*
avenue проспе́кт *m.*
average сре́дний
avoid, to избега́ть, -бежа́ть (*or* -бе́гнуть)
awake, to буди́ть, раз-; просыпа́ться, -сну́ться
away прочь
awful ужа́сный

B

back спина́ *f.*; спи́нка *f.*; *adj.* за́дний; *adv.* наза́д, обра́тно
bacon беко́н *m.*
bad плохо́й, дурно́й, скве́рный
bag мешо́к *m.*; су́мка *f.*
baggage бага́ж *m.*
balance бала́нс *f.*; весы́ *m. pl.*
balcony балко́н *m.*
ball шар *m.*; мяч *m.*; бал *m.*
ballet бале́т *m.*
banana бана́н *m.*
band ле́нта *f.*; ба́нда *f.*; орке́стр, *m.*
bank банк *m.*; бе́рег *m.* (*of a river*)
banknote ба́нковый биле́т *m.*, банкно́та *f.*
barber парикма́хер *m.*
barber shop парикма́херская *f.*
bare го́лый
bark, to ла́ять, за-
basic основно́й
basis осно́ва *f.*, основа́ние *n.*; ба́за *f.*
basket корзи́н(к)а *f.*
bath ва́нна *f.*
to bathe купа́ться, вы-
bathing *adj.* купа́льный
bathroom ва́нная *f.*
battle би́тва *f.*, бой *m.*
to be быть *imp.*

beach пляж *m.*
beam луч *m.*
beans фасо́ль *f.*
bear медве́дь *m.*
bear, to выноси́ть, вы́нести; терпе́ть, по-; нести́, по-
beard борода́ *f.*
beast зверь *m.*
beat, to бить, по-
beautiful краси́вый, прекра́сный
beauty красота́ *f.*
because потому́ что, так как
  ~ of из-за
become, to станови́ться, стать; де́латься, с-
bed крова́ть *f.*, посте́ль *f.*
  to go to ~ ложи́ться спать
bedroom спа́льня *f.*
bee пчела́ *f.*
beef говя́дина *f.*
beer пи́во *n.*
beet свёкла *f.*
before *prep.* пе́ред, до; *adv.* впереки́; *conj.* пре́жде чем
beg, to проси́ть, по-
beggar ни́щий *m.*
begin, to начина́ть(ся), -ча́ть(ся)
beginning нача́ло *n.*
behind за, позади́, сза́ди
being существо́ *n.*
belief ве́ра *f.*
believe, to ве́рить, по-
bell ко́локол *m.*; звоно́к *m.*
belly живо́т *m.*
belong, to принадлежа́ть *imp.*
below *prep.* под, ни́же; *adv.* внизу́
  from ~ сни́зу
belt по́яс *m.*
bench скаме́йка *f.*
benefit вы́года *f.*
berry я́года *f.*
beside ря́дом, во́зле, о́коло
besides кро́ме (того́)
best, the (наи)лу́чший
better *adj.* лучший; *adv.* лу́чше
between ме́жду
beyond сверх
big большо́й, кру́пный
bill счёт *m.*
billion миллиа́рд *m.*
bind, to свя́зывать, связа́ть
birch берёза *f.*
bird пти́ца *f.*
birthday день рожде́ния
biscuit пече́нье
bit кусо́чек *m.*
  not a ~ нисколько
bitter го́рький
black чёрный
blank бланк *m.*
blanket одея́ло *n.*
bleach, to бели́ть, вы́-
blind слепо́й
blonde блонди́н *m.*, блонди́нка *f.*
blood кровь *f.*
blot пятно́ *n.*
blouse блу́зка *f.*
blow уда́р *m.*
blow, to дуть *imp.*
blue си́ний, голубо́й
board доска́ *f.*, правле́ние *n.*; борт *m.*
board, to столова́ться *imp.*
boat ло́дка *f.*
body те́ло *n.*
boil, to кипе́ть, вс-; кипяти́ть(ся), вс-
bold сме́лый
bond связь *f.*
bone кость *f.*
book кни́га *f.*
bookcase кни́жный шкаф *m.*
book(let) кни́жка *f.*
boot сапо́г *m*, боти́нок *m.*
border грани́ца *f.*; край *m.*
born рождённый
boss нача́льник *m.*; хозя́ин *m.*
both о́ба
  ~ . . . and и . . . и
bottle буты́лка *f.*
bottom дно *n.*
bouillon бульо́н *m.*
bound свя́занный
box коро́бка *f.*, я́щик *m.*
boy ма́льчик *m.*
brag, to хва́стать(ся), по-
brain мозг *m.*
brake тормо́з *m.*
branch ветвь *f.*; о́трасль *f.*; отделе́ние *n.*
brandy коньяк *m.*, во́дка *f.*
brassiere ли́фчик *m.*
brave бра́вый, хра́брый

bread хлеб *m.*
breadth ширина́ *f.*
break, to лома́ть(ся), с-; разбива́ть, -би́ть; наруша́ть, -ши́ть
breakfast за́втрак *m.*
to have ~ за́втракать, по-
breast грудь *f.*
breathe, to дыша́ть *imp.*
breathing дыха́ние *n.*
bridge мост *m.*
brief кра́ткий
briefcase портфе́ль *m.*
briefly ко́ротко
bright я́ркий, све́тлый
brilliant блестя́щий
bring, to приноси́ть, -нести́; приводи́ть, -вести́
broad широ́кий
broadcast радиопереда́ча *f.*
brooch брошь *f.*
broom метла́ *f.*
brother брат *m.*
~-in-law зять *m.*
brow бровь *f.*
brown кори́чневый
brush щётка *f.*; кисть *f.*
bucket ведро́ *n.*
build, to стро́ить, по-
building зда́ние *n.*
burden бре́мя *n.*; но́ша *f.*
burn, to горе́ть, с-; сжига́ть, сжечь
bus авто́бус *m.*
bush куст *m.*
business де́ло *n.*, заня́тие *n.*
busy за́нятый
but *conj.* но, а; *prep.* кро́ме; *adv.* лишь
butcher мясни́к *m.*
butter ма́сло *n.*
butterfly ба́бочка *f.*
button пу́говица *f.*
button hole петля *f.*
buy, to покупа́ть, купи́ть
by *prep.* у, при, о́коло; *adv.* ря́дом; ми́мо
~ heart наизу́сть
~ and ~ вско́ре
~ the way кста́ти, ме́жду про́чим

C

cabbage капу́ста *f.*
cabin каю́та *f.*, каби́на *f.*
cable кана́т *m.*, ка́бель *m.*
cage клётка *f.*
cake торт *m.*, пиро́жное *n.*; кусо́к *m.*
calculation расчёт *m.*
calendar календа́рь *m.*
calf телёнок *m.*
call, to звать, по-; называть, -зва́ть
to ~ for тре́бовать, по-; заходи́ть, зайти́ за
to ~ up звони́ть, по-
to be ~ed называ́ться, -зва́ться
calm споко́йный
calm, to успока́ивать(ся), -ко́ить(ся)
camel верблю́д *m.*
camp ла́герь *m.*
can бидо́н *m.*, ба́нка *f.*
can мочь, с-
cancer рак *m.*
candle свеча́ *f.*
cane па́лка *f.*; камы́ш *m.*
cannon пу́шка *f.*
cap ша́пка *f.*, фура́жка *f.*
capable спосо́бный
capital столи́ца *f.*; капита́л *m.*
cape плащ *m.*; мыс *m.*
captain капита́н *m.*
capture, to захва́тывать, -ати́ть
car ваго́н *m.*; автомоби́ль *m.*
card ка́рта *f.*, ка́рточка *f.*
cardinal основно́й, гла́вный
care забо́та *f.*
to take ~ of забо́титься, по-
careful осторо́жный, тща́тельный
careless беззабо́тный; небре́жный
caress ла́ска *f.*
caress, to ласка́ть *imp.*
cargo груз *m.*
carpet ковёр *m.*
carrot(s) морко́вь *f.*
carry, to носи́ть *imp.*; нести́, по-
to ~ on продолжа́ть, -до́лжить

to ~ out выполня́ть, вы́полнить
cart теле́га *f.*
cartoon карикату́ра *f.*
case я́щик *m.*; слу́чай
in any ~ во вся́ком слу́чае
cashier касси́р *m.*
cast iron чугу́н *m.*
castle за́мок *m.*
cat кот *m.*, ко́шка *f.*
catch, to лови́ть, пойма́ть; схва́тывать, -ати́ть
to ~ cold простужа́ться, -уди́ться
cathedral собо́р *m.*
cattle скот m.
Caucasian кавка́зский
Caucasus Кавка́з *m.*
cauliflower цветна́я капу́ста *f.*
cause причи́на *f.*, по́вод *m.*
cause, to причиня́ть, -ни́ть
caviar икра́ *f.*
ceiling потоло́к *m.*
cellar подва́л *m.*
cemetery кла́дбище
center центр *m.*
central центра́льный
century век *m.*, столе́тие *n.*
certain определённый
a ~ не́который, не́кий
certainly непреме́нно, наве́рно
chain цепь *f.*
chair стул *m.*
chairman председа́тель *m.*
chalk мел *m.*
challenge, to вызыва́ть, вы́звать
chamber пала́та *f.*; ка́мера *f.*
champagne шампа́нское *n.*
chance возмо́жность *f.*, слу́чай *m.*
by ~ случа́йно
change переме́на *f.*; переса́дка *f.*; сда́ча *f.*
change, to меня́ть(ся), об-, по-; переменя́ть, -ни́ть; (*money*) разме́нивать, -меня́ть
chap па́рень *m.*
chapter глава́ *f.*
character хара́ктер *m.*
charge, free of беспла́тно
charming очарова́тельный, преле́стный
chatter, to болта́ть *imp.*
chauffeur шофёр *m.*
cheap дешёвый
cheaply дёшево
check чек *m.*; номеро́к *m.*
check, to проверя́ть, -ве́рить
to ~ the luggage сдава́ть, сдать бага́ж
cheek щека́ *f.*
cheerful бо́дрый, весёлый
cheese сыр *m.*
cherry ви́шня *f.*
chess ша́хматы *m. pl.*
chest грудь *f.*; я́щик *m.*
chestnut кашта́н *m.*
chicken ку́рица *f.*; цыплёнок *m.*
chief нача́льник *m.*, руководи́тель *m.*; *adj.* гла́вный
child ребёнок *m.*
childhood де́тство *n.*
childish де́тский
children де́ти *pl.*
chimney труба́ *f.*
china фарфо́р *m.*
chocolate шокола́д *m.*
choice вы́бор *m.*
choose, to выбира́ть, вы́брать
chop котле́та *f.*
Christmas рождество́ *n.*
church це́рковь *f.*
cigarette папиро́са *f.*
cinema кино́ *n.*
circle круг *m.*
circumstance обстоя́тельство *n.*
citizen граждани́н *m.*, -а́нка *f.*
city (большо́й) го́род *m.*
claim тре́бование *n.*; прете́нзия *f.*
claim, to тре́бовать, по-
class класс *m.*
clean чи́стый
clean, to чи́стить, вы-
to ~ up убира́ть, убра́ть
clear я́сный, све́тлый, поня́тный
clerk чино́вник *m.*, слу́жащий *m.*
clever у́мный
climb, to ла́зить *imp.*; лезть, по-
cloak-room ка́мера хране́ния
clock часы́ *m. pl.*
close бли́зкий
close, to закрыва́ть(ся), -кры́ть(ся)
cloth ткань *f.*; сукно́ *n.*; ска́терть *f.*

clothed одéтый
clothes одéжда *f.*, плáтье *n.*
cloud óблако *n.*, тýча *f.*
club клуб *n.*
coal ýголь *m.*
coast морскóй бéрег *m.*, побо-рéжье *n.*
coat пальтó *n. indecl.*
cocoa какáо *n*
coffee кофе *n. indecl.*
coincidence совпадéние *n.*
cold хóлод *m.*; простýда *f.*; *adj.* холóдный
it's ~ хóлодно
collapse обвáл *m.*, провáл *m.*
collar воротнúк *m.*
color цвет *m.*
colored цветнóй
comb грéбень *m.*; гребёнка *f.*
come, to приходúть, прийтú; приезжáть, -éхать
comedy комéдия *f.*
comfortable удóбный
comical смешнóй
command прикáз *m.*
command, to прикáзывать, -казáть; комáндовать *imp.*
commodity товáр *m.*
common óбщий
communicate, to сообщáть, -щúть
communication сообщéние *n.*
company óбщество *n.*
comparative сравнúтельный
compare, to срáвнивать, сравнúть
comparison сравнéние *n.*
compartment отделéние *n.*; купé *n.*
compassion сострадáние *n.*
compel, to заставлять, -áвить; вынуждáть, вы́нудить
compile, to составлять -áвить
complain, to жáловаться, по
complaint жáлоба *f.*
complete пóлный
completely совершéнно
complicated слóжный
compose, to составлять, -áвить
composer композúтор *m.*
comrade товáрищ *m.*
conceal, to скрывáть, скрыть
concerning касáтельно, относú-тельно
conclude, to заключáть, -чúть; дéлать, с- вы́вод
conclusion заключéние *n.*; вы́-вод *m.*
condition услóвие *n.*; состояние *n.*; *pl.* обстоятельства *n. pl.*
conductor кондýктор *m.*; дири-жёр *m.*
confess, to признавáться, -знáть-ся
confidence довéрие *n.*
confirm, to подтверждáть, -рдúть
conformity соответствие *n.*
congratulate, to поздравлять, -áвить
congress съезд *m.*, конгрéсс *m.*
connection связь *f.*
conquer, to завоёвывать, -воевáть
conscience сóвесть *f.*
consciousness сознáние *n.*
consent, to соглашáться, -асúться
consequently слéдовательно
consider, to считáть, счесть; рассмáтривать, -смотрéть
consideration, to take into прини-мáть, -нять во внимáние
consist of, to состоять *imp.* из
conspiracy зáговор *m.*
constant постоянный
construct стрóить, по-
contain, to содержáть *imp.*
content довóльный
contents содержáние *n.*
continue, to продолжáть(ся), -дóлжить(ся)
contract договóр *m.*
contrary протúвный
on the ~ наоборóт
convenient удóбный
conversation разговóр *m.*, бесé-да *f.*
convert, to превращáть, -атúть; обращáть, -атúть
convey, to перевозúть, -везтú
conviction убеждéние *n.*
convince, to убеждáть, убедúть
cook, to варúть, с-; готóвить *imp.*
cool прохлáдный
copper медь *f.*
copy-book тетрáдь *f.*
cord верёвка *f.*

cordial *adj.* серде́чный; ликёр *m.*
cork пробка *f.*
corkscrew што́пор *m.*
corn кукуру́за *f.*
corner у́гол *m.*
correct пра́вильный
correct, to поправля́ть, -а́вить
correspondence перепи́ска *f.*
corridor коридо́р *m.*
cost, to сто́ить *imp.*
costume костю́м *m.*
cottage да́ча *f.*
cotton хло́пок *m.*; *adj.* хлопчатобума́жный
cough ка́шель *m.*
cough, to ка́шлять, за-
council сове́т *m.*
counsel сове́т *m.*; совеща́ние *n.*
count, to счита́ть, счесть
to ~ on рассчи́тывать, -ита́ть
country страна́ *f.*; дере́вня *f.*
couple па́ра *f.*; чета́ *f.*
courage хра́брость *m.*
course курс *m.*; ход *m.*, тече́ние *n.*
of ~ коне́чно
court двор *m.*; суд *m.*; корт *m.*
cousin двою́родный брат *m.*; двою́родная сестра́ *f.*
cover, to покрыва́ть, -кры́ть
cow коро́ва *f.*
cozy ую́тный
cradle колыбе́ль *f.*
craftsman ремéсленник *m.*
crane жура́вль *m.*
crayfish рак *m.*
cream крем *m.*
create, to создава́ть, -да́ть
creation созда́ние *n.*
creature существо́ *n.*
criminal престу́пный
cross крест *m.*
cross, to переходи́ть, перейти́
crowd толпа́ *f.*
crown коро́на *f.*
cruel жесто́кий
cry крик *m.*; плач *m.*
cry, to крича́ть, кри́кнуть; пла́кать, за-
cucumber огуре́ц *m.*
culture культу́ра *f.*
cunning хи́трый
cup ча́шка *f.*
curiosity любопы́тство *n.*
curious любопы́тный; стра́нный
current тече́ние *n.*; ток *m.*; *adj.* теку́щий
curtain за́навес *m.*, за́навеска *f.*
cushion поду́шка *f.*
custom обы́чай *m.*
customary обыкнове́нный, обы́чный
custom-house тамо́жня *f.*
customs по́шлина *f.*
cut, to ре́зать, раз-, с-; руби́ть *imp.*; (hair) стричь *imp.*
to ~ out выреза́ть, вы-
cutlet котле́та *f.*
czar царь *m.*

D

daily ежедне́вный
damage вред *m.*; уще́рб *m.*
damp сыро́й, вла́жный
dance та́нец *m.*
dance, to танцева́ть, по-
danger опа́сность *f.*
dangerous опа́сный
dare, to сметь, по-
daring сме́лый, отва́жный
dark тёмный
darkness темнота́ *f.*
darling голу́бчик *m.*
date да́та *f.*; свида́ние *n.*
up to ~ совреме́нный
daughter дочь *f.*, до́чка *f.*
day день *m.*
~ off выходно́й день
dead мёртвый
deaf глухо́й
dealer торго́вец *m.*
dear дорого́й
death смерть *f.*
debate спор *m.*
debt долг *m.*
December дека́брь *m.*
decent прили́чный
decide, to реша́ть, -ши́ть
decision реше́ние *n.*
deck па́луба *f.*
declare, to заявля́ть, -ви́ть
deep глубо́кий
deeply глубоко́
deer оле́нь *m.*
defeat пораже́ние *n.*

defense защи́та *f.*
define, to определя́ть, -ли́ть
definite определённый
definitely реши́тельно
degree сте́пень *f.*; гра́дус *m.*
delay заде́ржка *f.*; опозда́ние *n.*
delight восто́рг *m.*
delightful восхити́тельный
deliver, to доставля́ть, -а́вить
deliverance избавле́ние *n.*
demand тре́бование *n.*; спрос *m.*
demand, to тре́бовать, по-
dense густо́й, пло́тный
dentist зубно́й врач *m.*
depart, to отбыва́ть, -бы́ть; уезжа́ть, уе́хать
department отде́л *m.*; минис-те́рство *n.*
department store универса́льный магази́н *m.*
departure отъе́зд *m.*
depend on, to зави́сеть *imp.* от
deposit зада́ток *m.*
depth глубина́ *f.*
describe, to опи́сывать, описа́ть
description описа́ние *n.*
desert пусты́ня *f.*
deserve, to заслу́живать, -ужи́ть
design за́мысел *m.*; чертёж *m.*; узо́р *m.*
desire жела́ние *n.*
desk пи́сьменный стол *m.*
despair отча́яние *n.*
dessert десе́рт *m.*
destiny судьба́ *f.*
destroy, to разруша́ть, -ши́ть
detachment отря́д *m.*
detail подро́бность *f.*, дета́ль *f.*
determine, to определя́ть, -ли́ть
develop, to развива́ть(ся), -ви́ть-(ся); (*photo*) проявля́ть, -ви́ть
devil чёрт *m.*
dictionary слова́рь *m.*
die, to умира́ть, умере́ть
differ, to отлича́ть(ся), -чи́ться
difference ра́зница *f.*
different разли́чный, ра́зный
difficult тру́дный
difficulty затрудне́ние *n.*
dignity досто́инство *n.*
diligent приле́жный
dimension разме́р *m.*
dine, to обе́дать, по-
dining car ваго́н-рестора́н *m.*
dinner обе́д *m.*
direct прямо́й
direct, to направля́ть, -а́вить
direction направле́ние *n.*
directly пря́мо; то́тчас
director дире́ктор *m.*
dirt грязь *f.*
dirty гря́зный
disappear, to исчеза́ть, -че́знуть
disappoint, to разочаро́вывать, -ова́ть
disaster несча́стье *n.*, бе́дствие *n.*
discount ски́дка *f.*
discovery откры́тие *n.*
dish блю́до *n.*
display, to выставля́ть, -а́вить; проявля́ть, -ви́ть
dispose, to располага́ть, -ложи́ть
disposition хара́ктер *m.*
distance расстоя́ние *n.*
distant отдалённый
distinct я́сный, отчётливый
distress го́ре *n.*; нужда́ *f.*; бе́дствие *n.*
distribute, to распределя́ть, -ли́ть
district о́бласть *f.*, райо́н *m.*, о́круг *m.*
disturb, to беспоко́ить, о-; меша́ть, по-
ditch кана́ва *f.*
divide, to дели́ть, по-, раз-
division деле́ние *f.*; разде́л *m.*
do, to де́лать, с-
how do you ~ здра́вствуйте
doctor врач *m.*, до́ктор *m.*
document докуме́нт *m.*
dog соба́ка *f.*
doll ку́кла
dollar до́ллар *m.*
domestic дома́шний
donkey осёл *m.*
door дверь *f.*
doorstep крыльцо́ *n.*
dot то́чка *f.*
double двойно́й
doubt сомне́ние *n.*
doubt, to сомнева́ться, усомни́ть-ся
down *adv.* вниз, внизу́; *prep.* вниз; по

downstairs вниз; внизу́
dozen дю́жина *f.*
draft сквозня́к *m.*
drag, to тащи́ть, вы́-
drama дра́ма *f.*
draw, to тяну́ть, по-
drawer я́щик *m.*
dream сон *m.*; мечта́ *f.*
dress пла́тье *n.*; оде́жда *f.*
dress, to одева́ть(ся), оде́ть(ся)
dressed оде́тый
dressmaker портни́ха *f.*
dried сушёный
drink питьё *n.*; напи́ток *m.*
drink, to пить, вы́-
drive пое́здка *f.*, езда́ *f.*
drive, to гнать, по-; е́хать, по-
driver води́тель *m.*
drop ка́пля *f.*
drop, to опуска́ть, -сти́ть
 to ~ by заходи́ть, зайти́
drugstore апте́ка *f.*
drunk пья́ный
dry сухо́й
dry, to суши́ть, вы́-
duck у́тка *f.*
due до́лжный
 ~ to благодаря́, всле́дствие
during во вре́мя, в тече́ние, в продолже́ние
dust пыль *f.*
duty долг *m.*; обя́занность *f.*; по́шлина *f.*
dwarf ка́рлик *m.*
dye, to кра́сить, о-

E

each ка́ждый
eagle орёл *m.*
ear у́хо *n.*
early ра́нний; *adv.* ра́но
earnest серьёзный
earth земля́ *f.*
earthly земно́й
east восто́к *m.*
eastern восто́чный
easily легко́
easy лёгкий
eat, to есть, съ-; ку́шать, по-
edible съедо́бный
educated образо́ванный
education образова́ние *n.*, воспита́ние *n.*
effort уси́лие *n.*
e.g. напр. (наприме́р)
egg яйцо́ *n*
 fried ~ яи́чница-глазу́нья
eight во́семь
eighteen восемна́дцать
eighth восьмо́й
eight hundred восемьсо́т
eighty во́семьдесят
either ... or и́ли ... и́ли
elastic рези́нка *f.*
elbow ло́коть *m.*
elect, to выбира́ть, вы́брать; избира́ть, -бра́ть
electric электри́ческий
elephant слоа *m.*
elpehant слон *m.*
elevator лифт *m.*
eleven оди́ннадцать
else ина́че; ещё
embassy посо́льство *n.*
embroidery вы́шивка *f.*
emergency exit запасно́й вы́ход
empire импе́рия *f.*
empty пусто́й
encounter встре́ча *f.*
encourage, to ободря́ть, -ри́ть
end коне́ц *m.*
end, to конча́ть(ся), ко́нчить(ся)
endeavor, to пыта́ться, по-; стара́ться, по-
endurance выно́сливость *f.*, терпе́ние *n.*
enemy враг *m.*
energy эне́ргия *f.*
engage, to нанима́ть, -ня́ть
 to be ~d быть за́нятым
engine мото́р *m.*, дви́гатель *m.*; парово́з *m.*
England А́нглия *f.*
English англи́йский
Englishman англича́нин *m.*
Englishwoman англича́нка *f.*
enjoy, to наслажда́ться, -ади́ться
enormous грома́дный
enough дово́льно, доста́точно
enter, to входи́ть, войти́; вступа́ть, -пи́ть
enterprise предприя́тие *n.*

entertain, to развлекáть, -влéчь; угощáть, угостúть
entire цéлый, весь
entirely вполнé, совершéнно
entrance вход *m.*
envelope конвéрт *m.*
envy зáвисть *f.*
epoch эпóха *f.*
equal рáвный
equality рáвенство *n.*
equipment оборýдование *n.*
escape, to бежáть *imp.* & *perf.*
especially осóбенно
essay óчерк *m.*; попы́тка *f.*
essence сýщность *f.*
esteem уважéние *n.*
esteem, to уважáть *imp.*
etc. и т.д., и т.п. (и так дáлее, и томý подóбное)
eternal вéчный
Europe Еврóпа *f.*
even дáже; рóвный
evening вéчер *m.*
in the ~ вéчером, по вечерáм
event собы́тие *n.*
ever когдá-либо
for ~ навсегдá
every кáждый, вся́кий
everybody кáждый, все *pl.*
everything всё
everywhere вездé, (по)всю́ду
evidently по-вúдимому
evil зло *n.*; *adj.* дурнóй
exactly тóчно, рóвно; úменно
examination экзáмен *m.*; осмóтр *m.*
examine, to осмáтривать, осмотрéть
example примéр *m.*; образéц *m.*
for ~ напримéр
excellent превосхóдный, отлúчный
except крóме
exception исключéние *n.*
excess, излúшек *m.*
exchange, to обмéнивать, -нúть *or* -ня́ть
exclaim, to восклицáть, -úкнуть
excuse, to извиня́ть, -нúть
exhausted измýченный
exhibition вы́ставка *f.*
exist, to существовáть *imp.*
existence существовáние *n.*
exit вы́ход *m.*
expect, to ожидáть *imp.*
expectation ожидáние *n.*
expense расхóд *m.*
expensive дорогóй
experience óпыт *m.*
experienced óпытный
expert знатóк *m.*, экспéрт *m.*
explain, to объясня́ть, -нúть
explanation объяснéние *n.*
export э́кспорт *m.*, вы́воз *m.*
express срóчный
express, to выражáть, вы́разить
expression выражéние *n.*
express train экспрéсс *m.*
expulsion исключéние *n.*
extend, to простирáться, -стерéться; протя́гивать(ся), -тянýть(ся); продлевáть, -длúть
extension продлéние *n.*
extent протяжéние *n.*
to what ~ до какóй стéпени
external внéшний
extraordinary чрезвычáйный
extremely чрезвычáйно, крáйне
eye глаз *m.*
eyebrow бровь *f.*
eyeglasses очкú *m. pl.*

F

face лицó *n.*
fact факт *m.*
factory фáбрика *f.*, завóд *m.*
fair справедлúвый; прекрáсный
fairy tale скáзка *f.*
faith вéра *f.*
faithful вéрный
fall óсень *f.*
fall, to пáдать, (у)пáсть
to ~ asleep засыпáть, -спáть
to ~ in love влюбля́ться, -бúться
false лóжный; фальшúвый
fame слáва *f.*
familiar знакóмый
family семья́ *f.*
famous знаменúтый, извéстный
far далёкий; *adv.* далекó
farmer фéрмер *m.*
fashion мóда *f.*

fast ско́рый, бы́стрый; *adv.* бы́стро
to be ~ (*watch*) спеши́ть
fasten, to прикрепля́ть, -пи́ть
fat жир *m.*, са́ло *n.*; *adj.* жи́рный; то́лстый
fate судьба́ *f.*, до́ля *f.*
father оте́ц *m.*
~-in-law тесть *m.*; свёкор *m.*
fault вина́ *f.*, оши́бка *f.*
favorable благоприя́тный
fear страх *m.*
feather перо́ *n.*
feature осо́бенность *f.*
February февра́ль *m.*
feeble сла́бый
feed, to корми́ть, на-
feel, to чу́вствовать(ся), по-
feeling чу́вство *n.*
fellow па́рень *m.*
female же́нский
feminine же́нский
ferry па́ром *m.*
fetch, to достава́ть, -та́ть; приноси́ть, -нести́
fever жар *m.*, лихора́дка *f.*
few мало
a ~ не́сколько
field поле *n.*; о́бласть *f.*
fifteen пятна́дпать
fifth пя́тый
fifty пятьдеся́т
fight бой *m.*, дра́ка *f.*
fight, to боро́ться, по-; дра́ться, по-
figure фигу́ра *f.*; ци́фра *f.*
fill, to наполня́ть(ся), -по́лнить(ся)
to ~ out заполня́ть -по́лнить
film плёнка *f.*; фильм *m.*
final коне́чный
finally наконе́ц
find, to находи́ть, найти́
to ~ in застава́ть, -ста́ть
to ~ out узнава́ть, узна́ть
to be found находи́ться, найти́сь
fine прекра́сный; ме́лкий
finger па́лец *m.*
finish, to конча́ть(ся) ко́нчить(ся
fir ель *f.*
fire ого́нь *m.*; пожа́р *m.*
firm фи́рма *f.*; *adj.* кре́пкий
first пе́рвый
at ~ снача́ло
in the ~ place во-пе́рвых
the ~ time впервы́е
fish ры́ба *f.*
fishing rod уди́лище *n.*
fist кула́к *m.*
fit, to годи́ться, при-; подходи́ть, подойти́
five пять
five hundred пятьсо́т
flag флаг *m.*
flame пла́мя *n.*
flashlight фона́рь *m.*
flee, to бежа́ть *imp.* & *perf.*
fleet фло́т *m.*
flight полёт *m.*; бе́гство *n.*
floor эта́ж *m.*; пол *m.*
flour мука́ *f.*
flower цвето́к *m.*
fluently свобо́дно, бе́гло
fly му́ха *f.*
fly, to лета́ть *imp.*; лете́ть. по-
fog тума́н *m.*
fold, to скла́дывать, сложи́ть
folk(s) люди *pl.*
follow, to сле́довать, по-
following сле́дующий
food пи́ща *f.*, еда́ *f.*
fool дура́к, *m.*, ду́ра *f.*
foolish глу́пый
foot нога́ *f.*
on ~ пешко́м
football футбо́л *m.*
for *prep.* для; из-за; на; в течение; за; *conj.* потому что, так как
forbid, to запреща́ть, -ети́ть
force си́ла *f.*
force, to заставля́ть, -а́вить
forehead лоб *m.*
foreign иностра́нный
foreigner иностра́нец, *m.*, иностра́нка *f.*
foreman ма́стер *m.*
forest лес *m.*
forget, to забыва́ть, -бы́ть
forgive, to проща́ть, прости́ть
fork ви́лка *f.*
form фо́рма *f.*; бланк *m.*; класс *m.*

form, to образо́вывать, -ова́ть
former пре́жний
formerly пре́жде, когда́-то
fortnight две неде́ли
fortunately к сча́стью
fortune состоя́ние *n.*
forty со́рок
forward вперёд; впредь
forward to отправля́ть, -а́вить
found, to осно́вывать, -ова́ть
fountain фонта́н *m.*
fountain pen автору́чка *f.*
four четы́ре; че́тверо
four hundred четы́реста
fourteen четы́рнадцать
fourth четвёртый
fox лиси́ца *f.*
France Фра́нция *f.*
free свобо́дный
 ~ of charge беспла́тный
freedom свобо́да *f.*
freeze, to замерза́ть, -мёрзнуть
freight груз *m.*
French францу́зский
frequently ча́сто
fresh све́жий
Friday пя́тница *f.*
friend друг *m.*, подру́га *f.*
friendly дру́жеский
friendship дру́жба *f.*
frighten, to пуга́ть, ис-
frightful стра́шный
from от, из, с; по
front пере́дняя сторона́; фронт *m.*; *adj.* пере́дний
 in ~ (of) впереди́, пе́ред
frontier грани́ца *f.*
frost моро́з *m.*
fruit фру́кты *m. pl.*
fry, to жа́рить, за-
fulfil, to исполня́ть, -по́лнить
fulfilment исполне́ние *n.*
full по́лный
fully вполне́, соверше́нно
function, to де́йствовать, по-
fund запа́с *m.*
fundamental основно́й
funeral по́хороны *f. pl.*
funny смешно́й, заба́вный; стра́нный
fur мех *m.*
furnish, to снабжа́ть, -бди́ть; мебли́ровать *imp.* & *perf.*
furniture ме́бель *f.*, обстано́вка *f.*
further да́льше; дальне́йший
future бу́дущее *n.*; *adj.* бу́дущий

G

gaily ве́село
gain, to выи́грывать, вы́играть
gallery галере́я *f.*
game игра́ *f.*
garage гара́ж *m.*
garden сад *m.*
gasoline бензи́н *m.*
gas station запра́вочный пункт *m.*
gate(way) воро́та *pl.*
gather, to собира́ть(ся), -бра́ть(ся)
gay весёлый
gear приспособле́ние *n.*
gender род *m.*
general генера́л *m.*; *adj.* о́бщий
generally, in general во́общем, вообще́
gentleman господи́н *m.*
genuine по́длинный, настоя́щий
geography геогра́фия *f.*
geometry геоме́трия *f.*
German не́мец *m.*, не́мка *f.*; *adj.* неме́цкий
Germany Герма́ния *f.*
get, to получа́ть, -чи́ть; достава́ть, -ста́ть; станови́ться, стать
 to ~ in входи́ть, войти́
 to ~ off сходи́ть, сойти́
 to ~ on пожива́ть *imp.*
 to ~ out выходи́ть, вы́йти
 to ~ up встава́ть, встать
giant велика́н *m.*
gift пода́рок *m.*, дар *m.*
girl де́вушка *f.*; де́вочка *f.*
give, to дава́ть, дать; подава́ть, -да́ть
 to ~ back отдава́ть, -да́ть
 to ~ in уступа́ть, -пи́ть
 to ~ up сдава́ть, сдать; броса́ть, бро́сить
glad рад
 to be ~ ра́доваться, об-

glance взгляд *m.*
glass стекло́ *n.*; стака́н *m.*; *pl.* очки́ *m. pl.*
glide, to скользи́ть, -зну́ть
glitter, to блесте́ть, -сну́ть
globe шар *m.*
glorious сла́вный
glory сла́ва *f.*
glow, to пыла́ть, вос-
go, to ходи́ть *imp.*; итти́ (идти́), пойти́; е́хать, по-
to ~ away уходи́ть, уйти́; уезжа́ть, уе́хать
to ~ in входи́ть, войти́
to ~ on продолжа́ть, -до́лжить
to ~ out выходи́ть, вы́йти
to ~ up поднима́ться, -ня́ться
God бог *m.*
gold зо́лото *n.*
golden золото́й
good хоро́ший; до́брый
goods това́ры *m. pl.*
goose гусь *m.*
government прави́тлеьство *n.*
grade сте́пень *f.*; сорт *m.*; класс *m.*
gradually постепе́нно
grand замеча́тельный
granddaughter вну́чка *f.*
grandfather де́душка *m.*
grandmother ба́бушка *f.*
grandson вну́к *m.*
grape виногра́д *m.*
grass трава́ *f.*
grateful благода́рный
grave моги́ла *f.*
gray се́рый, седо́й
grease жир *m.*; сма́зка *f.*
grease, to сма́зывать, смаза́ть
great большо́й, вели́кий
greedy жа́дный
green зелёный
greet, to приве́тствовать *imp.*; кла́няться, поклони́ться
greeting приве́т *m.*, покло́н *m.*
grief го́ре *n.*
grocer бакале́йщик *m.*
ground по́чва *f.*; основа́ние *n.*
ground floor ни́жний эта́ж
group группа *f.*
grow, to расти́, вы́- ; выра́щивать, вы́растить; станови́ться, стать
grown-up взро́слый
growth рост *m.*
guarantee гара́нтия *f.*
guarantee, to гаранти́ровать *imp.* & *perf.*
guard сто́рож *m.*; стра́жа *f.*; *pl.* гва́рдия *f.*
guess, to уга́дывать, угада́ть; полага́ть *imp.*
guest гость *m.*
guide руководи́тель *m.*; провод-ни́к *m.*, гид *m.*; путеводи́тель *m.*
guilt вина́ *f.*
guilty винова́тый
guitar гита́ра *f.*
gum каме́дь *f.*; рези́на *f.*
gun ору́дие *n.*, пу́шка *f.*; ружьё *n.*; револьве́р *m.*

H

habit привы́чка *f.*, обы́чай *m.*
hailing, it is идёт град
hair во́лос *m.*; во́лосы *m. pl.*
hairdresser парикма́хер *m.*
half полови́на *f.*
hall зал *m.*; пере́дняя *f.*
ham ветчина́ *f.*
hammer молото́к *m.*
hand рука́ *f.*
hand, to передава́ть, -да́ть; вруча́ть, -чи́ть
handbook спра́вочник *m.*
handicraft ремесло́ *n.*
handkerchief носово́й плато́к *m.*
handsome краси́вый
hang, to висе́ть *imp.*
to ~ up ве́шать, пове́сить
happen, to случа́ться, -чи́ться
happiness сча́стье *n.*
happy счастли́вый, ра́достный
hard твёрдый, жёсткий; тру́дный, тяжёлый; суро́вый; *adv.* си́льно; усе́рдно
hardly едва́ (ли); с трудо́м
hare за́яц *m.*
harm вред *m.*
harmless безоби́дный
harmony гармо́ния *f.*
harsh жёсткий, грубый, ре́зкий
hasten, to торопи́ть(ся), по-
hastily поспе́шно

hat шля́па *f.*
hate, to ненави́деть, воз-
hatred не́нависть *f.*
have, to име́ть *imp.*; получа́ть, -чи́ть;
I ~ to go я до́лжен итти́
he он
head голова́; глава́
headache головна́я боль *f.*
headlight фа́ра *f.*
health здоро́вье *n.*
healthy здоро́вый
hear, to слы́шать, у-
hearing слух *m.*
heart се́рдце *n.*
by ~ наизу́сть
hearty серде́чный
heat жара́ *f.*, тепло́ *n.*
heaven не́бо *n.*
heavy тяжёлый; *adv.* тяжело́
heel каблу́к *m.*
height высота́ *f.*; вышина́ *f.*
hell ад *m.*
hello! алло!
help по́мощь *f.*; прислу́га *f.*
help, to помога́ть, -мо́чь
her её; свой
here здесь, тут
(to) ~ сюда́
from ~ отсю́да
~ you are вот, пожа́луйста
hereby, herewith э́тим; при сём
hero геро́й *m.*
hide шку́ра *f.*
hide, to пря́тать(ся), с-; скрыва́ть(ся), скры́ть(ся)
high высо́кий; *adv.* высоко́
highly весьма́
high school сре́дняя шко́ла *f.*
highway автостра́да *f.*
hill холм *m.*
hinder, to меша́ть, по-
hire, to нанима́ть, -ня́ть
for ~ напрока́т
his его́; свой
historic(al) истори́ческий
history исто́рия *f.*
hit, to ударя́ть, удари́ть; попада́ть, -па́сть
hoarse хри́плый
to hold держа́ть(ся), по-
to ~ out выде́рживать, вы́держать
to ~ up заде́рживать, -держа́ть
hole дыра́, ды́рка
holiday пра́здник *m.*; *pl.* кани́кулы *f. pl.*
holy свято́й
home дом *m.*; *adj.* дома́шний; *adv.* домо́й
honest че́стный
honey мёд *m.*
honor честь *f.*
hook крючо́к *m.*
hope наде́жда *f.*
hope, to наде́яться *imp.*
horizon горизо́нт *m.*
horror у́жас *m.*
horse ло́шадь *f.*, конь *m.*
horseback, on верхо́м
hospital больни́ца *f.*, го́спиталь *m.*
host хозя́ин *m.*
hostess хозя́йка *f.*
hot горя́чий; жа́ркий
hotel гости́ница *f.*
hour час *m.*
house дом *m.*; пала́та *f.*
housekeeping (дома́шнее) хозя́йство *n.*
housewife дома́шняя хозя́йка *f.*
how как, каки́м о́бразом
~ many, ~ much ско́лько
however одна́ко, всё-таки
huge огро́мный
human челове́ческий
humanity челове́чество *n.*
humor ю́мор *m.*
hundred сто; со́тня
hundredth со́тый
hunger го́лод *m.*
hungry голо́дный
hunt охо́та *f.*
hurry, in a второпя́х
hurry, to спеши́ть, по-; торопи́ть(ся), по-
~ up! скоре́е!
hurt, to причиня́ть, -ни́ть боль; боле́ть *imp.*
husband муж *m.*
hydrogen водоро́д *m.*

I

I я
ice лёд *m.*
ice cream моро́женое *n.*
idea иде́я *f.*, мысль *f.*, поня́тие *n.*
identical одина́ковый
i.e. т.е. (то́-есть)
if е́сли
ill больно́й
illness боле́знь *f.*
image о́браз *m,*
imagine, to представля́ть, -а́вить себе́
immediately неме́дленно
immense огро́мный
import и́мпорт *m.*, ввоз *m.*
important ва́жный
impossible, it is невозмо́жно
impression впечатле́ние *n.*
imprisonment заключе́ние *n.*
improbable, it is ма́ло вероя́тно, вря́д ли
improve, to улучша́ть(ся), улу́чшить(ся)
impulse поры́в *m.*, побужде́ние *n.*
in *prep.* в, во; *adv.* внутри́; внутрь
inadequate недоста́точный
inasmuch as поско́льку
incapable неспосо́бный
inclination скло́нность *f.*
include, to включа́ть, -чи́ть
incomprehensible непоня́тный
incorrect непра́вильный
indeed в са́мом де́ле, действи́тельно
increase, to увели́чивать(ся), -и́чить(ся)
indicate, to ука́зывать, указа́ть
indirect ко́свенный
individual ли́чный
inflammation воспале́ние *n.*
influence влия́ние *n.*
inform, to сообща́ть, -щи́ть
information спра́вка *f.*, све́дения *n. pl.*
inhabitant обита́тель *m.*
ink черни́ла *n. pl.*
inn тракти́р *m.*
inner вну́тренний
innocent неви́нный
innumerable бесчи́сленный
inquire, to спра́шивать, спроси́ть
insane душевнобольно́й
inscription на́дпись *f.*
insect насеко́мое *n.*
inside внутри́, внутрь
insolent де́рзкий, на́глый
inspect, to осма́тривать, осмотре́ть
inspection осмо́тр *m.*
inspiration вдохновле́ние *n.*
install to устра́ивать, -ро́ить
instalments, by в рассро́чку
instance, for наприме́р
instant мгнове́ние *n.*
instantly сейча́с же
instead of вме́сто; вме́сто того́, что́бы
institution учрежде́ние *n.*
instructive поучи́тельный
instrument прибо́р *m.*, инструме́нт *m.*
insufficiently недоста́точно
insult оби́да *f.*; оскорбле́ние *n.*
insurance страхова́ние *n.*
insure, to страхова́ть, за-
intelligent у́мный, толко́вый
intend, to намерева́ться *imp.*
intention наме́рение *n.*
interest интере́с *m.*
interest, to заинтересо́выва́ть, -сова́ть
to be ~ed интересова́ться *imp.*
interesting интере́сный
internal вну́тренний
international междунаро́дный
interpreter перево́дчик *m.*
interrupt, to перебива́ть, -би́ть; прерыва́ть, -рва́ть
interview интервью́ *n.*
intimate инти́мный; бли́зкий
into, в, во
introduce, to вводи́ть, ввести́; представля́ть, -а́вить; знако́мить, (п)о-
introduction введе́ние *n.*
invasion вторже́ние *n.*, наше́ствие *n.*
investigate, to иссле́довать *imp.* & *perf.*
investigation иссле́дование *n.*

investment (капитало)вложе́ние *n.*
invisible неви́димый
invitation приглаше́ние *n.*
invite, to приглаша́ть, -аси́ть
involuntarily нево́льно
iron желе́за *f.*; утю́г *m.*
iron, to гла́дить, вы́-
ironic(al) ирони́ческий
irregular непра́вильный
irritate, to раздража́ть, -жи́ть
island, isle о́стров *m.*
issue вы́ход *m.*; вы́пуск *m.*
it он, она́, оно́; э́то
item пункт *m.*; статья́ *f.*; но́мер *m.*
itinerary путеводи́тель *m.*
its его́, её; свой

J

jacket жаке́т *m.*, ку́ртка *f.*
jam варе́нье *n*
January янва́рь *m.*
jar ба́нка *f.*; кувши́н *m.*
jewel драгоце́нный ка́мень *m.*
job рабо́та *f.*, слу́жба *f.*
join, to присоединя́ть(ся), -ни́ть(ся)
joke, шу́тка *f.*
joke, to шути́ть, по-
journal журна́л *m.*
journalist журнали́ст *m.*
journey путеше́ствие *n.*; пое́здка *f.*
joy ра́дость *f.*
joyful ра́достный
jubilee юбиле́й *m.*
judge судья́ *m.*
judge, to суди́ть *imp.*
juice сок *m.*
July ию́ль *m.*
jump, to пры́гать, -гнуть
 to ∼ up вска́кивать, вскочи́ть
junction у́зел *m.*, узлова́я ста́нция *f.*
June ию́нь *m.*
just *adj.* справедли́вый; *adv.* то́чно, и́менно, как раз; то́лько что
 ∼ now сейча́с
justify, to опра́вдывать, -вда́ть

K

keep, to держать(ся), по-; сохраня́ть(ся), -ни́ть(ся)
key ключ *m.*
kill, to убива́ть, уби́ть
killer уби́йца *m.* & *f.*
kind сорт *m.*, вид *m.*, род *m.*
kind любе́зный, до́брый, ми́лый
kindly ла́сково, любе́зно
king коро́ль *m.*
kingdom короле́вство *n.*, ца́рство *n.*
kiss поцелу́й *m.*
kiss, to целова́ть, по-
kitchen ку́хня *f.*
knee коле́но *n.*
knife нож *m.*
knit, to вяза́ть, с-
knock, to стуча́ть, по-
 to ∼ down сбива́ть, сбить с ног
know, to знать *imp.*
knowledge зна́ние *n.*
kopek копе́йка *f.*

L

label ярлы́к
labor труд *m.*, рабо́та *f.*
lace кру́жево *n.*
lack отсу́тствие *n.*, недоста́ток *m.*
ladder ле́стница *f.*
lady да́ма *f.*
lake о́зеро *n.*
lamb ягнёнок *m.*
lamp ла́мпа *f.*
land страна́ *f.*; земля́ *f.*
land, to приземля́ться, -ли́ться
landlady хозя́йка *f.*
landlord хозя́ин *m.*
lane переу́лок *m.*
language язы́к *m.*
lantern фона́рь *m.*
large большо́й, кру́пный
last после́дний; про́шлый
 at ∼ наконе́ц
last, to дли́ться, про-
late по́здно
 to be ∼ опа́здывать, опозда́ть
lately неда́вно, за после́днее вре́мя
later по́зже, пото́м

latest после́дний
laugh, to смея́ться, за-
laughter смех *m.*
laundry пра́чечная *f.*
lavatory убо́рная *f.*
law зако́н *m.*
lawn лужа́йка *f.*, га́зо́н *m.*
lawyer адвока́т *m.*, юри́ст *m.*
lay, to класть, положи́ть
lazy лени́вый
lead, to води́ть *imp.*; вести́, по-; руководи́ть *imp.*
leader вождь *m.*, руководи́тель *m.*
leaf лист *m.*
lean, to наклоня́ться, -ни́ться
  to ~ out высо́вываться, вы́сунуться
leap year високо́сный год *m.*
learn, to учи́ть(ся), на-; узнава́ть, узна́ть
leather ко́жа *f.*; ко́жаный *adj.*
leave, to покида́ть, -ки́нуть; уходи́ть, уйти́; уезжа́ть, уе́хать; оставля́ть, -а́вить
  to ~ for отправля́ться, -а́виться
  to ~ out пропуска́ть, -сти́ть
lecture ле́кция *f.*
left ле́вый; *adv.* нале́во, сле́ва
leg нога́ *f.*
leisure до́суг *m.*
lemon лимо́н *m.*
lemonade лимона́д *m.*
length длина́ *f.*
lengthen, to удлиня́ть(ся), -ни́ть(ся)
less ме́нее, ме́ньше
lesson уро́к *m.*
let, to пуска́ть, пусти́ть
  to ~ in впуска́ть, -сти́ть
  to ~ out выпуска́ть, вы́пустить
  to ~ know сообща́ть, -щи́ть
  to ~ pass пропуска́ть, -сти́ть
letter бу́ква *f.*; письмо́ *n.*
  ~ of credit аккредити́в *m.*
lettuce сада́т *m.*
liberate, to освобожда́ть, -оди́ть
liberty свобо́да *f.*
library библиоте́ка *f.*
license лице́нзия *f.*
lie ложь *f.*
lie, to лга́ть, со-; врать, со-
lie, to лежа́ть, по-
  to ~ down ложи́ться, лечь
life жизнь *f.*
lift лифт
  to give a ~ подвози́ть, -везти́
lift, to поднима́ть, -ня́ть
light свет *m.*; *adj.* светлый; лёгкий
light, to зажига́ть(ся). -же́чь(ся)
lighter зажига́лка *f.*
lightning мо́лния *f.*
like похо́жий, подо́бный; *adv.* как
like, to люби́ть *imp.*
  I ~ мне нра́вится
  I would ~ я хоте́л бы
likely вероя́тно
limb член *m.*
lime ли́па *f.*
limit, to ограни́чивать, -чить
line ли́ния *f.*; строка́ *f.*; черта́ *f.*
linen полотно́ *n.*; бельё *n.*; *adj.* полотня́ный
link звено́ *n.*
lion лев *m.*
lip губа́ *f.*
liquid жи́дкий
list спи́сок *m.*
listen, to слу́шать, по-
literature литерату́ра *f.*
little ма́ленький; ма́ло
  a ~ немно́го
live, to жить *imp.*
lively живо́й
liver пе́чень *f.*; печёнка *f.*
living room гости́ная *f.*
load, to заряжа́ть, -ряди́ть
lobster ома́р *m.*, рак *m.*
local ме́стный
lock замо́к *m.*
lock, to запира́ть(ся), -пере́ть(ся)
lonely одино́кий
long дли́нный; до́лгий; *adv.* до́лго
  ~ ago давно́
longing тоска́ *f.*
look взгляд *m.*
look, to смотре́ть, по-; вы́глядеть *imp.*
  to ~ after забо́титься, по-

to ~ around, back огля́дываться, -яну́ться
to ~ for иска́ть, по-
to ~ like каза́ться, по-
to ~ on наблюда́ть *imp.*
to ~ out остерега́ться, -ре́чься
to ~ over просма́тривать, -смотре́ть
to ~ up справля́ться, -а́виться
lorry грузови́к *m.*
lose, to теря́ть, по-; прои́грывать, -игра́ть
to ~ one's way заблужда́ться, -уди́ться
loss поте́ря *f.*; убы́ток *m.*
lost, to get пропада́ть -па́сть
lot жре́бий *m.*; до́ля *f.*
a ~ of мно́жество
loud гро́мкий; шу́мный
love любо́вь *f.*
in ~ with влюблённый в
love, to люби́ть *imp.*
low ни́зкий
lower ни́зший; ни́жний
lower, to опуска́ть, -сти́ть
lucky счастли́вый, уда́чный
luggage бага́ж *m.*
luggage room ка́мера хране́ния
lump кусо́к *m.*
lunch второ́й за́втрак *m.*
lung лёгкое *n.*
luxury ро́скошь *f.*

M

machine маши́на *f.*
mad сумасше́дший
magazine журна́л *m.*
mail по́чта *f.*
main гла́вный, основно́й
mainly гла́вным о́бразом
maintain, to подде́рживать, -держа́ть; содержа́ть *imp.*
maintenance содержа́ние *n.*
majority большинство́ *n.*
make, to де́лать, с-; заставля́ть, -а́вить
to ~up one's mind реша́ться, реши́ться
man мужчи́на *m.*; челове́к *m.*
manage, to управля́ть, -а́вить; заве́довать *imp.*; суме́ть *perf.*
manager заве́дующий *m.*, дире́ктор *m.*
manicure маникю́р *m.*
mankind челове́чество *n.*
manner спо́соб
in this ~ таки́м о́бразом
manual ручно́й
manufacture произво́дство *n.*
manuscript ру́копись *f.*
many мно́гие, мно́го
map ка́рта *f.*
March март *m.*
mark знак *m.*
market ры́нок *m.*
married жена́тый; заму́жняя
marry, to жени́ть(ся) *imp.* & *perf.*; выходи́ть, вы́йти за́муж; выдава́ть, вы́дать за́муж; венча́ть(ся), об-
marvelous чу́дный, чуде́сный
masculine мужско́й
mass ма́сса *f.*
massage масса́ж *m.*
master ма́стер *m.*; хозя́ин *m.*
master, to овладева́ть, -де́ть
masterpiece шеде́вр *m.*
match спи́чка *f.*; (*sports*) матч *m.*, состяза́ние *n.*
material материа́л *m.*; мате́рия *f.*
mathematics матема́тика *f.*
matter де́ло *n.*, вопро́с *m.*
what 's the ~? в чём де́ло?
as a ~ of fact на са́мом де́ле
it doesn't ~ нева́жно, ничего́
mattress матра́ц *m.*
May май *m.*
may мочь *imp.*
maybe мо́жет быть
meadow луг *m.*
meal еда́ *f.*, тра́пеза *f.*
mean, to зна́чить *imp.*
meaning значе́ние *n.*; смысл *m.*
means сре́дство *n.*
by ~ of посре́дством
by all ~ во что бы то ни ста́ло
by no ~ ни в ко́ем слу́чае
meantime, in the ме́жду тем, тем вре́менем
measure ме́ра *f.*
measure, to измеря́ть, -ме́рить

meat мя́со *n.*
mechanic меха́ник *m.*
medicine лека́рство *n.*
meet, to встреча́ть(ся), -е́тить(ся)
meeting встре́ча *f.*; собра́ние *n.*
melody мело́дия *f.*
melon ды́ня *f.*
member член *m.*
memory па́мять *f.*
mention, to упомина́ть, -мяну́ть
don't ~ it не сто́ит благода́рности
menu меню́ *n. indecl.*
mercy ми́лость *f.*
merely то́лько, про́сто
merry весёлый
message сообще́ние *n.*, посла́ние *n.*
metal мета́лл *m.*
meter метр *m.*
method ме́тод *m.*, спо́соб *m.*
midday по́лдень *m.*
middle середи́на; *adj.* сре́дний
in the ~ of среди́
Middle Ages сре́дние века́ *m. pl.*
middleman посре́дник *m.*
midnight по́лночь *f.*
mighty могу́щественный
mild кро́ткий; мя́гкий
mile ми́ля *f.*
military вое́нный
milk молоко́ *n.*
million миллио́н *m.*
mind ум *m.*, ра́зум *m.*
to bear in ~ име́ть в виду́
mind, to возража́ть, -ази́ть
never ~! ничего́!
mineral минера́льный
minute мину́та *f.*
miracle чу́до *n.*
mirror зе́ркало *n.*
miserable жа́лкий
misfortune го́ре, *n.*, несча́стье *n.*
miss, to прома́хиваться, -махну́ться; не попада́ть, не попа́сть; пропуска́ть, -сти́ть; скуча́ть *imp.* по
missing недостаю́щий
mist тума́н *m.*
mistake оши́бка *f.*
mistress хозя́йка *f.*
misunderstanding недоразуме́ние *n.*
mixture смесь *f.*
modern совреме́нный
modest скро́мный
moment моме́нт *m.*
Monday понеде́льник *m.*
money де́ньги *f. pl.*
money order де́нежный перево́д *m.*
monkey обезья́на *m.*
month ме́сяц *m.*
monthly ежеме́сячный
monument па́мятник *m.*
mood настрое́ние *n.*
moon луна́ *f.*
moral нра́вственный
morals нра́вы *m. pl.*
more бо́лее, бо́льше
morning у́тро *n.*
most, the наибо́лее; са́мый
mostly чаще *or* бо́льше всего́
mother мать *f.*
~-in-law тёща *f.*; свекро́вь *f.*
motion ход *m.*, движе́ние *n.*
in ~ на ходу́
motor дви́гатель *m.*, мото́р *m.*
motorboat мото́рная ло́дка
motorcar автомаши́на *f.*
motorcycle мотоци́кл *m.*
motor ship теплохо́д *m.*
mountain гора́ *f.*
mournful печа́льный
mouse мышь *f.*
moustache усы́ *m. pl.*
mouth рот *m.*
move, to дви́гать(ся), дви́нуть(ся); переезжа́ть, -е́хать
movement движе́ние *n.*
movies кино́ *n.*
Mr. господи́н *m.*
Mrs. госпожа́ *f.*
much мно́го; гора́здо
how much ско́лько
so much сто́лько
mud грязь *f.*
muddy гря́зный
multiply, to умножа́ть, -о́жить
municipal городско́й
murder уби́йство *n.*
muscle му́скул *m.*, мы́шца *f.*
museum музе́й *m.*

mushroom гриб *m.*
music му́зыка *f.*
must до́лжен
mustard горчи́ца *f.*
mute немо́й
mutton бара́нина *f.*
mutual взаи́мный
my мой, моя́, моё; мои́
mysterious таи́нственный
mystery та́йна *f.*

N

nail но́готь *m.*
naked го́лый
name и́мя *n.*; назва́ние *n.*
family ~ фами́лия *f.*
name, to называ́ть, -зва́ть
to be ~d называ́ться, -зва́ться
namely то́-есть, и́менно
napkin салфе́тка *f.*
narrow у́зкий
nasty га́дкий, проти́вный
nation наро́д *m.*, на́ция *f.*
national наро́дный
native родно́й
~ land ро́дина *f.*
natural есте́ственный
nature приро́да *f.*
naughty, to be шали́ть *imp.*
navy (вое́нный) флот *m.*
near бли́зко, о́коло
nearly почти́
necessary необходи́мый, ну́жный
necessity необходи́мость *f.*
neck ше́я *f.*
necklace ожере́лье *n.*
necktie га́лстук *m.*
need нужда́ *f.*
need, to нужда́ться *imp.*
needle иго́лка *f.*; игла́ *f.*
negative негати́в *m.*; *adj.* отрица́тельный
neglect, to пренебрега́ть, -бре́чь
negotiations перегово́ры *m.pl.*
neighbor сосе́д *m.*, сосе́дка *f.*
neighboring сосе́дний
neither . . . nor ни . . . ни
nephew племя́нник *m.*
nervous не́рвный
nest гнездо́ *n.*
never никогда́
nevertheless тем не ме́нее
new но́вый
news но́вость *f.*
newspaper газе́та *f.*
next бу́дущий; сле́дующий; ближа́йший; *adv.* по́сле э́того
~ to ря́дом
nice прия́тный, хоро́ший
niece племя́нница *f.*
night ночь *f.*; *adj.* ночно́й
at ~ но́чью
nightingale солове́й *m.*
nine де́вять
nine hundred девятьсо́т
nineteen девятна́дцать
ninety девяно́сто
ninth девя́тый
nitrogen азо́т *m.*
no нет
noble благоро́дный
nobody никто́
nod, to кива́ть, кивну́ть (голово́й)
noise шум *m.*
nominate, to назнача́ть, -а́чить
none никако́й; ни оди́н
nonsense вздор *m.*, чепуха́ *f.*, ерунда́ *f.*
noon по́лдень *m.*
norm но́рма *f.*
normal норма́льный
north се́вер *m.*
northern се́верный
nose нос *m.*
not не
not at all во́все не(т)
note запи́ска *f.*
nothing ничто́, ничего́
notice, to замеча́ть, -ме́тить
notify, to извеща́ть, -вести́ть уведомля́ть, уве́домить
notion поня́тие *n.*
notwithstanding несмотря́ на
novel рома́н *m.*
November ноя́брь *m.*
now тепе́рь, сейча́с
~ and then вре́мя от вре́мени
just ~ то́лько что
nowhere нигде́; никуда́
number число́ *n.*; но́мер *m.*
numerous многочи́сленный

nurse медсестра́ *f.*; ня́ня *f.*
nut оре́х *m.*

O

oak дуб *m.*
oat(s) овёс *m.*
obedient послу́шный
obey, to слу́шаться, по-
object предме́т *m.*
object, to возража́ть, -рази́ть
objection возраже́ние *n.*
obliged обя́занный
observe, to наблюда́ть *imp.*
obstacle препя́тствие *n.*
obtain to получа́ть, -чи́ть
obviously очеви́дно
occasionally случа́йно
occupation заня́тие *n.*
occupy, to занима́ть, -ня́ть
occur, to случа́ться, -чи́ться; приходи́ть, прийти́ на ум
October октя́брь *m.*
odd стра́нный
off с, со
hands ~! ру́ки прочь!
offend, to обижа́ть, оби́деть
offer предложе́ние *n.*
offer, to предлага́ть, -ложи́ть
office конто́ра *f.*, бюро́ *n.*
officer офице́р *m.*
official официа́льный
often ча́сто
oil ма́сло n.; нефть *f.*
oil, to сма́зывать, смаза́ть
okay ла́дно
old ста́рый
how old are you? ско́лько вам лет?
omelette омле́т *m.*
omit, to опуска́ть, -сти́ть
on на; в
once раз; одна́жды; когда́-то
~ more ещё раз
at ~ сра́зу
one оди́н; не́кто
~ another друг дру́га
~ and a half полтора́, -ры́
oneself (самого́) себя́; -ся
onion лук *m.*
only *adv.* то́лько; *adj.* еди́вствен-ный
open откры́тый
open, to открыва́ть, -кры́ть
opera о́пера *f.*
operation опера́ция *f.*; де́йст-вие *n.*
opinion мне́ние *n.*
opponent проти́вник *m.*
opportunity возмо́жность *f.*
opposite *prep.* напро́тив
or и́ли
orange апельси́н *m.*
orchard фрукто́вый сад *m.*
orchestra орке́стр *m.*
order зака́з *m.*; прика́з *m.*; строй *m.*
to be in ~ быть в поря́дке
in ~ to с тем, что́бы
order, to прика́зывать, -каза́ть; зака́зывать, -каза́ть
ordinary обыкнове́нный, обы́ч-ный
ore руда́ *f.*
organ о́рган *m.*
organization организа́ция *f.*
organize, to организо́вывать, -ова́ть
origin исто́чник *m.*; происхож-де́ние *n.*
original оригина́льный
orphan сирота́ *m.* & *f.*
other друго́й, ино́й
the ~ day на-днях
otherwise ина́че
ought to до́лжен; сле́дует
our наш, на́ша, на́ше; на́ши
out из; вне; нару́жу
he is ~ его́ нет до́ма
outburst вспы́шка *f.*
outfit обору́дование *n.*
outline о́черк *m.*
output произво́дство *n.*
outside *adv.* снару́жи
outstanding выдаю́щийся
outward вне́шний
over над; че́рез; на, по; за
the work is ~ рабо́та око́нчена
overcoat пальто́ *n. indecl.*
oversea за́ морем; *adj.* замо́р-ский
overshoe гало́ша *f.*
owing to благодаря́
own со́бственный; родно́й
own, to владе́ть *imp.*, облада́ть *imp.*

owner владе́лец *m.*
ox бык *m.*; вол *m.*
oxygen кислоро́д *m.*

P

pace шаг *m.*
pack, to упако́вывать, -кова́ть
package па́чка *f.*, паке́т *m.*
page страни́ца *f.*
pain боль *f.*
paint кра́ска *f.*
paint, to кра́сить, о-
painter живопи́сец *m.*
painting жи́вопись *f.*; карти́на *f.*
pair па́ра *f.*; чета́ *f.*
palace дворе́ц *m.*
pale бле́дный
palm ладо́нь *f.*; па́льма *f.*
pants брю́ки *f. pl.*
paper бума́га *f.*
paragraph абза́ц *m.*; пара́граф *m.*
parcel посы́лка *f.*; паке́т *m.*
parents роди́тели *m. pl.*
park парк *m.*
part часть *f.*; роль *f.*
participate, to уча́ствовать *imp.*
participation уча́стие *n.*
particular осо́бенный
partly отча́сти
partner партнёр *m.*
party па́ртия *f.*; гру́ппа *f.*; вечери́нка *f.*
pass про́пуск *m.*
pass, to проходи́ть, пройти́; проезжа́ть, -е́хать; передава́ть, -да́ть
  to ~ an examination сдать *perf.* экза́мен
passage прое́зд *m.*, прохо́д *m.*
passenger пассажи́р *m.*
passer-by прохо́жий
passion страсть *f.*
passionate стра́стный
passport па́спорт *m.*
past про́шлый; прошло́е *n.*
paste те́сто *n.*; па́ста *f.*
paste to, кле́йть, с-
pastry пиро́жное *n.*
path тропи́нка *f.*; путь *m.*
patience терпели́вость *f.*; терпе́ние *n.*
patient пацие́нт *m.*, больно́й *m.*; *adj.* терпели́вый
pattern образе́ц *m.*, модель *f.*
pause па́уза *f.*
pavement мостова́я *f.*
paw ла́па *f.*
pay пла́та *f.*
pay, to плати́ть, за-; опла́чивать, -ати́ть
  to ~ attention обраща́ть, -ати́ть внима́ние
payment упла́та *f.*, платёж *m.*
pea горо́х *m.*
peace мир *m.*
peaceful споко́йный, ми́рный
peach пе́рсик *m.*
peacock павли́н *m.*
peak верши́на *f.*
pear гру́ша *f.*
pearl же́мчуг *m.*
peasant крестья́нин *m.*
peculiar осо́бенный
peculiarity осо́бенность *f.*
pedestrian пешехо́д *m.*
pen перо́ *n.*
pencil каранда́ш *m.*
penetrate, to проника́ть, -ни́кнуть
people наро́д *m.*; лю́ди *pl.*
pepper пе́рец *m.*
per че́рез, посре́дством; в, на
per cent проце́нт *m.*
perfect соверше́нный
perform, to исполня́ть, -по́лнить
performance исполне́ние *n.*; представле́ние *n.*
perfume духи́ *m.pl.*
perhaps мо́жет быть
period пери́од *m.*
perish, to погиба́ть *imp.*; ги́бнуть, по-
permanent постоя́нный
  ~ wave шестиме́сячная зави́вка *f.*
permission разреше́ние *n.*
permit про́пуск *m.*
permit, to разреша́ть, -ши́ть; позволя́ть, -о́лить
perpetual постоя́нный
perseverance насто́йчивость
person лицо́ *n.*, осо́ба *f.*, челове́к *m.*
personal ли́чный
personality ли́чность *f.*

perspiration пот *m.*
perspire, to потéть, вс-
persuade, to убеждáть, убедúть
petticoat нúжняя юбка
pharmacy аптéка *f.*
photograph фотогрáфия *f.*, снúмок *m.*
phrase фрáза *f.*
physician врач *m.*
piano пианúно *n.*
grand ~ роя́ль *m.*
pick up, to подбирáть, подобрáть
picture картúна *f.*
pie пирóг *m.*
piece кусóк *m.*; штýка *f.*
pig свинья́ *f.*
pigeon гóлубь *m.*
pike щýка *f.*
pile кýча *f.*, грýда *f.*
pillow подýшка *f.*
pilot лётчик *m.*
pin булáвка *f.*
pincers клещú *f.pl.*; шипцы́ *m.pl.*
pine соснá *f.*
pineapple ананáс *m.*
pink рóзовый
pipe трубá *f.*; трýбка *f.*
pitiful жáлкий
pity сожалéние *n.*, жáлость *f.*
place мéсто *n.*
to take ~ имéть мéсто
place, to помещáть, -местúть
plain я́сный; простóй
plan план *m.*
plan, to планúровать *imp.* & *perf.*
planet планéта *f.*
plank доскá *f.*
plant растéние *n.*; завóд *m.*
plant, to сажáть, посадúть
plate тарéлка *f.*
platform площáдка *f.*, платфóрма *f.*
play игрá *f.*; пьéса *f.*
play, to игрáть, сыгрáть
pleasant прия́тный
please пожáлуйста
pleased довóльный
pleasure удовóльствие *n.*
plenty (of) óчень мнóго
plot зáговор *m.*
plum слúва *f.*
pocket кармáн *m.*
pocketbook бумáжник *m.*
poem поэ́ма *f.*; стихотворéние *n.*
poet поэ́т *m.*
point тóчка *f.*; пукнт *m.*
the ~ is дéло в том
point out, to укáзывать, указáть
poison яд *m.*
poisonous, ядовúтый
pole столб *m.*
police полúция *f.*
policeman полицéйский *m.*
policy полúтика *f.*
polite вéжливый, любéзный
political политúческий
politics полúтика *f.*
pond пруд *m.*
pool лýжа *f.*
poor бéдный
popular нарóдный, популя́рный
population населéние *n.*
porcelain фарфóр *m.*
pork свинúна *f.*
porridge кáша *f.*
port порт *m.*
porter носúльщик *m.*
portrait портрéт *m.*
position положéние *n.*
to be in a ~ быть в состоя́нии
positive положúтельный
possess, to владéть *imp.*; обладáть *imp.*
possibility возмóжность *f.*
possible возмóжный
post пóчта *f.*
postal почтóвый
postcard откры́тка *f.*
poster афúша *f.*
postman почтильóн *m.*; листонóсец *m.*
post office пóчта *f.*, почтóвое отделéние *n.*
postpone, to отклáдывать, отложúть
pot горшóк *m.*
potato картóфель, *m.*, картóшка *f.*
poultry домáшняя птúца *f.*
pound фунт *m.*
pour out, to наливáть, -лúть
powder пýдра *f.*
power власть *f.*; сúла *f.* держáва *f.*
powerful сúльный, мóщный
practical практúческий

practice пра́ктика *f.*
prairie степь *f.*
praise, to хвали́ть, по-
pray, to моли́ться, по-
precede, to предше́ствовать *imp.*
precise то́чный
preface предисло́вие *n.*
prefer, to предпочита́ть, -че́сть
preparation подгото́вка *f.*
prepare, to пригота́вливать(ся), -то́вить(ся)
prescription реце́пт *m.*
presence прису́тствие *n.*
present пода́рок *m.*; настоя́щее вре́мя *n.*
present тепе́решний; настоя́щий; прису́тствующий
at ~ в да́нное вре́мя
for the ~ пока́
present, to представля́ть, -а́вить
presently вско́ре
preserve, to сохраня́ть, -ани́ть
president председа́тель *m.*; президе́нт *m.*
press печа́ть *f.*
press, to нажима́ть, -жа́ть; гла́дить, вы́-
pressure давле́ние *n.*
pretty хоро́шенький; *adv.* дово́льно
previous предыду́щий
price цена́ *f.*
pride го́рдость *f.*
prince принц *m.*, князь *m.*
principal гла́вный
print, to печа́тать, на-
prison тюрьма́ *f.*
private ча́стный; ли́чный
probably вероя́тно
problem пробле́ма *f.*
proceed, to продолжа́ть, -до́лжить; происходи́ть, -изойти́
process проце́сс *m.*
produce, to производи́ть, -вести́
production произво́дство *n.*
professor профе́ссор *m.*
profit вы́года *f.*; при́быль *f.*
profound глубо́кий
program програ́мма *f.*
progress успе́хи *m.pl.*
prohibit, to воспреща́ть, -ети́ть
prolong, to продлева́ть, -дли́ть
prolongation продле́ние *n.*
prominent ви́дный, выдаю́щийся
promise, to обеша́ть *imp.* & *perf.*
prompt бы́стрый, ско́рый, неме́дленный
pronounce, to произноси́ть, -нести́
pronunciation произноше́ние *n.*
proper до́лжный; со́бственный
properly как сле́дует
propose, to предлага́ть, -ложи́ть
prose про́за *f.*
protection защи́та *f.*
protest проте́ст *m.*
proud го́рдый
to be ~ of горди́ться *imp.*
prove, to дока́зывать, -каза́ть; ока́зываться, оказа́ться
proverb посло́вица *f.*
provide, to снабжа́ть, -бди́ть
provoke, to вызыва́ть, вы́звать
public пу́блика *f.*
public публи́чный; обще́ственный
publish, to издава́ть, -да́ть
publisher изда́тель *m.*
publishing house изда́тельство *n.*
pull, to тяну́ть *imp.*; тащи́ть, вы́-
pump насо́с *m.*
punish, to нака́зывать, -каза́ть
pupil учени́к *m.*
purchase поку́пка *f.*
pure чи́стый
purpose цель *f.*, наме́рение *n.*
on ~ наро́чно
push, to толка́ть, -кну́ть
put, to класть, положи́ть; ста́вить, по-;
to ~ down запи́сывать, -писа́ть
to ~ in вставля́ть, -а́вить
to ~ off откла́дывать, отложи́ть
to ~ on надева́ть, -де́ть
to ~ out туши́ть, по-

Q

quality ка́чество *n.*
quantity коли́чество *n.*
quarter че́тверть *f.*; кварта́л *m*
quay на́бережная *f.*
queen короле́ва *f.*
question вопро́с *m.*

questionnaire анкéта *f.*
queue óчередь *f.*
quick бы́стрый
be ~! скорée!
quickly бы́стро
quiet спокóйный, ти́хий
quite вполнé, совсéм, совершéнно

R

rabbit крóлик *m.*
race рáса *f.*; гóнка *f.*
radiator радиáтор *m.*
radio рáдио *n.*
railroad желéзная дорóга *f.*
rain дождь *m.*
raincoat дождеви́к *m.*
raining, it is дождь идёт
raise, to поднимáть, -ня́ть
raisins изю́м *m.*
ram барáн *m.*
random, at наугáд
range предéл *m.*
rapid скóрый, бы́стрый
rare рéдкий
raspberry мали́на *f.*
rat кры́са *f.*
rate нóрма *f.*; стáвка *f.*
at any ~ во вся́ком спу́чае
~ of exchange курс *m.*
rather довóльно; скорée; лу́чше
raw сырóй
~ material сырьё *n.*
ray луч *m.*
razor бри́тва *f.*
reach, to достигáть, -сти́чь; доходи́ть, дойти́; доезжáть, -éхать; доставáть, -стáть
reaction реáкция *f.*
read, to читáть, про- (*or* прочéсть)
reader читáтель *m.*
ready готóвый
~ money нали́чные дéньги
real настоя́щий, действи́тельный
reality действи́тельность *f.*
realization осуществлéние *n.*
realize, to осуществля́ть, -ви́ть; представля́ть, -áвить себé
really действи́тельно, на сáмом дéле
reason причи́на *f.*, пóвод *m.*
reasonable разу́мный
recall, to отзывáть, отозвáть; вспоминáть, вспóмнить
receipt получéние *n.*; распи́ска *f.*; квитáнция *f.*
receive, to получáть, -чи́ть; принимáть, -ня́ть
recently недáвно *f.*
reception приём *m.*
recipe рецéпт *m.*
reckon on, to рассчи́тывать, -итáть на
recognize, to признавáть, -знáть; узнавáть, узнáть
recollection воспоминáние *n.*
recommend, to редомендовáть *imp.* & *perf.*; совéтовать, по-
reconstruct, to восстанáвливать, -нови́ть
reconstruction восстановлéние *n.*
record пласти́нка *f.*; рекóрд *m.*
recover поправля́ться, -áвиться
recovery выздоровлéние *n.*
recreation óтдых *m.*
red крáсный
reduction снижéние *n.*; ски́дка *f.*
refer, to ссылáться, сослáться на; относи́ться, -нести́сь
reference спрáвка *f.*; ссы́лка *f.*
with ~ to относи́тельно
reflection отражéние *n.*
refreshment room буфéт *m.*
refusal откáз *m.*
refuse, to откáзываться, -казáться
regards привéт *m.*, поклóн *m.*
regiment полк *m.*
region óбласть *f.*
registered letter заказнóе письмó
regret сожалéние *n.*
regret, to жалéть, по-
regular прáвильный; регуля́рный
rejoice, to рáдовать(ся), об-
relate, to расскáзывать, -азáть
relation отношéние *n.*
relative рóдственник *m.*; *adj.* сравни́тельный
relax, to отдыхáть, -дохну́ть
release, to освобождáть, -оди́ть
reliable надёжный
religion религия *f.*
reluctantly неохóтно
remain, to оставáться, остáться

remainder оста́ток *m.*
remaining остально́й
remark, to замеча́ть, -ме́тить
remarkable замеча́тельный
remember, to по́мнить *imp.;* вспомина́ть, вспо́мнить
remind, to напомина́ть, -по́мнить
reminiscence воспомина́ние *n.*
remote отдалённый
remove, to устраня́ть, -ни́ть; снима́ть, снять
render, to ока́зывать, оказа́ть
renew, to возобновля́ть, -ви́ть
renounce отка́зываться, -каза́ться
rent, to нанима́ть, -ня́ть
repair почи́нка *f.,* ремо́нт *m.*
repair, to исправля́ть, -а́вить; чини́ть, по-
repeat, to повторя́ть, -ри́ть
replace, to заменя́ть, -ни́ть
replacement заме́на *f.*
reply отве́т *m.*
reply, to отвеча́ть, -ве́тить
report докла́д *m.*; отчёт *m.*; акт *m.*
report, to сообща́ть, -щи́ть; докла́дывать, доложи́ть
repose о́тдых *m.*
represent, to представля́ть, -а́вить
representative представи́тель *m.*
reproach, to упрека́ть, -кну́ть
reproduction репроду́кция *f.,* воспроизведе́ние *n.*
reptile пресмыка́ющее *n.*
republic респу́блика *f.*
repulsive отта́лкивающий
request про́сьба *f.*
request, to проси́ть, по-
rescue, to спаса́ть, спасти́
research иссле́дование *n.*
resembling похо́жий
resentment возмуще́ние *n.*
reserve запа́с *m.*
reserve, to резерви́ровать, за-
reside, to прожива́ть, -жи́ть
residence местожи́тельство *n.*
resist, to сопротивля́ться, -ви́ться
resistance сопротивле́ние *n.*
resolution реше́ние *n.*
respect уваже́ние *n.*
  in ~ to в отноше́нии к
respect, to уважа́ть *imp.*
respective соотве́тственный
responsibility отве́тственность *f.*; обя́занность *f.*
responsible отве́тственный
  to be ~ for отвеча́ть, -ве́тить за
rest о́тдых *m.,* поко́й *m.*; оста́ток *m.*
rest, to отдыха́ть, -дохну́ть
restaurant рестора́н *m.*
restless беспоко́йный
restriction ограниче́ние *n.*
result результа́т *m.,* сле́дствие *n.*
retire, to удаля́ться, -ли́ться
retreat, to отступа́ть, -пи́ть
return возвраще́ине *n.*
return, to возвраща́ть(ся), -врати́ть(ся); верну́ть(ся) *perf.*
revenue годово́й дохо́д *m.*
reverse обра́тный
review обзо́р *m.*; журна́л *m.*
revolution револю́ция *f.*; оборо́т *m.*
revolve, to враща́ться *imp.*
reward награ́да *f.*
rich бога́тый
rid of, to get избавля́ться, -ба́виться
riddle зага́дка *f.*
ride езда́ *f.*
ride, to е́здить *imp.*; е́хать, по-
right пра́во *n.*; *adj.* пра́вый; пра́вильный; *adv.* ве́рно; пря́мо
  turn to the ~ поверни́те напра́во
  all ~ хорошо́, пра́вильно
  ~ away сейча́с же
ring круг *m.*; кольцо́ *n.*
ring (up), to звони́ть, по-
rise, to встава́ть, встать; поднима́ться, -ня́ться
risk, to рискова́ть, -кну́ть
river река́ *f.*
road доро́га *f.*
roar, to реве́ть, про-
roast, to жа́рить, из-
roastbeef ро́стбиф *m.*
role роль *f.*

roll свёрток *m.*; рулóн *m.*; бýлочка *f.*
roll, to катúть(ся), по-
roof крыша *f.*
room кóмната *f.*
root кóрень *m.*
rope верёвка *f.,* канáт *m.*
rose рóза *f.*
rough грýбый
round крýглый; *adv.* вокрýг
row ряд *m.*
royal королéвский
rubber резúна *f.*; каучýк *m.*; *pl.* галóши *f. pl.*
ruble рубль *m.*
rug ковёр *m.,* кóврик *m.*
rule прáвило *n.*; правлéние *n.*
as a ∼ обычно
rumor слух *m.*
run, to бéгать *imp.*; бежáть, по-
to ∼ away убегáть, убежáть
rush, to мчáться *imp.*
to ∼ into врывáться, ворвáться
rust, to ржавéть, за-
Russia Россúя *f.*
Russian рýсский *m.,* рýсская *f.*; *adj.* рýсский
rye bread ржанóй хлеб *m.*

S

sack мешóк *m.*
sad печáльный, грýстный
safety безопáсность *f.*
sailboat пáрусная лóдка *f.*
salad салáт *m.*
salary жáлованье *n.*
sale продáжа *f.*
salesgirl продавщúца *f.*
salesman продавéц *m.*
salmon лососúна *f.*
salt соль *f.*
salt shaker солóнка *f.*
same тот же (сáмый), одинáковый
it's all the ∼ to me мне э́то безразлúчно
sample образéц *m.*
sand песóк *m.*
satisfaction удовлетворéние *n.*
satisfactory удовлетворúтельный
satisfied довóльный
satisfy удовлетворя́ть, -рúть
Saturday суббóта *f.*
saucer блю́дце *n.*
sausage колбасá *f.*
savage дúкий
save, to спасáть, спастú; экономить, с-
savings-bank сберегáтельная кáсса *f.*
say, to говорúть, сказáть
scarcely едва; вряд ли
scene сцéна *f.*
scent зáпах *m.*
schedule расписáние *n.*; грáфик *m.*
scheme схéма *f.*
scholar учёный *m.*
school шкóла *f.*
schoolboy шкóльник *m.*
science наýка *f.*
scientific наýчный
scientist учёный *m.*
scissors нóжницы *f. pl.*
scold, to ругáть, вы-
scratch, to царáпать(ся), -пнуть(ся)
scream, to кричáть, крúкнуть
screen экрáн *m.*
screw винт *m.*
scrupulous щепетúльный
sculptor скýльптор *m.*
sculpture скульптýра *f.*
sea мóре *n.*
seagull чáйка *f.*
seal печáть *m.*
seam шов *m.*
season сезóн *m.*
seasick, to be страдáть морскóй болéзнью
seat стул *m.,* сидéнье *n.*
to take a ∼ садúться, сесть
second вторóй
secondly во-вторы́х
secret тайна *f.*; *adj.* тáйный
secretary секретáрь *m.*
∼ of State минúстр инострáнных дел
section отдéл *m.*; отделéние *n.*
secure, to обеспéчивать, -пéчить; закрепля́ть, -пúть
sediment осáдок *m.*
see, to вúдеть, у-
to ∼ off провожáть, -водúть
let me ∼ дáйте подýмать
I ∼ понимáю

seed се́мя *n.*
seek, to иска́ть, по-
seem, to каза́ться, по-
seize, to схва́тывать, -ати́ть
seldom ре́дко
selection вы́бор *m.*
self сам, себя́
sell, to продава́ть, -да́ть
send, to посыла́ть, -сла́ть
to ~ for посыла́ть за
to ~ off отправля́ть, -а́вить
senior ста́рший
sensation ощуще́ние *n.*
sense чу́вство *n.*; смысл *m.*
sense, to чу́вствовать, по-
sensitive чувстви́тельный
sentence фра́за *f.*, предложе́ние *n.*; пригово́р *m.*
sentimental сентимента́льный
separate отде́льный
separate, to разъединя́ть, -ни́ть
September сентя́брь *m.*
sergeant сержа́нт *m.*
series се́рия *f.*
serious серьёный, ва́жный
serve, to служи́ть, по-; подава́ть, -да́ть
service слу́жба *f.*; услу́га *f.*
session се́ссия *f.*; заседа́ние *n.*
set набо́р *m.*; компле́кт *m.*
settle, to поселя́ть(ся), -ли́ть(ся); ула́живать(ся), ула́дить(ся)
settlement поселе́ние *n.*; реше́ние *n.*
seven семь
seven hundred семьсо́т
seventeen семна́дцать
seventh седьмо́й
seventy се́мьдесят
several не́сколько
severe суро́вый, стро́гий
sex пол *m.*
sexual полово́й
shade тень *f.*; што́ра *f.*
shadow тень *f.*
shake, to трясти́, тряхну́ть
shallow ме́лкий
shame стыд *m.*, позо́р *m.*
shampoo шампу́нь *m. or f.*
shape фо́рма *f.*
share до́ля *f.*
sharp о́стрый, ре́зкий
shave, to бри́ть(ся), по-
shawl шаль *f.*, плато́к *m.*
she она́
shed, to пролива́ть, -ли́ть
sheep овца́ *f.*
sheet простыня́ *f.*; (*of paper*) лист *m.*
shelf по́лка *f.*
shelter прию́т *m.*; убе́жище *n.*
shepherd пасту́х *m.*
shine, to свети́ть, по-; сия́ть *imp.*; блесте́ть, -сну́ть
ship су́дно *n.*, кора́бль *m.*
ship, to отправля́ть, -а́вить
shipment груз *m.*; погру́зка *f.*
shirt руба́шка *f.*, соро́чка *f.*
shiver to дрожа́ть, дро́гнуть
shoe боти́нок *m.*, ту́фля *f.*, башма́к *m.*
shoemaker сапо́жник *m.*
shoot, to стреля́ть *imp.*; застрели́ть *perf.*
shop ла́вка *f.*, магази́н *m.*
shopping, to go де́лать поку́пки
shore бе́рег *m.*
short коро́ткий
shorthand стеногра́фия *f.*
shortly вско́ре
shorts тру́сики *m. pl.*
shortsighted близору́кий
shoulder плечо́ *n.*
shout, to крича́ть, кри́кнуть
show вы́ставка *f.*; спекта́кль *m.*
show, to пока́зывать(ся), -каза́ться
to ~ in вводи́ть, ввести́
to ~ off хва́статься, по-
shrink, to сади́ться, сесть
shut, to закрыва́ть(ся), -кры́ть(ся)
to ~ in запира́ть, -пере́ть
to ~ out выключа́ть, вы́ключить
shutter ста́вень *m.*; затво́р *m.*
shy ро́бкий
sick больно́й
I am ~ of мне надое́ло
sickness боле́знь *f.*
side сторона́ *f.*; бок *m.*
~ by ~ ря́дом
sidewalk тротуа́р *m.*
sieve решето́ *n.*
sigh, to вздыха́ть, вздохну́ть
sight зре́ние *n.*; вид *m.*; *pl.* достопримеча́тельности

sign знак *m.*; при́знак *m.*
sign, to поди́сывать(ся), -писа́ть(ся)
signature по́дпись *f.*
significance значе́ние *n.*
silence молча́ние *n.*, тишина́ *f.*
silent безмо́лвный
to be ~ молча́ть, за-
silk шёлк *m.*
silken шёлковый
silly глу́пый
silver серебро́ *n.*; *adj.* серебряный
similar подо́бный
simple просто́й
simply про́сто
simultaneous одновре́менный
sin грех *m.*
since *prep.* с; *conj.* с тех пор как; так как; *adv.* с тех пор
sincere и́скренний
sing, to петь, с-
singer певе́ц *m.*, певи́ца *f.*
single еди́нственный; отде́льный
sink, to тону́ть, у-; топи́ть, у-
sister сестра́ *f.*
~-in-law неве́стка *f.*
sit, to сиде́ть, по-
to ~ down сади́ться, сесть
situation положе́ние *n.*
six шесть
six hundred шестьсо́т
sixteen шестна́дцать
sixth шесто́й
sixty шестьдеся́т
size разме́р *m.*
skate, to ката́ться *imp.* на конька́х
ski, to ходи́ть *imp.* на лы́жах
skilled квалифици́рованный; иску́сный
skin, ко́жа *f.*; шку́ра *f.*
skirt ю́бка *f.*
sky не́бо *n.*
skyscraper небоскрёб *m.*
slang жарго́н *m.*
slave раб *m.*
sled са́ни *f. pl.*
sleep сон *m.*
sleep, to спать, по-
sleeping car спа́льный ваго́н *m.*
sleepy со́нный
sleeve рука́в *m.*
slender то́нкий, стро́йный
slice ло́мтик *m.*
slide скользи́ть, -зну́ть
slightly слегка́
slip скольже́ние *n.*; оши́бка *f.*, прома́х *m.*; бума́жка *f.*
slipper ту́фля *f.*
slow ме́дленный
my watch is ~ мои́ часы́ отстаю́т
slowly ме́дленно
sly хи́трый
small ма́ленький
smart наря́дный
smash, to разбива́ть, -би́ть
smell за́пах *m.*
smell, to па́хнуть *imp.*
smile улы́бка *f.*
smile, to улыба́ться, -бну́ться
smoke дым *m.*
smoke, to кури́ть, за-
smoker куря́щий *m.*
snack заку́ска *f.*
snake змея́ *f.*
snatch, to хвата́ть(ся), (с)хвати́ть(ся)
sneeze, to чиха́ть, -хну́ть
snow снег *m.*
snowing, it is снег идёт
so так; таки́м о́бразом; ита́к
~ far до сих пор
~ long! пока́!
~ that так что; что́бы
soap мы́ло *n.*
soccer футбо́л *m.*
social обще́ственный; социа́льный
society о́бщество *n.*
sock носо́к *m.*
sofa дива́н *m.*
soft мя́гкий
soil земля́ *f.*, по́чва *f.*
soldier солда́т *m.*
sold out распро́данный
sole подо́шва *f.*; *adj.* еди́нственный
solemn торже́ственный
solid кре́пкий; соли́дный
solution реше́ние *n.*
solve, to (раз)реша́ть, -ши́ть
some како́й-нибудь; не́который; не́сколько
somebody кто́-то

somehow ка́к-нибудь
someone кто́-то
something что́-нибудь, что́-то, ко́е-что
sometimes иногда́
somewhere где́-нибудь; куда́-нибудь
son сын *m.*
song пе́сня *f.*
son-in-law зять *m.*
soon вско́ре, ско́ро
as ~ as как то́лько
sore чувстви́тельный
sorrow го́ре *n.*; скорбь *f.*
sorry, to be жале́ть, по-
I'm ~ винова́т, извини́те, прости́те
sort сорт *m.*, вид *m.*
soul душа́ *f.*
sound звук *m.*; *adj.* здоро́вый
soup суп *m.*
sour ки́слый
source исто́чник *m.*
south юг *m.*
Soviet сове́тский
~ Union Сове́тский Сою́з
southern ю́жный
sow, to се́ять, за-
space простра́нство *n.*
spare запасно́й
spare, to щади́ть, по-; эконо́мить, с-
sparrow воробе́й *m.*
speak, to говори́ть, по-
special специа́льный; осо́бый
spectacle зре́лище *n.*
spectator зри́тель *m.*
speech речь *f.*
speed ско́рость *f.*
spend, to тра́тить, по-; проводи́ть, -вести́
spider пау́к *m.*
spinach шпина́т *m.*
spirit дух *m.*
spiritual духо́вный
spit, to плева́ть, плю́нуть
spite of, in несмотря́ на
splendid блестя́щий, великоле́пный
spoil, to по́ртить(ся), ис-; балова́ть, из-
sponge гу́бка *f.*
spoon ло́жка *f.*
sport спорт *m.*
spot пятно́ *n.*; ме́сто *n.*
spring весна́ *f.*; пружи́на *f.*
spring, to пры́гать, -гнуть; вска́кивать, вскочи́ть
spy шпио́н *m.*
square пло́щадь *f.*; *adj.* квадра́тный
squeeze, to выжима́ть, вы́жать
stability усто́йчивость *f.*; про́чность *f*, сто́йкость *f.*
stadium ста́дион *m.*
stagnation засто́й *m.*
stage сце́на *f.*
stain пятно́ *n.*
staircase ле́стница *f.*
stairs ле́стница *f.*
stamp (почто́вая) ма́рка *f.*
stand стоя́нка *f.*; сто́йка *f.*; стэнд *m.*
stand, to стоя́ть, по-; выде́рживать, вы́держать
standard зна́мя *n.*; станда́рт *m.*
standpoint то́чка зре́ния
star звезда́ *f.*
starch, to крахма́лить, на-
start, to начина́ть(ся), -ча́ть(ся); отправля́ться, -а́виться; (motor) заводи́ть, -вести́
state госуда́рство *n.*; состоя́ние *n.*; *adj.* госуда́рственный
statement заявле́ние *n.*
station ста́нция *f.*; вокза́л *m.*
statue па́мятник *m.*
stay, to остава́ться, оста́ться; остана́вливаться, -нови́ться
steady постоя́нный
steak бифште́кс *m.*
steal, to красть, у-
steam пар *m.*
steamship парохо́д *m.*
steel сталь *f.*; *adj.* стально́й
step шаг *m.*; ступе́нька *f.*
step, to ступа́ть, -пи́ть; шага́ть, шагну́ть
steppe степь *f.*
stick па́лка *f.*
stick, to втыка́ть, воткну́ть; прикле́ивать(ся), -е́ить(ся)
to ~ in застрева́ть, -стря́ть
to ~ to приде́рживаться, -держа́ться
stiff жёсткий

still *adj.* ти́хий; *adv.* ещё, всё ещё; всё-таки, всё же
stimulate, to побужда́ть, -буди́ть
stir, to шевели́ть(ся), -льну́ть(ся); разме́шивать, -меша́ть
stocking чуло́к *m.*
stomach желу́док *m.*
stone ка́мень *m.*; ко́сточка *f.*; *adj.* ка́менный
stool табуре́тка *f.*
stop остано́вка *f.*
stop, to остана́вливать(ся), -нови́ть(ся); прекраща́ть(ся), -крати́ть(ся); затыка́ть, -ткну́ть
stopper про́бка *f.*
storage хране́ние *n.*
store склад *m.*; магази́н *m.*
stork а́ист *m.*
storm бу́ря *f.*
stormy бу́рный
story расска́з *m.*; исто́рия *f.*; эта́ж *m.*
stout то́лстый, по́лный; кре́пкий
stove печь *f.*, пе́чка *f.*
straight прямо́й
  ~ ahead пря́мо
strange стра́нный
stranger незнако́мец *m.*; посто-ро́нний челове́к *m.*
strawberries клубни́ка *f.*
stream пото́к *m.*; тече́ние *n.*
stream, to течь *imp.*
street у́лица *f.*
streetcar трамва́й *m.*
strength си́ла *f.*
stress, to подчёркивать, -черкну́ть
stretch, to протя́гивать, -тяну́ть; растя́гивать(ся), -тяну́ть(ся); тяну́ться, по-
strict стро́гий; то́чный
strike ста́чка *f.*, забасто́вка *f.*
strike, to ударя́ть(ся), уда́рить(ся); поража́ть, -рази́ть; бить, про-; бастова́ть, за-
  to ~ a match зажига́ть, -же́чь спи́чку
string *верёвка f.*; струна́ *f.*
strip, to раздева́ть(ся), -де́ть(ся)
stripe полоса́ *f.*
striped полоса́тый
strive, to стара́ться, по-
strong си́льный; кре́пкий
struggle борьба́ *f.*
struggle, to боро́ться, по-
student студе́нт *m.*
study изуче́ние *n.*; кабине́т *m.*
study, to изуча́ть, -учи́ть
stuff веществ́о *n.*, материа́л *m.*
stupid глу́пый
style стиль *m.*, слог *m.*
subject предме́т *m.*, те́ма *f.*
  to be ~ to подверга́ться, -ве́ргнуться; подлежа́ть *imp.*
subscribe, to подпи́сываться. -писа́ться
subsequently зате́м, пото́м
substance веществ́о *n.*
substitute замести́тель *m.*
substitute, to заменя́ть, -ни́ть
subtract вычита́ть, вы́честь
suburb при́город *m.*; *pl.* предме́стье *n.*
subway метро́ *n.*
succeed, to удава́ться, уда́ться
  I ~ed in мне удало́сь
success успе́х *m.*
successful уда́чный
such тако́й
suddenly вдруг, внеза́пно
suffer, to страда́ть, по-
suffering страда́ние *n.*
sufficient доста́точный
sugar са́хар *m.*
suggest, to предлага́ть, -ложи́ть
suggestion предложе́ние *n.*
suicide самоуби́йство *n.*
suit костю́м *m.*
suit, to годи́ться, при-
suitable подходя́щий
suitcase чемода́н *m.*
sum су́мма *f.*
summer ле́то *n.*; *adj.* ле́тний
summit верши́на *f.*
sun со́лнце *n.*
Sunday воскресе́нье *n.*
sunny со́лнечный
sunrise восхо́д со́лнца
sunset зака́т *m.*
superfluous (из)ли́шний
superior вы́сший, лу́чший
superiority превосхо́дство *n.*
supper у́жин *m.*
  to have ~ у́жинать, по-

supply снабже́ние *n.*; запа́с *m.*
support, to подде́рживать, -держа́ть; содержа́ть *imp.*
suppose, to (пред)полага́ть, -ложи́ть
supreme верхо́вный
sure уве́ренный; надёжный
surely несомне́нно
surface пове́рхность *f.*
surname фами́лия *f.*
surprise удивле́ние *n.*
surprise, to удивля́ть, -ви́ть
to be ∼d удивля́ться, -ви́ться
surprising удиви́тельный
surround, to окружа́ть, -жи́ть
surroundings окре́стности *f. pl.*
survey обзо́р *m.*
suspect, to подозрева́ть *imp.*
suspenders подтя́жки *f. pl.*
suspicion подозре́ние *n.*
suspicious подозри́тельный
swallow, to прогла́тывать, -глоти́ть
swan ле́бедь *f.*
swear, to кля́сться, по-; присяга́ть, -гну́ть
sweat пот *m.*
sweater сви́тер *m.*
sweet сла́дкий
swell, to распуха́ть, -пу́хнуть; вздува́ться, взду́ться
swim, to пла́вать *imp.*; плыть, по-
swimmer плове́ц *m.*
swing, to кача́ть(ся), качну́ть(ся); разма́хивать, -махну́ть
switch, to переключа́ть, -чи́ть
to ∼ off выключа́ть, вы́ключить
to ∼ on включа́ть, -чи́ть
sword меч *m.*
symbol си́мвол *m.*
sympathy сочу́вствие *n.*
system систе́ма *f.*

T

table стол *m.*; табли́ца *f.*
tablecloth ска́терть *f.*
tail хвост *m.*
tailor портно́й *m.*
take, to брать, взять
to ∼ away убира́ть, убра́ть
to ∼ off снима́ть, снять
to ∼ out вынима́ть, вы́нуть
to ∼ over принима́ть, -ня́ть
tale расска́з *m.*, по́весть *f.*
talent тала́нт *m.*
talk разгово́р *m.*, бесе́да *f.*
talk, to говори́ть, по-; разгова́ривать *imp.*
tall высо́кий
tan, to загора́ть, -ре́ть
tank бак *m.*, цисте́рна *f.*, резервуа́р *m.*; танк *m.*
tap кран *m.*
task зада́ча *f.*
taste вкус *m.*
taste, to про́бовать, по-; име́ть (при́)вкус
tax нало́г *m.*
taxi такси́ *n.*
tea чай *m.*
teach, to учи́ть, на- *or* вы́-; обуча́ть, -учи́ть; преподава́ть *imp.*
teacher учи́тель *m.*, учи́тельница *f.*; преподава́тель *m.*
team кома́нда *f.*
teapot ча́йник *m.*
tear слеза́ *f.*
tear, to рва́ть(ся), по-; раздира́ть, разодра́ть
tease, to дразни́ть, по-
teaspoon ча́йная ло́жка *f.*
technical техни́ческий
technique те́хника *f.*
telegram телегра́мма *f.*
telegraph, to телеграфи́ровать, *imp.* & *perf.*
telephone телефо́н *m.*; *adj.* телефо́нный
telephone directory телефо́нная кни́га *f.*
telephone number но́мер телефо́на
telephone receiver тру́бка
telephone, to звони́ть, по- по телефо́ну
television телеви́дение *n.*
televison set телеви́зор *m.*
tell, to говори́ть, сказа́ть; расска́зывать, -аза́ть
temper хара́ктер *m.*; настрое́ние *n.*
temperature температу́ра *f.*
temple висо́к *m.*

temporary вре́менный
temptation искуше́ние *n.*, собла́зн *m.*
ten де́сять; деся́ток *m.*
tenant жи́тель *m.*; жиле́ц *m.*
tendency скло́нность *f.*
tender не́жный
tennis те́ннис *m.*
tent пала́тка *f.*
tenth деся́тый
term срок *m.*; те́рмин *m.*; *pl.* усло́вия *n. pl.*
terrible стра́шный, ужа́сный
terror у́жас *m.*; терро́р *m.*
test, to испы́тывать, -пыта́ть
text текст *m.*
textbook уче́бник *m.*
textile тексти́льный
than чем
thank, to благодари́ть, по-
  ~ you!, ~ s! спаси́бо
thankful благода́рный
thanks to благодаря́ (чему́-либо)
that *pron.* (э́)тот, (э́)та, (э́)то; кото́рый; *conj.* что; что́бы
  ~ is то́-есть
the more the better чем бо́льше, тем лу́чше
theater теа́тр *m.*
their(s) их; свой
then тогда́; зате́м, пото́м
theory тео́рия *f.*
there там; туда́
  from ~ отту́да
  ~ is есть, име́ется
therefore поэ́тому
these э́ти
they они́
thick то́лстый; пло́тный; густо́й
thief вор *m.*
thin то́нкий; худо́й
thing вещь *f.*; де́ло *n.*
think, to ду́мать, по-
third тре́тий
  a ~ треть *f.*
thirsty, to be хоте́ть пить
thirteen трина́дцать
thirty три́дцать
this э́тот, э́та, э́то
thorough тща́тельный
those те
though хотя́
  as ~ как бу́дто бы
thought мысль *f.*
thousand ты́сяча
thread ни́тка *f.*
threat угро́за *f.*
threaten, to грози́ть, по-; угрожа́ть *imp.*
three три; тро́е
three hundred три́ста
threshold поро́г *m.*
throat го́рло *n.*
through че́рез, сквозь; посре́дством
throw, to броса́ть, бро́сить; кида́ть, ки́нуть
thunder гром *m.*
thunderstorm гроза́ *f.*
Thursday четве́рг *m.*
thus так, таки́м о́бразом
ticket биле́т *m.*; ярлы́к *m.*
ticket window ка́сса *f.*
tie связь *f.*; га́лстук *m.*
tie, to свя́зывать, связа́ть; привя́зывать, -вяза́ть
tiger тигр *m.*
tight те́сный; туго́й
till *prep.* до; *conj.* до тех пор пока́, пока́ не
time вре́мя *n.*; срок *m.*; раз *m.*
  at that ~ тогда́
  for the ~ being пока́; в настоя́щее вре́мя
  on ~ во́-вре́мя
timetable расписа́ние *n.*
timid ро́бкий
tin о́лово *n.*; же́сть *f.*; ба́нка *f.*
tip чаевы́е *pl.*; сове́т *m.*
tiptoe, on на цы́почках
tire ши́на *f.*
tired уста́лый
  I am ~ я уста́л
  to get ~ устава́ть, уста́ть
tiresome утоми́тельный
title загла́вие *n.*; ти́тул *m.*
to к, в, на
tobacco таба́к *m.*
today сего́дня
  ~'s сего́дняшний
toe па́лец ноги́
together вме́сте
toilet убо́рная *f.*
tomato помидо́р *m.*
tomorrow за́втра
  day after ~ послеза́втра

ton то́нна *f.*
tone тон *m.*
tongue язы́к *m.*
tonight сего́дня ве́чером *or* но́чью
too та́кже, то́же; сли́шком
tool ору́дие *n.*, инструме́нт *m.*
tooth зуб *m.*
toothache зубна́я боль *f.*
toothbrush зубна́я щётка *f.*
tooth paste зубна́я па́ста *f.*
tooth powder зубно́й порошо́к *m.*
top верх *m.*; верши́на *f.*; *adj.* ве́рхний
on ~ наверху́
topic предме́т *m.*, те́ма *f.*
tortoise черепа́ха *f.*
torture пы́тка *f.*; му́ка *f.*
total ито́г *m.*; *adj.* весь; по́лный
touching тро́гательный
tourist тури́ст *m.*, тури́стка *f.*
toward к
towel полоте́нце *n.*
tower ба́шня *f.*
town го́род *m.*
toy игру́шка *f.*
trace след *m.*
tractor тра́ктор *m.*
trade торго́вля *f.*
traffic движе́ние *n.*
tragedy траге́дия *f.*
tragic траги́ческий
train по́езд *m.*
training обуче́ние *n.*; трениро́вка *f.*
traitor преда́тель *m.*
transaction де́ло *n.*, сде́лка *f.*
translate, to переводи́ть, -вести́
translation перево́д *m.*
transmission переда́ча *f.*
transparent прозра́чный
transport перево́зка *f.*; тра́нспорт
transport, to перевози́ть, -везти́
trap лову́шка *f.*
travel путеше́ствие *n.*
travel to путеше́ствовать *imp.*
travel bureau бюро́ путеше́ствий
traveler путеше́ственник *m.*
treasure сокро́вище *n.*
treat, to обраща́ться, обрати́ться; угоща́ть, угости́ть; лечи́ть, вы-
tree де́рево *n.*
tremble, to дрожа́ть, дро́гнуть
tremendous огро́мный
trial про́бный
trick фо́кус *m.*
trifle ме́лочь *f.*, пустя́к *m.*
trip пое́здка *f.*, экску́рсия *f.*
triumph торжество́ *n.*
trolley bus тролле́йбус *m.*
tropical тропи́ческий
trouble забо́та *f.*, хло́поты *f. pl.*; го́ре *n.*, беда́ *f.*
trousers брюки *f. pl.*
truck грузови́к *m.*
true и́стинный; по́длинный; ве́рный
truly, yours с уваже́нием
trumpet труба́ *f.*
trump ко́зырь *m.*
trunk сунду́к *m.*
trust, to ве́рить, по-; доверя́ть, -ве́рить
truth пра́вда *f.*
truthful правди́вый
try, to пыта́ться, по-; стара́ться, по-; про́бовать, по-
to ~ on примеря́ть, -ме́рить
to ~ out испы́тывать, -пыта́ть
tube тру́бка *f.*; тю́бик *m.*
Tuesday вто́рник *m.*
tumbler стака́н *m.*
tunnel тунне́ль *m.*
turkey индю́к *m.*
turn поворо́т *m.*; о́чередь *f.*
turn, to верте́ть(ся) *imp.*; крути́ть(ся) *imp.*; враща́ть(ся) *imp.*; повора́чивать(ся), поверну́ть(ся); обора́чивать(ся), оберну́ть(ся); обраща́ть(ся), обрати́ть(ся); де́латься, с-; станови́ться, стать
to ~ off (*tap*) закрыва́ть, -кры́ть
to ~ on (*tap*) открыва́ть, -кры́ть; (*light*) включа́ть, -чи́ть
to ~ out (*light*) выключа́ть, вы́ключить
to ~ pale побледне́ть *perf.*
twelve двена́дцать
twenty два́дцать
twice два́жды
~ as вдво́е

twilight сумерки *f. pl.*
twins близнецы *m. pl.*
two два, две; двое
∼ and a half два с половиной
two hundred двести
type тип *m.*
typewriter пишущая машинка *f.*
typist машинистка *f.*

U

ugly безобразный, отталкивающий
Ukraine Украина *f.*
Ukrainian украинец *m.*, -нка *f.*; *adj.* украинский
umbrella зонтик *m.*
uncle дядя *m.*
uncomfortable неудобный
unconscious бессознательный
under под; при
underclothes (нижнее) бельё *n.*
undergo, to подвергаться, -вергнуться
understand, to понимать, понять
undertake, to преприниматъ, -нять
undertaking предприятие *n.*
underwear (нижнее) бельё *n.*
undress, to раздевать(ся), -деться
unemployment безработица *f.*
unexpectedly неожиданно
unfinished незаконченный
unfortunately к сожалению
unhappy несчастный
uniform форма *f.*, мундир *m.*
union союз *m.*; объединение *n.*
unit единица *f.*
united соединённый, объединённый
United Nations Объединённые Нации
United States Соединённые Штаты
universal универсальный
university университет *m.*
unknown незнакомый, неизвестный
unless если не
unlimited неограниченный
unnecessary (из)лишний, ненужный
unpleasant неприятный
until *prep.* до; *conj.* пока не
unusual необыкновенный
unwillingly неохотно
up наверх, вверх
∼ and down вверх и вниз; взад и вперёд
∼ to now до сих пор
upbringing воспитание
upon на; в
upper верхний; высший
upright прямой; *adv.* прямо
upset огорчённый, расстроенный
upside down вверх ногами
upstairs наверх; наверху
upward вверх
urgent срочный
use польза *f.*; употребление *n.*
use, to употреблять, -бить; пользоваться, вос-; использовать *imp.* & *perf.*
used to, to get привыкать, -выкнуть
useful полезный
usual обычный, обыкновенный
usually обычно, обыкновенно
utmost крайний

V

vacant пустой; свободный
vacation отпуск *m.*
vacuum cleaner пылесос *m.*
vain, in напрасно
valid действительный
valley долина *f.*
valuable ценный
valuables драгоценности *f. pl.*
value стоимость *f.*; ценность *f.*
van багажный вагон *m.*
vanish, to исчезать, -чезнуть; пропадать, -пасть
various разный, различный
vast обширный
veal телятина *f.*
vegetables зелень *f.*
vein вена *f.*, жила *f.*
velvet бархат *m.*
verb глагол *m.*
verse стих *m.*
very очень, весьма
vessel судно *n.*
vest жилет *m.*
victim жертва *f.*

victory побе́да *f.*
view вид *m.*; взгляд *m.*
point of ~ то́чка зре́ния
vigorous си́льный
village дере́вня *f.*, село́ *n.*
vinegar у́ксус *m.*
violin скри́пка *f.*
visa ви́за *f.*
visible ви́димый
vision зре́ние *n.*
visit визи́т *m.*
visit, to посеща́ть, -сети́ть; наве-ща́ть, -вести́ть
visitor посети́тель *m.*, гость *m.*
vodka во́дка *f.*
voice го́лос *m.*
volume объём *m.*; том *m.*
voluntary доброво́льный
vote, to голосова́ть, про-
vow обе́т *m.*, кля́тва *f.*
voyage путеше́ствие *n.*

W

wages за́работная пла́та *f.*
waist та́лия *f.*
wait, to ждать, подо-
waiter официа́нт *m.*
waiting room зал ожида́ния
waitress официа́нтка *f.*
wake up, to буди́ть, раз-; про-бужда́ть(ся), -буди́ть(ся); просыпа́ться, -сну́ться
walk прогу́лка *f.*
walk, to гуля́ть, по-; итти́, пойти́ пешко́м
wall стена́ *f.*
wallpaper обо́и *m. pl.*
waltz вальс *m.*
want нужда́ *f.*
want, to жела́ть, по-; хоте́ть, за-; нужда́ться *imp.*
war война́ *f.*; *adj.* вое́нный
wardrobe гардеро́б *m.*
warehouse склад *m.*
warm тёплый
warn, to предупрежда́ть, -еди́ть
wash, to мыть(ся), по-; стира́ть-(ся), вы́-
waste, to тра́тить, по-; (*time*) теря́ть, по-
watch часы́ *m. pl.*
watch, to наблюда́ть *imp.*; сле-ди́ть *imp.*
watchmaker часовщи́к *m.*
water вода́ *f.*
waterfall водопа́д *m.*
watermelon арбу́з *m.*
waterproof непромока́емый
wave волна́ *f.*
wave, to маха́ть, махну́ть; (*hair*) завива́ть, -ви́ть
way доро́га *f.*, путь *m.*; на-правле́ние *n.*; спо́соб *m.*
~ out вы́ход *m.*
by the ~ ме́жду про́чим
we мы
weak сла́бый
weakness сла́бость *f.*
wealth бога́тство *n.*
weapon ору́жие *n.*
wear, to носи́ть(ся) *imp.*
to ~ out изна́шивать(ся), -носи́ть(ся)
weather пого́да *f.*
wedding сва́дьба *f.*; *adj.* сваде́б-ный
Wednesday среда́ *f.*
weed сорня́к *m.*
week неде́ля *f.*
weekly еженеде́льный
weep, to пла́кать, за-
weigh, to ве́сить, вз-
weight вес *m.*; тя́жесть *f.*
welcome! добро́ пожа́ловать!
well хорошо́; *interjection* ну
as ~as и ... и, как ..., так и
well-known изве́стный
west за́пад *m.*
western за́падный
wet мо́крый
what что; како́й
wheat пшени́ца *f.*
wheel колесо́ *n.*
when когда́
whence отку́да
where где; куда́
~ from отку́да
whereas тогда́ как
whether ли; и́ли
which кото́рый; како́й
~ of you кто из вас
while вре́мя *n.*; *conj.* в то вре́мя как
whisper, to шепта́ть, шепну́ть
whistle, to свисте́ть, сви́стнуть
white бе́лый

who кто
whole весь; це́лый
whose чей
why почему́, заче́м
wide широ́кий, обши́рный
widow вдова́ *f.*
widower вдове́ц *m.*
wife жена́ *f.*
wild ди́кий
will во́ля *f.*
win, to выи́грывать, вы́играть
wind ве́тер *m.*
wind, to (*watch*) заводи́ть, -вести́
window окно́ *n.*; *adj.* око́нный
wine вино́ *n.*
wing крыло́ *n.*
winner побе́дитель *m.*
winter зима́ *f.*
wire про́волока *f.*, про́вод *m.*; телегра́мма *f.*
wisdom му́дрость *f.*
wise му́дрый
wish жела́ние *n.*
best ~es! наилу́чшие пожела́ния!
wish, to жела́ть, по-
with с
withdraw, to отдёргивать, -рнуть; брать, взять наза́д
within внутри́; в тече́ние
without без
witness свиде́тель *m.*
wolf волк *m.*
woman же́нщина *f.*
wonder чу́до *n.*
no ~ не удиви́тельно
wonder, to удивля́ться, -ви́ться
wonderful чуде́сный, удиви́тельный
wood ле́с *m.*; де́рево *n.*
wooden деревя́нный
wool шерсть *f.*
woolen шерстяно́й
word сло́во *n.*
work рабо́та *f.*; труд *m.*
work, to рабо́тать, по-; де́йствовать, по-
worker рабо́тник *m.*, -ница *f.*; рабо́чий *m.*; трудя́щийся *m.*
works заво́д *m.*
workshop мастерска́я *f.*; цех *m.*
world мир *m.*; свет *m.*; *adj.* мирово́й
world war мирова́я война́ *f.*
worm червь *m.*, червя́к *m.*
worry, to беспоко́ить(ся), о-
worse ху́же
worth, be сто́ить *imp.*
worthy досто́йный
wound ра́на *f.*
wrap, to завёртывать, -верну́ть; запако́вывать, -кова́ть
wrestle, to боро́ться, по-
wrist watch ручны́е часы́ *m. pl.*
write, to писа́ть, на-
to ~ down запи́сывать, -писа́ть
writer писа́тель *m.*
writing paper пи́счая бума́га *f.*
wrong непра́вильный; не тот
something is ~ что́-то не в поря́дке

X

X-ray рентге́новские лучи́ *m. pl.*

Y

year год *m.*
yearly ежего́дный
yeast дро́жжи *pl.*
yell, to вопи́ть *imp.*
yellow жёлтый
yes да
yesterday вчера́
day before ~ позавчера́
~'s вчера́шний
yet ещё; всё ещё; одна́ко, всё-таки
you вы, ты
young молодо́й, ю́ный
your(s) ваш, твой
youth мо́лодость *f.*; молодёжь *f.*

Z

zero нуль *m.*
zone зо́на *f.*; райо́н *m.*
zoo зоопа́рк *m.*

ILS
INSTITUTE FOR LANGUAGE STUDY